SNOWSHOE ROUTES

SNOWSHOE ROUTES

New England

Massachusetts

Vermont

New Hampshire

Maine

DIANE BAIR AND PAMELA WRIGHT

THE MOUNTAINEERS BOOKS

We'd like to thank our snowshoeing buddies, who made researching this book such fun: Nancy Bergeron, Lisa Hollis, Connor Bair-Cucchiaro, Travis Kelley, Jarrett Kelley, Carroll Jones, Sadie Wright-Ward, Jared Wright-Ward, Angela Mangini, and Megan and Alex Morouse. Diane would like to give special thanks to outdoorsman extraordinaire Paul Kelley, who proved once again that he's got game. Pam says big thanks to good sport and hubby Chuck Ward, who makes all her life's adventures more fun.

THE MOUNTAINEERS BOOKS
is the nonprofit publishing arm of The Mountaineers Club, an organization founded in 1906 and dedicated to the exploration, preservation, and enjoyment of outdoor and wilderness areas.

1001 SW Klickitat Way, Suite 201, Seattle, WA 98134

© 2006 by Diane Bair and Pamela Wright

First edition, 2006

Manufactured in the United States of America

Acquiring Editor: Christine Hosler
Project Editor: Christine Hosler
Copy Editor: Jane Crosen
Cover and Book Design: The Mountaineers Books
Layout: Elizabeth Cromwell/Books in Flight
Cartographer: Pease Press Cartography
Photographer: All photos by Diane Bair and Pamela Wright

Cover photograph: *Snowshoer leaving behind tracks* © Don Mason/Corbis
Frontispiece: *Snowshoeing on the trail up Bromley Mountain*

Library of Congress Cataloging-in-Publication Data

Bair, Diane.
  Snowshoe routes New England / by Diane Bair and Pamela Wright.—1st ed.
    p. cm.
  Includes index.
  ISBN 0-89886-849-1
  1. Snowshoes and snowshoeing—New England—Guidebooks. I. Wright, Pamela. II. Title.
  GV853.B35 2006
  796.9'20974—dc22
                      2006012643

 Printed on recycled paper

Contents

MASSACHUSETTS

VERMONT

MAP KEY

═══════	divided highway	Ⓟ	parking
───────	highway	⅄	campground
───────	road	⋔	picnic area
═══════	unplowed road	■	building or point of interest
- - - - - - -	main trail	▲	mountain peak
··············	alternate trail	🌑	body of water
- - - - - - - -	other trail	∿	river or stream
—+—+—+—	railroad	∼	small stream
(91)	interstate highway	⤬	waterfall or cascade
(7)	U.S. highway	) (	pass
(3)	state highway	⊶	gate
[259]	forest service road	— - - —	boundary (park or wilderness area)
→	directional indicator		private property

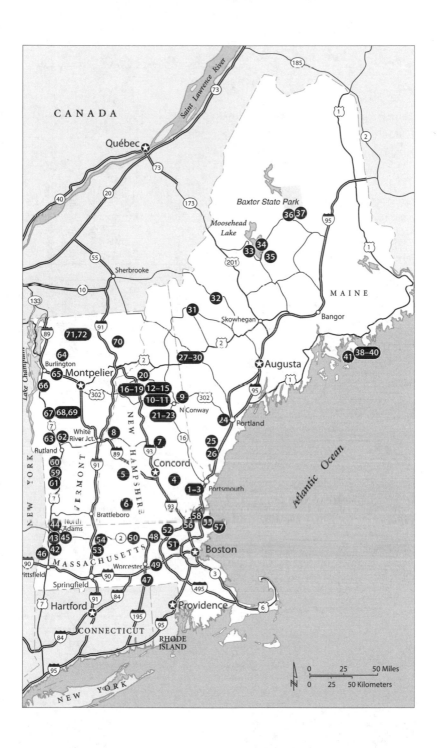

Quick Reference to the Trails

Trail number and name	Water and ice features	Magical meadow	Interesting rock formations	Awesome views	Family outing	Summit climb	Birds/wildlife signs	Historic feature
NEW HAMPSHIRE								
1. Great Bay National Wildlife Refuge	X	X		X	X		X	
2. Adams Point	X	X		X	X		X	X
3. Odiorne Point State Park	X	X		X	X		X	X
4. Bear Brook State Park	X		X	X	X			X
5. Norsk Center/Low Plain Wildlife Area	X	X			X		X	
6. Mount Monadnock				X		X		
7. Hamlin Recreation and Conservation Area	X	X	X	X	X			X
8. Mount Cardigan				X	X	X		
9. Peaked Mountain				X	X	X		
10. Mount Willard				X		X		X
11. Mount Washington	X		X	X		X		X
12. Pinkham Notch	X		X	X				
13. Arethusa Falls	X			X	X			
14. Carter Notch	X			X		X		
15. Tuckerman Ravine	X		X	X		X		X
16. The Flume	X		X	X	X			
17. Bald Mountain and Artists Bluff				X	X		X	
18. Lonesome Lake	X			X	X			
19. Falling Waters	X		X	X				
20. Zealand Falls	X			X	X			
21. Lincoln Woods	X				X			
22. Champney Falls	X			X	X			
23. Greeley Ponds	X	X			X			
MAINE								
24. Scarborough Marsh	X	X			X		X	
25. Gilsland Farm		X			X		X	
26. Harris Farm Cross-Country Ski Center		X			X			
27. Caribou Mountain				X		X		
28. Carter's Cross-Country Ski Center			X	X	X	X		
29. Sunday River Cross-Country Ski Center			X	X	X	X		
30. Table Rock			X	X			X	
31. Piazza Rock			X	X		X		
32. Burnt Mountain				X		X		
33. Mount Kineo	X		X	X	X	X		X

Trail number and name	Water and ice features	Magical meadow	Interesting rock formations	Awesome views	Family outing	Summit climb	Birds/wildlife signs	Historic feature
34. Lily Bay State Park	X			X	X		X	
35. Gulf Hagas			X	X				
36. Lost Pond	X		X					
37. Chimney Pond	X		X	X				
38. Cadillac Mountain			X	X		X		
39. Eagle Lake	X				X			
40. Gorham Mountain			X	X		X		
41. Day Mountain			X	X	X			
MASSACHUSETTS								
42. Hoosic River/Ashuwillticook Trail	X			X				
43. Mount Greylock	X			X		X		
44. Pine Cobble	X		X	X				
45. Spruce Hill	X	X	X		X	X		
46. Pleasant Valley Wildlife Sanctuary	X	X		X		X		
47. Douglas State Forest	X		X	X				
48. Oxbow National Wildlife Refuge	X			X		X		
49. Upton State Forest			X	X				
50. Wachusett Mountain State Reservation			X	X		X	X	
51. Walden Pond State Reservation	X			X				X
52. Great Brook Farm State Park	X	X		X				X
53. Mount Holyoke/Skinner State Park				X		X		X
54. Mount Toby	X			X		X		X
55. Bradley Palmer State Park	X	X		X				X
56. Weir Hill Reservation	X	X		X		X		
57. Ravenswood Park	X		X	X		X		X
58. Harold Parker State Forest	X			X		X		
VERMONT								
59. Griffith Lake and Baker Peak	X			X		X		
60. White Rocks Recreation Area	X			X				
61. Bromley Mountain			X	X		X		
62. Mountain Top Inn		X		X		X		
63. Mount Tom, Woodstock	X			X	X	X		
64. Smugglers Notch				X	X			
65. Little River State Park	X			X				X
66. Mount Philo State Park			X	X		X	X	
67. Robert Frost Interpretive Trail	X			X				X
68. Hogback Mountain/Blueberry Hill		X		X	X			
69. Mount Moosalamo	X			X		X		
70. Mount Pisgah	X			X		X		
71. Sugar Hill		X		X	X	X		X
72. Burnt Mountain				X		X		

Introduction

Snowshoeing is—believe it or not—positively trendy. Hard to imagine that tromping around in deep snow on giant shoes is cool, but it's a fact. Snowshoeing is America's *fastest-growing winter sport*. (Yes, that includes snowboarding!) A dozen years ago, you couldn't find a snowshoe in a sporting goods store if you scoured every aisle; now, they're everywhere. Ski resorts are adding moonlight snowshoe tours and wildlife watching routes to their arsenal of winter fun activities, and cross-country ski centers are stocking up on rental snowshoes for kids and adults. "We've seen steady growth in the popularity of snowshoeing for several years," says Rob Burbank, spokesperson for the Appalachian Mountain Club. "It's a great wintertime activity for people of just about any age or level of ability."

FLOATING ON SNOW

What's old is new again. Snowshoes were first used about 6000 years ago, when ancient people used them to trek the snowy tundra of what is now central Asia. Archeologists believe that the first tribes who journeyed across the Bering Strait to present-day North America developed this unique, float-on-the-snow footwear.

The earliest models were simply pieces of wood, lashed to the bottom of the feet. Those first snowshoes varied in shape, according to the snow conditions faced by the wanderers who wore them, but they had one thing in common: decking made of the treated rawhide of moose or caribou.

These days, you can still find those traditional snowshoes, made of wood (often, varnished ash), and so beautifully designed they're like works of art. You can also find lightweight aluminum models that are easy to use, and built for everything from meandering woods and valleys to tackling rugged peaks.

Random snowmen are among the surprises one might encounter along the trail.

WHY SNOWSHOE?

So what's the attraction? If you're reading this book, you get it. Everyone trumpets the fact that snowshoeing has no learning curve and is as easy as walking, but in our view, "easy" doesn't come close to explaining the appeal of this sport.

Snowshoeing is all about serenity. You're not thinking about the next hill, or if your wax is right, as you do on Nordic skis. It's just you and winter, in all of her sparkling, white-on-white glory. You slip over the snow, effortlessly at times, and skim under a lacy canopy of ice-slicked branches. You make the first tracks up a mountain summit, without the distraction of mossy rocks and tangly roots underfoot. You take in the grandeur of white-cloaked peaks against a backdrop of bluer-than-blue sky. The stark beauty of it all is truly humbling. And in winter, you may well have the mountaintop all to yourself.

Snowshoeing offers its own unique rewards. When the mercury drops and snowflakes fall, the summer's vibrant landscapes are transformed into places of hushed silence and pristine beauty. Even the most familiar places take on a fresh, new look with winter's blustery arrival. While researching this book, we've realized that winter in the North Country has an allure we never fully appreciated until we strapped on a pair of snowshoes.

We've hiked deep into snow-blanketed woods, skirting icy beaver ponds and frozen waterfalls. We've snowshoed to an ice cave at the top of a mountain and watched as stars lit up a glittery winterscape. Yet, as with most things in life, some of our most pleasurable moments have been the simplest: an easy meander across a sun-dappled farm field; a short walk along a snow-banked shoreline; an invigorating tromp through a nearby nature preserve, where animal tracks crisscrossed our path and streams gurgled softly under icy surfaces.

If you truly want to find a reason to love winter, this is your sport. You'll stay warm, provided you dress appropriately. You'll tune into winter's secret beauties, zeroing in on things you'd never notice if you were shushing past on skis: tiny frozen berries on a bush, and the gorgeous crackly patterns of wetlands shrouded in ice. You'll see more wildlife than you'll ever see in summertime. You'll experience the joy of discovering the fresh tracks of a white-tailed deer, and perhaps see wild turkeys strutting in the snow, and snowshoe hares at play.

Besides fun and fresh air, snowshoeing is a great workout—better exercise than your typical walk in the park or jog on the treadmill. The winter air (metabolic rates increase in cold weather), the added weight of the shoe, and the resistance of moving through snow, together produce mega-calorie burn. According to a recent University of Vermont study, traveling 4 miles an hour in snowshoes on packed trails burns the same number of calories as jogging at 6 miles per hour on a treadmill. In fact, the study showed that after a six-week training period, a group of snowshoers showed a higher fitness level than that of a group of runners. Add a couple of hills, fresh, untracked snow, and poles for upper-body movement, and you really get a workout. According to the same study, a typical 140-pound woman can burn from 400 to 800 calories in a single hour of snowshoeing. An added benefit: the sport is low impact; the snow is a soft cushion and the shoe acts as a shock absorber.

SNOWSHOEING TECHNIQUE

One of the reasons snowshoeing has become so popular is that it has a satisfy ingly fast learning curve. You may have heard the saying, "If you can walk, you can snowshoe." It's true. We found that learning to walk in snowshoes took less time than learning how to put them on. There are, however, a few basic techniques to mastering the sport.

First, take a slightly wider stance to avoid hitting the shoes against each other as you walk. Be sure to lift your feet (don't drag them) so you can plant the claws of the shoes firmly into the snow.

When you climb up a hill, keep your feet flat, use the claws to really dig into the snow, and stay upright; don't lean forward or backward. It also helps to take a shorter stride while walking up an incline.

When you climb down a hill, take bigger steps, plant your claws, and stand straight (try not to lean forward). Backing up can be awkward; it's best to take small, circular steps to turn around. Using poles will also help you maintain rhythm, balance, and traction.

Most people get the knack for it within an hour or two on the trail. Even kids as young as three or four can snowshoe, and most major manufacturers make tyke-sized shoes for kids seventy pounds and under.

You can snowshoe on just about any patch of snow that's four inches or more deep. Well-traveled, packed snow trails are the easiest to hike. In fresh, deep snow, you'll work harder as you sink a few inches and lift the snow with every step. But as the AMC's Burbank explains, "For the most part, you can travel on top of deep snow, so you move through the woods at a much greater height than you do when hiking in the summer." We've also discovered that many trails are easier to navigate in the winter, when they're covered with a soft blanket of snow, not littered with roots and rocks.

SHARING THE TRAIL

Sometimes, you'll have the delightful experience of making first tracks on virgin powder. (We don't have to tell you to be mindful of walking of private property.)

At other times, though, you'll be sharing the area with the skinny-ski crowd, since many Nordic ski centers have opened up their trails to snowshoers. Good etiquette can make this a happy situation for all. Here are some tips:

- Do not snowshoe on top of ski trails. Walk along an established snowshoe trail or make your own trail, beside the ski tracks.
- Yield to Nordic skiers (easier for you to get out of the way than for them, especially if they're going downhill). Ditto for snowmobiles, should you encounter one, for obvious reasons!
- Listen for the schussing sounds of skis and the whine of snowmobiles, especially if you're approaching an intersection.
- Step off the side of the trail when resting.

WHY NEW ENGLAND IS A PRIME SNOWSHOE DESTINATION

Our region is justifiably famous for its classic, postcard-perfect winter scenes, all white-steepled churches, horse-drawn sleighs and antique farmhouses. Snowshoers quickly discover that the surrounding pasturelands, old logging roads, and craggy peaks are an inviting playground, peaceful and often unexplored.

Plenty of snow. Winter in New England is truly spectacular, and a snowshoe hike is the best way to pay your respects. True, our annual snowfall amounts are wildly unpredictable. The fact is, the snow gods are notoriously fickle in New England. An unusually snowy winter in Massachusetts might be a near snow-drought in Vermont. Snow can be early, with heaps and heaps in December, or it can be late, or even nonexistent. But when we have snow, the opportunities to get out and explore are virtually endless.

Generally, you'll find the most reliable snowfall in the west and northern tiers of the region. Even when Boston is bereft of white stuff, you can often find it in central Massachusetts and the Berkshire Hills. The Green Mountains of Vermont, along with the Northeast Kingdom (bordering Canada) and New Hampshire's White Mountains, are also good bets for snowfall, typically in January and February. In Maine, you'll usually find ample snow in the Western Mountains, Rangeley and Sugarloaf, Moosehead, and Baxter regions.

Rainfall in southern New England often translates as snowfall a couple of hours north, hooray. You can't count on this, though. Therefore, nothing beats checking out the weather conditions before you go, online at *www.weather.com* or by calling ahead, if you're staying in the area.

Wicked awesome snowshoeing. If you're new to the region, you'll quickly discover what the rest of us take for granted: New England is an amazing outdoor playground in any season. In this book, we've included a variety of destinations, from the popular, must-see spots to quieter places located off the beaten track.

One of the pure joys of snowshoeing is pristine powder, without a soul in sight.

In addition to many hikes in New England's mountainous hinterlands, we've also selected destinations for this book that are close to cities and urban areas. If we get really hammered with white stuff, as we have in recent years, you can head to nearly any country inn or bed-and-breakfast and find a couple of worthy snowshoe trails nearby. Add some tasty provisions, a wonderful dinner, a roaring fire, a fit, friendly companion, and you have the makings of a perfect winter weekend in New England.

For many beginners, Nordic centers and ski resorts are appealing, because they offer rental gear and well-marked trails. Other destinations include mountain lodges, state parks, national parks, snow-covered golf courses, city and state conservation land, and much more. To the south, especially in Massachusetts and southern to central Vermont, you'll find a choice of marked trail systems. Travel northward, and undiscovered backcountry paths await.

We've discovered that the best way to tap into the coolest local haunts is to simply ask around. People we've met on the trail have shared their favorites with us, and many of those hidden gems are featured here. Nothing beats insider knowledge, especially when you're exploring an area you're not familiar with. These same folks have also been invaluable when it comes to revealing the places not to go.

Wonderful wild places. Thanks to the region's strong focus on preservation, New England is rich with state parks, wildlife preserves, and protected land. In spite of soaring property values, you'll find plenty of property that looks much as it did a century ago. The farmhouses might be gone, but miles of stone walls and ghostly foundations remain. Families and other private landowners have turned over property (or development rights) to the Trustees of Reservations, local chapters of the National Audubon Society, land trusts, and other groups devoted to preserving green space—all the better for those of us who want to gently enjoy it!

Some properties encompass private lands (typically abutting state parks and forests) whose owners generously allow snowshoe hikers to trespass. Others are state forests and reservations or federally managed areas. Most do not charge fees in winter, but signage runs the gamut from "great" to "nonexistent." Generally, don't expect restrooms to be open in winter or felled trees to be removed. While many state parks offer maps on-site, you can't count on these, but you can find them online or by using the information contacts listed in this book.

If you're heading far out of town, especially to the mountains, it pays to ask ahead about current conditions before setting out, in case roads or trails have become impassable or hazardous due to recent snowmelts, for example. When you're planning to ski in parks and state reservations, your best resource, always, is a park ranger. You'll find contact information for the appropriate local authority or land manager at the beginning of each hike.

Variety of terrain. Our region has it all when it comes to variety, snowshoe-style, from shoreside rambles, to lovely walks into the woodlands, to adrenalin-pumping mountain climbs. We're blessed with intriguing wetlands, and more than our fair share of humpy mountains. They may not be Tetons, but even Mount Greylock in Massachusetts is a worthy piece of work on snowshoes.

Granite summits. The fact that our craggy granite summits are easier to navigate on snowshoes with crampons is just a bonus. Many times, hiking in summer, we've missed our snowshoes. How enjoyable to leap up a summit trail atop a fluffy cushion of white stuff!

Not to mention, those views! You'll really appreciate New England's rocky spine when you're enjoying wide-open vistas of surrounding peaks and valleys. Okay, we'll say it: New England rocks. The giant-sized granite boulders you'll see as you hike throughout the region are glacial erratics, left behind by receding glaciers in the last ice age. Wander Vermont, and you'll see chunks of quartz. In many places in the state, powder-white marble is camouflaged by snow.

Backcountry and winter camping. If you're into extremes, our region offers long-distance hikes and backcountry camping excursions—and a population of hardy outdoorspeople who can't wait to take 'em on! We've featured several possibilities for winter camping here, but we could write a whole book on the subject. AMC huts are a great way to go if you're a newbie to winter camping (see sidebar "AMC Winter Huts" following Hike 20). If you're experienced, you'll find several options along backcountry trails (especially in northern areas) and near long-distance trails. For details, check with the information contacts included here (often available online).

Snowshoeing buddies. With so many colleges and universities, our population is on the youngish side, making New England the perfect place to find snowshoe hiking buddies. Like the idea of meeting like-minded outdoorsy types? Join a local outdoor sports group, and you're sure to find snowshoeing companions and some great guided snowshoe treks to the region's choicest spots.

The beauty part is, you can enjoy this sport no matter what your age demographic. Local chapters of the National Audubon Society, the Appalachian Mountain Club, the Green Mountain Club, neighborhood YMCAs, hiking clubs, and birding groups all offer guided snowshoe hikes and group trips to great places. Local newspapers feature outdoors listings, as do the websites of outdoor recreation–affiliated groups like the AMC.

Winter Driving in New England

Narrow country roads, black ice, sudden thawing and freezing—we have it all. The most dangerous aspect of your snowshoe trip will most likely be the drive to and from the trailhead. To get to most of the hikes in this book, you'll need a vehicle with four-wheel drive or all-wheel drive. Another good feature for winter driving is anti-lock brakes. It's best to stick to cars and SUVs; avoid pickup trucks, as they tend to fishtail and spin unless well-weighted in the back. There's nothing more discouraging than driving for hours to a great hike, and not being able to make it up the last stretch of unpaved road to the trailhead. For safe winter driving, here are some key tips:

- Put on snow tires.
- Check your antifreeze level.
- Make sure your battery is charged and that your wiper blades are working properly. Pack extra wiper fluid and antifreeze.
- Use lightweight motor oil.
- Keep these items in your vehicle, just in case: tire chains, a tow strap, jumper cables, a shovel, an ax, a backpacking stove and lighter, a pot, some dried food, a jug of water, a sleeping bag(s) and pad(s). (Also see sidebar "The Ten Essentials.")
- Drive at a safe speed for road conditions.

EQUIPMENT

The introduction of smaller and lighter shoes and increased affordability have helped to open the sport up to the ranks. Today, nylon and neoprene have replaced rawhide lacing; frames are made of high-tech aluminum or lightweight molded plastics. Are you planning to trek up steep mountains and rugged terrain? Or, are you a recreational/day hiker? Generally, a good snowshoe—perfect for day hikes—costs a couple hundred bucks or so.

How to Choose the Right Snowshoes

Vermont-based Tubbs Snowshoes offers the following advice for selecting the right snowshoe. For more information, visit *www.tubbssnowshoes.com.*

These are the main things to pay attention to when choosing a snowshoe:

Flotation. Perhaps the number one benefit of snowshoes is the ability to "walk on snow." For the right balance of flotation, maneuverability, and comfort, manufacturers recommend different sizes for different user weights. (Typically, a heavier person needs a bigger snowshoe to have the same flotation experience as a lighter person in similar snow conditions.) Be sure to factor in the weight of your clothes and gear as well as your own body weight.

21" = 80–150 lbs
25" = 120–200 lbs
30" = 170–250 lbs
36" = 220–300 lbs

If your weight, with gear, puts you "on the fence" between two sizes, or you are trying to choose between two sizes, consider the following:

RACE YOU TO THE TOP!

Got the itch to compete? As the sport of snowshoe racing and competition becomes ever more popular (and snowshoe enthusiasts gain more expertise), the number of events is mushrooming, both regionally and nationally. And what could be more fun than participating in a snowshoe event when you travel?

To see what's happening, check out the listings on the United States Snowshoe Association website (*www.snowshoeracing.com*). Another good source of activities nationwide, including event calendars and snowshoe club information, is *www.snowshoemag.com*. The snowshoe manufacturers hold racing events throughout the winter months; Redfeather, Atlas, and Tubbs stage a majority of the events in the United States. Also, check out snowshoe events organized by Winter Trails (*www.wintertrails.org*), REI, and EMS.

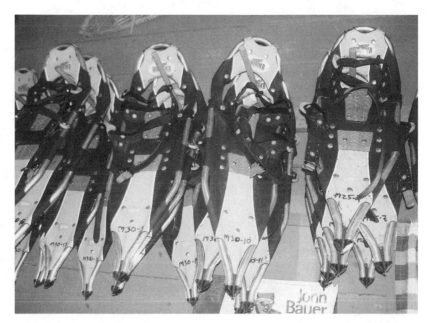

Rental snowshoes at Smuggler's Notch Nordic Ski and Snowshoe Center

- Selecting the smaller size will generally give you more maneuverability.
- Choosing the larger size will increase the amount of flotation.
- More surface area or flotation is usually desirable for use in powder snow conditions; less is needed for packed snow.

Articulation. A tough word, but an easy concept. It's the amount of movement your foot and ankle require for maximum comfort as the snowshoe terrain varies. Snowshoes rotate under the ball of the foot, and generally the more rotation, the more stability, control, and comfort on a variety of terrain. Full rotation gives the snowshoe hiker more traction on steep terrain and minimizes fatigue in powder conditions by allowing the snow to drop off the shoe's tail.

Comfort. Snowshoe weight, shape, and pivot point all combine with binding fit to impact your overall comfort and enjoyment. The binding is often considered the heart of the snowshoe, as this is where the user meets and interfaces with the snowshoe. Choosing a binding depends on the intended use. For steep ascents and extreme terrain, rigid binding materials will provide proper stability. For day hikes in varying terrain, more flexible bindings offer a comfortable, secure fit.

Women's snowshoes. Companies like Tubbs and MSR offer snowshoes engineered specifically for women. All models, whether for hiking/backpacking or recreation/fitness use, feature a smaller binding scaled to custom-fit a women's size 5 to 9 boot of any style. Women's snowshoes are shaped differently, too, with an ergonomic frame for a comfortable, natural stride.

Traction. Sure-footed traction is the expectation of every snowshoe hiker. While there are many crampon styles, for optimal traction snowshoes should come equipped with front and rear crampon systems, located directly under the key areas of impact – the ball of the foot and the heel. This ensures traction in the key areas of impact and through the entire walking stride. Tubbs measures traction by the depth of crampon penetration on uphill, sidehill, and downhill slopes as well as variable snow conditions. What type of traction system you need depends upon your intended use.

And Don't Forget the Ski Poles

Some love 'em, some hate 'em, but they can be useful. Ski poles will help you keep your balance on uneven terrain, and they'll help you get up when you fall down. You may also use them as a rack for your mittens, and they are handy for probing the terrain immediately ahead to detect unstable conditions.

CLOTHING AND WARMTH

You'll also need warm winter clothing (wicking polypropylene fabrics are best), a windbreaker, and a pair of good, waterproof boots. Remember to dress in layers; you will get hot! The trick is to shed layers before you begin to sweat too much and to pile them back on when you cool down.

First, we'll tell you what *not* to wear: scarves, turtlenecks, and pullovers. They tend to stifle ventilation, causing you to overheat. Skip the waterproof shells, too, since they'll make you sweat profusely and, well, yuck! No cotton or wool, since they dry slowly. Nothing too tight, because tight-fitting clothing will restrict your circulation, causing you to chill. Do not wear polypropylene glove liners inside your mittens. (We learned this the hard way.) Mittens keep you warm because they allow your fingers to touch each other.

Here's more advice, from snowshoe designer (for MSR) and ultimate mountain climber/outdoorsman Bill Forrest, who has snowshoed more than 1700 miles while developing snowshoes for MSR.

Wear synthetic materials. They dry quickly and will keep you much drier than natural fibers. Look for: nylon, polyester, polypropylene, and acrylic.

Think ventilation. High-tech, breathable fabrics will help keep you warm as well as dry. Wearing lightweight layers of clothing will enable you to add or remove clothing to keep you at an optimum temperature. Says Forrest, "When the weather is cold, people tend to overdress, and they ventilate only after they are thoroughly soaked with sweat. Stay dry to stay warm, and as soon as you start to sweat, ventilate!"

Dress in layers. Adding or removing a cap or pair of mittens is a simple way to control body temperature. (Tip: Bring extra mittens in your pack; they always get wet.) It won't hurt to bring an extra pair of wool socks as well, lest your boots leak or your feet perspire. Be sure that all of your upper layers of clothing can be fully opened. If you just open up your front layers, you can avoid the need to peel off clothing.

Don't forget the fuel. Remember, your body has a heating system that is powered by an engine which requires large amounts of food and water to function. Forrest says, "If you start to get cold, cover your ears with an ear band, zip up the front of your jacket, munch on some trail mix, and have a healthy drink of water." At minimum, you should drink a quart of water for every four hours that you're on the trail. Carry a small backpack to stow extra clothing, snacks, more water than you think you'll need, and a first aid kit.

Here's a list of what Forrest calls the "right stuff" to wear while snowshoeing:

Next to the skin—
- Medium-weight polypro long john bottoms
- Synthetic athletic-type bra (women)
- Medium-weight, button or zip-front polyester shirt (microfleece)
- Acrylic pile socks
- Five-finger polypro gloves (do not wear these inside your mittens)
- Acrylic or polyester headband
- Waterproof/breathable wide-brimmed sun hat for sunny and rainy days
- Wool or fleece hat
- Sunscreen and sunglasses
- Reliable wristwatch

THE TEN ESSENTIALS: A SYSTEMS APPROACH
1. Navigation (map and compass)
2. Sun protection (sunglasses and sunscreen)
3. Insulation (extra clothing)
4. Illumination (headlamp or flashlight)
5. First-aid supplies
6. Fire (firestarter and matches/lighter)
7. Repair kit and tools (including knife)
8. Nutrition (extra food)
9. Hydration (extra water)
10. Emergency shelter

—The Mountaineers

Second layer—
- Shell pants (typically nylon)
- Polyester vest (microfleece)
- Shell mittens (insulated with polyester pile or down)
- Boots, waterproof and breathable. Rubber-bottom/leather-top boots, with felt insulated liners, are excellent. Insulated leather hunting boots are okay, too. Your summer hiking boots will be fine if they keep the water out, but if you won't be constantly on the move, you may want a boot with insulation. Be sure your boots fit comfortably and that they have plenty of wiggle room in the toes.

Third (outer) layer—
- Nylon jacket with hood
- Gaiters (if you're not wearing high-top boots), to keep the snow out of your boots
- Bandanna (this can be cotton), cooler than a neck warmer and good for runny noses, tying up broken straps, etc.

HOW TO USE THIS BOOK

Here are a few things to consider as you look for the snowshoe hike that best suits you.

Rating. In some cases, rating the trails is tough, because some of them are fairly flat but have a couple of challenging steep stretches. We've rated trails based on their overall difficulty level, and pointed out places where they might offer some challenge; we've also pointed out easier alternatives when available. The ratings are as follows:

Easy trails are great for novices who want to get a feel for the sport, and for those early-season outings when you want to get your "snowshoe legs." They're also good for families. Many are, simply, beautiful walks in the woods. To make them more challenging, you can always head off trail. Typically, elevation gain or loss is slight.

Moderate trails generally require a bit more climbing. They may be somewhat steep and narrow in places, with some lengthy but gradual uphill slopes. They may have some of the features of a difficult trail, but the moderate trail is often shorter, with less up-and-down and a lower elevation gain. Some previous snowshoe experience is useful, as is a good level of cardiovascular fitness.

Difficult trails usually feature a climb to a ridge top. Often, the path is narrow and steep. You may be required to take off your snowshoes and crawl up a difficult segment of the trail. These are among the longer hikes, with higher total elevation gain. Good experience and familiarity with snowshoeing is essential, and a good, up-to-date map is a must. Some winter survival skills are a plus.

Backcountry routes follow topography rather than trails or roads, so skill with a map and compass is essential. You may encounter a variety of conditions along backcountry routes, including steep elevation gains and losses. Injuries, a sudden storm, and getting lost are all possibilities, so bring safety gear that will enable you to survive outdoors for one night (see "The Ten Essentials"). You may not be comfortable, but you will survive. Bill Forrest advises bringing the following extra gear (about two pounds' worth) when heading into the backcountry: a firestarting kit; a small pot with packets of soup, oatmeal, and a spoon; a lightweight plastic survival shelter or space blanket; extra food; and spare, dry clothing. He also recommends adding these items to your pack: a waterproof stuff sack with spare clothing, food, water, and TP; a compass and topo map of the area; a first-aid kit, headlamp, pocket knife, repair kit (duct tape, baling wire), small pliers, anti-fog solution, sunscreen, sunglasses, and a whistle.

Round Trip. These distances are not absolute. In some cases, you'll be going off trail to avoid wet or marshy areas, or areas where snow cover isn't so great. Use the round trip figures for total distance as an estimate only.

Hiking Time. We all move at different speeds. If you normally cover 3 miles per hour when you hike through the mountains in summer, you will generally cover the same terrain on snowshoes at 2 miles per hour, depending upon weather and snow conditions. If the trail is well packed, you may come close to your normal summer hiking speed. If you spend an hour breaking trail through deep powder or climbing a steep hill, you may not even travel 1 mile! Most people find that they move 30 to 50 percent slower in snow than they do on a bare trail. That slower rate, combined with short winter days, means you should plan to do fewer miles in winter than in summer or fall. Cut your mileage in half, to be on the safe side.

Elevation Gain. This is the total elevation gain from the trail's start to its high point.

High Point. This is the elevation at the highest point on the route.

Maps. The map illustrations in this book are not designed for route finding, but as locator maps, so you can find the route on a good topographic map. At the beginning of each hike description, we've recommended USGS topos and other maps we found useful. In some cases, the map supplied by the state park or reservation is perfectly fine and up-to-date, especially when the trails are easy, well marked, and used by cross-country skiers and others.

Sun-dappled woodlands after a snowfall

However, you can't count on getting a map once you get to a park. Supplies do run out. You may be able to print out a map online, from the state park website. Even so, it's always a good idea to back up the park's map with a second one, from a commercial source. The Appalachian Mountain Club, Green Mountain Club, and DeLorme all make good maps of key recreation areas and parks covered in this book.

Information. We've listed local contacts here, along with websites, so you can read more about the trails and facilities at each location. Call ahead to ask about trail conditions (type and amount of snow), driving conditions, and whether lakes are frozen enough to safely walk on, if appropriate.

Getting there. Wherever you're coming from, our directions will get you from a major state highway or Interstate to the nearest town, so you can extrapolate from there. A good road atlas is a necessity in New England, and the DeLorme state atlases are among the best and most detailed. And you can always ask a friendly local or knowledgeable innkeeper to point you in the right direction.

SAFETY

Although many people like the peacefulness and escape-from-the-crowds aspect of snowshoeing, it's always a good idea to snowshoe with a friend or partner. What if you slipped and broke an ankle? It happens. Don't think your cell phone will save you—the White Mountain National Forest is full of stories of people who ran out of daylight without adequate food and water, and later paid thousands of dollars to cover the cost of rescue efforts. And this is a happy ending!

Please, please don't take chances. Give yourself ample daylight, keeping in mind that darkness falls very early in the Northeast in winter. Before you leave the trailhead, decide on a turnaround time and stick to it. Pick a time that will get you back to the trailhead well before dark, and keep an eye on your wristwatch. Don't take on a hill you can't handle. If it becomes harder than you expected and you can't hike it without gasping for breath, turn back. This is supposed to be about fun, not misery! Likewise, if conditions change quickly   and they do in New England, particularly in the mountains—turn back. Do not try to out-run a storm. White-out conditions can be deadly. Don't risk it; the mountain will still be there on another day. Head in, have a bowl of chowder, and plan your next adventure.

And, although it sounds like a no-brainer, bring maps. Outdoor divas that we think we are, we've been lost on trails close to home, trails we've hiked in summer and thought we knew well, because we went out map-less. Think you can't possibly *miss* a mountain? Believe us, you can! Without a well-worn trail to follow, and blazes that have vanished under snowfall, you really are flying blind on snowshoes. Those landmarks you count on in summer, like the nice pile of cairns or the bronze plaque that marks Hermits Cave or some other can't-miss natural feature, are likely hidden under the snow. Don't assume that another snowshoe hiker will have been there first, blazed the trail for you and left some tracks, or that you can always follow your own tracks back out. We're constantly astonished to find that the most popular, most heavily used trails in summer and fall are virtual ghost towns after the snow flies. Consider bringing a global positioning system (GPS) device and a compass to help better navigate remote and wooded areas—provided, of course, you know how to use them.

Avalanche Safety

And, need we say this? Backcountry snowshoeing can be dangerous due to the potential for avalanche conditions. Avalanche hazard is greatest during the first 24 to 48 hours after snow has fallen, says Bill Forrest of MSR. "At this time, the snow has not yet consolidated, and is most prone to shifting and sliding," he explains. Snowshoeing is also more difficult right after a snowstorm. The snow has not yet settled, so you will sink more deeply than on older snow. Generally, the centers of broad valleys, stands of old-growth timber, and ridges are avalanche-free, Forrest says, but any slope that is greater than 15 degrees could pose an avalanche hazard. If you've never done any winter mountaineering, we recommend a course run by the Appalachian Mountain Club (AMC). They offer a spectrum of winter outdoors classes including snow shelter building, winter camping, and avalanche safety. Read more at *www.outdoors.org*, or contact your local chapter.

Safety on Ice

One of the joys of snowshoeing is walking on water—hiking across a lake or pond, or around a shoreline, to explore. Use caution here. Each winter, New England newspapers are full of sad tales of ice-related mishaps, some fatal. The safest months to trek across the ice are January and February, generally speaking, but a "January thaw" of fifty-degree temps can make even that a dicey proposition.

The experts recommend waiting to walk on ice until it is at least two inches thick (four inches is better). Snowy ice is less sturdy than clear, hard ice. Stay away from icy rivers. Be cautious while crossing ice near lake and pond inlets and outlets, mouths of tributary streams, bridges, islands, points of land, and over springs; current typically causes ice to be thinner around these areas. Beware of currents and weak ice under lake bridges, too. Stay off the ice if it has melted away from shore; this is a sign that melting is underway, and ice can shift position as wind direction changes.

If you're heading out for a walk along a lake or pond, confirm ice thickness and safety with the local Fish and Wildlife Department, a park ranger, or the folks at a local bait shop (since this is a big issue for ice-fishing enthusiasts).

What to Do If You're Lost in the Woods

Everyone gets lost occasionally. Even the most experienced snowshoe hiker can miss a trail intersection, or look for a landmark, such as a brook crossing,

For safety's sake, check the edges of lakes and ponds for ice melt before you venture onto the water.

that has disappeared under the cloak of winter. Signs fall off trees, and blazes painted on rocks are obliterated by white stuff in winter. And that lovely directional signal that every hiker counts on in summertime—the path made by other people's feet—is gone, gone when the snow flies! Snowshoe hikers often have to be good sleuths when it comes to finding and following a trail.

So, if you're lost, don't panic—this usually isn't as dire as it seems, even if you're out in the middle of nowhere-land. Here's some advice from the Appalachian Mountain Club (AMC). The first thing to do is to stop. Go back over your route slowly, leaving markers as you go, until you find a sure indication of the trail. That should reveal where you made your mistake. If, after a hard look, you still can't find the trail, do one of two things. If you are on a mountain, you can usually reach the road in a few hours or less by simply going downhill until you reach a brook or stream. Then, follow it downward. If you are hiking in a wooded, flat area, take a compass bearing and follow it until you reach a road. If you know your general position on a map, the decision of which direction to travel will be easier.

Hiking with a group? Take pains to stay within sight of the next person. If you get too spread out, the odds are that someone will take a wrong turn. Always make sure the slowest hiker in the group has a buddy, so he or she doesn't lag behind. If you're separated from the pack, stay in one place. Signal your location by blowing your whistle three times, periodically, or shouting three times in a row, as often as necessary.

A NOTE ABOUT SAFETY

Safety is an important concern in all outdoor activities. No guidebook can alert you to every hazard or anticipate the limitations of every reader. Therefore, the descriptions of roads, trails, routes, and natural features in this book are not representations that a particular place or excursion will be safe for your party. When you follow any of the routes described in this book, you assume responsibility for your own safety. Under normal conditions, such excursions require the usual attention to traffic, road and trail conditions, weather, terrain, the capabilities of your party, and other factors. Keeping informed on current conditions and exercising common sense are the keys to a safe, enjoyable outing.

—*The Mountaineers Books*

Views from atop Peaked Mountain

NEW HAMPSHIRE

SOUTHERN, SEACOAST, AND LAKES REGION

-- 1 --
Great Bay National Wildlife Refuge

Rating: Easy
Round trip: 2 miles
Hiking time: 1 hour
Elevation gain: 100 feet
High point: 100 feet
Map: Great Bay National Wildlife Refuge map
Information: U.S. Fish and Wildlife Service, Great Bay National Wildlife Refuge, 100 Merrimac Drive, Newington, NH 03801; 603-431-7511; *www.northeast.fws.gov/nh/gtb*

Getting there: From Portsmouth, take the Spaulding Turnpike (Route 16) west to exit 1 and follow signs to the Pease International Tradeport. Take a right onto Arboretum Drive; follow refuge signs for 3 miles to refuge parking lot, office, and trails.

This is one of our favorite, easy-to-do walks in New Hampshire's seacoast area. This local gem, one of more than 580 national wildlife refuges across the country, protects more than 1000 acres and 6.5 miles of shoreline along the picturesque Great Bay in Newington. Keep your eyes cast in the tall pines or

Shoreline overlooking Great Bay

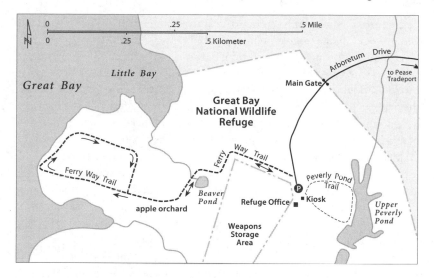

overhead for bald eagles; the refuge is the wintering habitat for bald eagles, as well as a variety of migratory birds. Many state-protected species use the refuge, including common loon, pied-billed grebe, osprey, common tern, northern harrier, and upland sandpiper. Wildlife is plentiful, too. On our snowshoe hikes, we've seen wild turkey, white-tailed deer, and red fox. The refuge also serves as New Hampshire's major wintering habitat for black ducks. It's always a treat to catch a glimpse of wildlife in natural settings and habitats. But we enjoy our hikes at the refuge as much for the serene and scenic setting.

The refuge features two main snowshoeing trails. A shorter, half-mile trail meanders gently through woods to picture-perfect Upper Peverly Pond. We especially like this easygoing route after a soft snowstorm, when the trees are draped in a white blanket and the woods cloaked in winter silence. The longer Ferry Way Trail, however, is our favorite. The 2-mile trail takes about an hour to snowshoe and travels through woods, along intertidal mud flats, frozen ponds and bogs, and out to the open waters of Great Bay.

The trail begins as a wide path, along a very ugly fence, remnants of the military weapons storage area that was once housed here. Don't let this deter you; the trail quickly enters a forest of mixed hardwoods and evergreens. The velvety, burnt-red tops of wintering sumac and the chalky trunks of white birch trees stand out against snow-covered grounds and blue skies. The trail follows an abandoned dirt road and passes by a beaver pond; dead trunks and snags stick out of the frozen bog like ancient grave markers. Thick fuzz graces the tops of the dormant cattails that surround the bog. You'll pass a wooden footpath leading to an open meadow; here, you could snowshoe across the meadow to the shores of Great Bay or continue on the path. Either way, you'll end up covering the same ground; the path is a two-way loop.

Continue through the woods to an old apple orchard, a grouping of winter skeletons with twisty branches reaching out and up to the sky. To your right is a bench overlooking the open meadow, a peaceful place to stop for a rest. Across the field, through a break in the woods, you'll have a glimpse of Little Bay.

Continue on the path, lined with tall, shagbark hickories and the remains of a lichen-covered stone wall, until you reach the small viewing deck overlooking Great Bay. This is a great spot to linger, breathe in the briny smell of the sea, and poke around the driftwood and shell-strewn shoreline. Directly across the bay, you'll see the Jackson Estuarine Research Laboratory at Adams Point. Long-needled red pines dot the woods, often casting eerie shadows on the shoreline path. Walk the shoreline for a short distance, with sweeping views of Great Bay, before heading back into the woods.

Circling back toward the refuge headquarters at the trailhead, you'll snowshoe through sparse woods showcasing the straight trunks of white birch and red pines. The path passes through a pretty salt marsh, then traverses the open field. You'll get one more glimpse of the beaver pond before backtracking your way to the trailhead parking lot.

The refuge office is open Monday through Friday, 8:00AM–4:30PM. Trails are open year-round, dawn to dusk. Note: No pets are allowed at the refuge.

--2--
Adams Point

Rating:	Easy
Round trip:	1.3 miles
Hiking time:	1 hour
Elevation gain:	300 feet
High point:	300 feet
Map:	Great Bay National Estuarine Research Reserve map
Information:	Great Bay National Estuarine Research Reserve, New Hampshire Fish and Game Department, Marine Fisheries Division, 225 Main Street, Durham, NH 03824; 603-868-1095

Getting there: In Durham, take Route 108 south to Durham Point Road. Follow Durham Point Road 3.7 miles to the Jackson Estuarine Research Laboratory sign on the left. Turn left on Adams Point Road and follow it to the end.

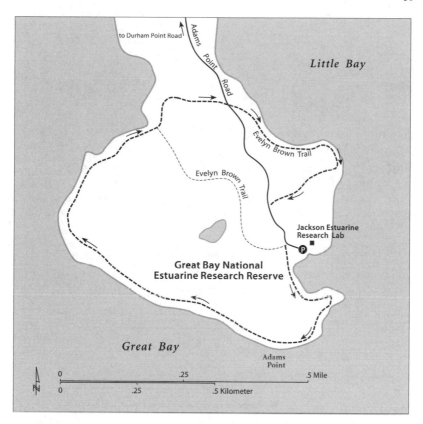

The lusty, briny smell of the sea, the sounds of honking geese, the sight of a soaring eagle, and stunning water views may greet you on this wintry walk along spectacular Great Bay. There are a couple of narrow, steep spots along the water's edge, but generally this is a short, easy hike, perfect for young and old.

Adams Point is a jutting peninsula on Great Bay, where freshwater rivers and ocean tides converge in a picturesque, pristine basin. The 80-acre site divides Little Bay to the north and Great Bay to the south. Much of the surrounding land is protected as part of the Great Bay National Estuarine Research Reserve, including about 4500 acres of tidal waters and wetlands and 3000 acres of coastal land. The estuary is refuge for twenty-three species of threatened or endangered animals and plants, including the common tern and osprey. The refuge also supports a winter population of about a dozen bald eagles. There's an eagle-watching platform at Adams Point; if you're lucky, you may catch a glimpse of one of these magnificent birds of prey as you snowshoe along the trail.

Rocky shoreline along Little Bay

The trailhead begins across the road from the Jackson Estuarine Research Laboratory, built in 1970 as a field station for scientists at the University of New Hampshire. Here you can pick up a brochure and map detailing significant sites and historic spots along the self-guided interpretive trail. You'll have two choices: you can head right across the field, following the Evelyn Brown Trail, or you can turn left and head out to the waters of Great Bay; this is the longer route and the one we always take because it provides the best water views. The trails converge and end up following the same route along Little Bay.

You'll walk a short distance through an open field, skirting the water's edge, to a high point overlooking Great Bay. Two benches beckon hikers to stop for a rest and take in the rocky shoreline and open water views. This is a favorite spot for geese and ducks to congregate, feeding in the shallow, nutrient-rich waters. The trail continues to skirt Great Bay; there are several places where you can venture down the hill, climbing over snow-covered rocks to reach the driftwood-strewn shoreline. You're likely to see oyster and horseshoe crab shells that have washed up to shore. The estuary is also home to softshell clams, green crabs, lobster, herring, eel, smelt, and flounder. Scientists have uncovered evidence suggesting that native Americans once fished the abundant waters off Adams Point; one recently excavated site reveals that the area was used as a base camp between A.D. 650 and 800.

Follow the shoreline trail as it loops around Great Bay and intersects with the Evelyn Brown Trail. You can turn right here and head across the field, back to the parking area. Along the way, you'll see a tall obelisk that marks the tomb of the Adams family, former residents of Adams Point. John Adams, of the same family that boasts two U.S. presidents, held popular Methodist revival meetings at his homestead on Adams Point.

Or continue along the trail as it enters the woods, then skirts an open salt marsh. The trail meanders a flat section through sparse woods, of young oak, birch, shagbark hickory, and poplar trees. You'll cross Adams Point Road, then loop around the shoreline of Little Bay. Is it low tide? If so, you'll get a peek at the rocky shingle beach. The trail drops you back on the access road, a short distance from the parking area.

--⟩--
Odiorne Point State Park

Rating: Easy
Round trip: 3.25 miles
Hiking time: 2 hours
Elevation gain: 20 feet
High point: 20 feet
Map: Odiorne Point State Park map
Information: Odiorne Point State Park, Route 1A, Rye, NH 03870; 603-436-7406; *www.nhstateparks.org*

Getting there: Take I-95 in New Hampshire to the Portsmouth Traffic Circle (exit 5). Take first exit off the circle to Route 1 south. Take a left onto 1A south at the traffic lights at Elwyn Road. Follow Route 1A south for about 5 miles; Odiorne Point State Park will be on the left.

Odiorne Point State Park in Rye, between Portsmouth and Rye Beach on New Hampshire's sliver of coastline, is a perfect place to be after fresh snow falls on the southern seacoast. (Get there quickly, because the snow never lasts long along the shore!) A network of walking paths skirt the scenic shoreline, wind through upland forests and meadows, and twist around freshwater and saltwater marshes and a pond. This is a great snowshoe hike for families, with added bonuses: tidepooling at the park is fantastic, and the on-site Science Center (with special programs, exhibits, and touch tanks) is open year-round.

The pristine, 300-acre park was once the site of a well-to-do summer colony and resort hotel. Today, it is the largest undeveloped stretch of shore on New Hampshire's 18-mile coast and home to a variety of habitats. Standing on the rocky shoreline, you'll face the edge of the Gulf of Maine and the mouth of the Piscataqua River. The Gulf of Maine is a semi-enclosed sea bounded to the south and east by tall underwater banks of land that form a barrier to the North Atlantic. It is said to be one of the world's most biologically productive

environments, home to more than 300 animals and thousands of invertebrate
and plant species. With a little patience and a keen eye, we've been able to
spot a number of these fascinating sea creatures in the Odiorne tide pools. On
clear days, you'll get a glimpse of the Isles of Shoals in the distance and sweeping views of the Atlantic Ocean. And, at low tide, the rock-lined puddles and
pools teem with sea life.

At the parking lot, look for the Odiorne Point trailhead which begins to
your right, as you look to the ocean. Follow the path through open fields to the
coast, where you'll have splendid views of the rocky shoreline. If you're lucky,
your snowy hike will coincide with low tide—perfect for exploring the pockets
of seawater and deep pools surrounded by weather-worn rocks. You're likely
to notice the mussels and barnacles first. You might also spot limpets (they
look like small Oriental straw hats) and periwinkles hugging the side of the
rocks, and bug-like amphipods skidding about in the water. The tide pools are
like magic pictures; the more you stare into them, the more you'll see!

Take your time along the coast, then follow the footpath around the
point, along the shoreline—with open ocean views—to the Seacoast Science

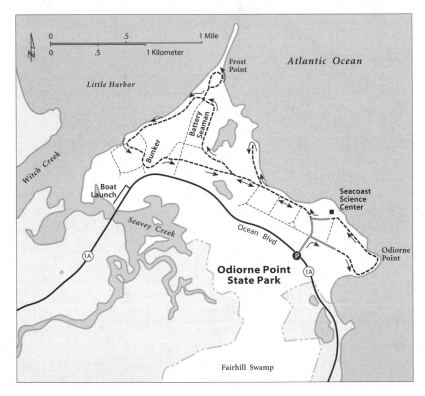

Center. If you like, stop in here to warm up. Admission is charged for entry into the museum exhibit area (well worth it, especially if you have kids in tow), but you'll also find a small (and heated) lobby area, gift shop, and restrooms.

Continue on the path that now leads north along the rocky shoreline, then across an open field following the Battery Seaman Loop trail. You'll have views of two freshwater ponds. Take the side path that enters to your right, leading to Frost Point, overlooking Little Harbor. Stay to your right as you loop around, following the coast. Turn left at the next junction and walk to the historic World War II bunker site. Loop around the bunker and head back across the field, back to the parking lot.

Of course, you might want to take another stroll out to the ocean for one more look into those magical tide pools.

--4--
Bear Brook State Park

Rating: Easy/more difficult
Round trip: 2.5 miles
Hiking time: 2 hours
Elevation gain: 0
High point: 200 feet
Map: Trail Guide for Bear Brook State Park, New Hampshire Division of Parks and Recreation
Information: Bear Brook State Park, 157 Deerfield Road, Allenstown, NH 03275; 603-485-9874; *www.nhparks.state.nh/us /ParkPages*

Getting there: Take I-93 to exit 9N (Hooksett). Follow Route 28 north for 11 miles to Deerfield Road. The park tollbooth is 1 mile down. Winter parking area is 2 miles beyond the tollbooth, off Podunk Road.

This is New Hampshire's largest developed state park and one of the best for snowshoeing. The park encompasses more than 10,000 acres, including marshes, bogs, mountain summits, and ponds, and a spider web of trails—more than 40 miles in all. You'll find something to suit all ages, abilities, and energy levels. We've spent several winter days exploring the trails that crisscross the forest, fields, and slopes of this southern New Hampshire preserve, and still haven't seen it all. It's heavily used in summer; there's hiking, biking, swimming, fishing, camping, a twenty-station fitness course, archery range, and a small museum

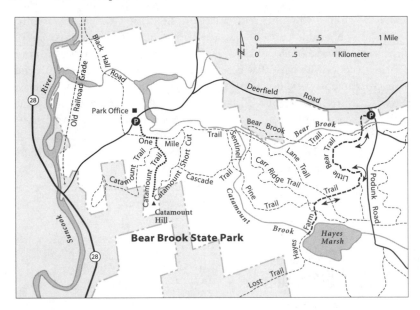

complex. While Bear Brook State Park slows down when the mercury drops and the snow flies, it still gets a fair amount of use from cross-country skiers, snowshoers, snowmobilers, and hard-core (read: crazy!) mountain bikers. The park campground closes in mid-October, but if you'd like to spend a few days exploring the park, check out nearby Circle 9 Ranch. The 125-site campground stays open all winter, offering entertainment and heated bathrooms.

Note of caution: It is really, really easy to get lost in this park; we've done it several times. Trails go here and there and everywhere, and after a while it can all look the same. Be sure to pick up a trail map at the park tollbooth when you come in. Study it and pay extra attention to landmarks, turns, and directions along the way. It's not likely to be dangerous; there are often people around to lead you in the right direction, but you could end up on a much longer hike than you anticipated.

Little Bear Trail is a popular winter jaunt, a gentle up-and-down hike leading through snow-covered woods. The trail roughly parallels Podunk Road (popular with snowmobilers). You can connect with three other short trails to visit Hayes Marsh, a pretty site, especially in winter when the grasses are ice-tipped and glistening in the sun.

Park your car in the winter lot, off Podunk Road, and walk back up the road and look for the Bear Brook Trail on your left. Follow the Bear Brook Trail for about 0.5 mile to connect with the Little Bear Trail. You'll follow Little Bear as it weaves through the woods. In about a mile, you'll reach the junction with the Hayes Farm Trail; take this to your right. Continue on Hayes Farm Trail, past three trail junctions: first the Lane Trail, then the Sentinel Pine Trail, and the Carr Ridge Trail.

Within a few yards past the Carr Ridge Trail junction, you'll reach the edge of Hayes Marsh. The marsh is a summer hangout for beavers, muskrats, and great blue herons. Quiet and serene in the winter, the marsh is a nice place to linger. Then backtrack on the Hayes Farm Trail to Little Bear, and out to the parking area.

Looking for a more strenuous hike, with a bit of altitude? Try the Catamount Hill Trail. Park at the office near the tollbooth and head to the One-Mile Trail, which is accessed from a small connecting trail located next to the toll booth. Follow One-Mile Trail for about 0.5 mile before reaching Catamount Trail. Follow the trail to the left and climb (steeply in spots) 0.5 mile to the top of 721-foot Catamount Hill. You'll have some open views from the summit and bare ledge.

Little Bear Trail, Bear Brook State Park

-- 5 --
Norsk Center/Low Plain Wildlife Area

Rating: Easy
Round trip: 5.4 miles
Hiking time: 4 hours
Elevation gain: 490 feet
High point: 1250 feet
Maps: Norsk Cross-Country Ski Trail Map and Trail Map; Esther Currier Wildlife Management Area at Low Plain, Conservation Commission, Town of New London

Information: Norsk Cross-Country Ski Center, Country Club Lane, New London, NH 03257; 603-526-4685 or 800-426-6775; *www.skinorsk.com* and Esther Currier Wildlife Management Area at Low Plain, Conservation Commission, Town of New London, P.O. Box 240, 375 Main Street, New London, NH 03257; 603-526-4821; *www.nl-nh.com*

Getting there: Take I-89 to exit 11, New London. Head east on Route 11 for about 2 miles to Country Club Lane. Take a right at the light, and Norsk will be 0.5 mile in front of you. To reach the Esther Currier Wildlife Management Area, continue east on Route 11 a mile or so, to the parking area on the right.

There are several reasons why we're including this well-established cross-country center in New Hampshire's mid-state region. The setting is gorgeous:

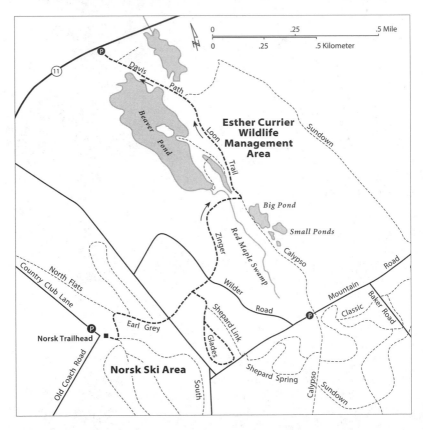

forty-eight trails spread across the rolling hills and open fields of the Lake Sunapee Country Club. The 47 miles of groomed and ungroomed trails, in the shadows of 2937-foot Mount Kearsage, lead to ponds and marshes, wild-life areas and preserves. Also, when other parts of the region may be receiving early- and late-season sleet and rain, odds are that this area is getting snow. If you have a cross-country skier in your group, this is a great place to spend the day. It's also a good place for folks to try snowshoeing. The center rents snowshoes, and several trails are easygoing enough for beginners. An added benefit is that snowshoers (and skiers who appreciate ungroomed terrain) can hike to the Esther Currier Wildlife Management Area at Low Plain, where they'll find a spiderweb of trails around a large, active beaver pond and low-land marshes.

Stop by the ski shop to pick up maps and to chat with the owners about trails. You'll have plenty to choose from, but the following 5.4-mile, up-and-back hike is one of our favorites.

Heading out of the shop, you'll pass the country club, with its pretty gran-ite steps and walls and an old, beautifully shaped sugar maple. Pick up the Earl Grey Trail, crossing an open field, where you'll have expansive valley and mountain views. In an easy third-of-a-mile, you'll see the intersection for the Glades Trail. This 0.5-mile loop leads through a pretty forest of white and yel-low pine trees and chalky-white birches.

After completing the side loop (it's worth it), take the Zinger Trail head-ing toward the Low Plain Wildlife Area. The narrow, ungroomed path climbs gradually, crossing Wilder Road, and heading back into the woods. Follow this a half mile and then turn left onto the Loon Trail heading northwest toward the wildlife area. This soon turns into Davis Path.

This is a great place to explore. Pick a spot and head left into the frozen swamps, bogs, and marshlands. Short paths also lead to observation blinds, overlooking the beaver pond. Along the way, there are several places to get off the main path and travel the shoreline of the pond. Of course, use caution (see Introduction for general safety rules) as there could be some seeps along the shore where one could break through the ice. On the north end of the pond, you'll find a small overlook; grab a seat on the bench and enjoy the view. Dead tree trunks and snags stand like soldiers in the frozen pond, casting eerie shad-ows in the midday sunlight.

If you continue northwest on the Davis Path, you'll reach an informa-tion kiosk (with interpretive trail maps) and the wildlife parking area, off Route 11. Tip: If you'd like to snowshoe around the wildlife area only (and not on any of the Norsk Center trails), you can park here, off Route 11, and save yourself trail fees.

--6--

Mount Monadnock

Rating: More difficult
Round trip: 4.2 miles
Hiking time: 4 hours
Elevation gain: 1800 feet
High point: 3165 feet
Map: Monadnock State Park Hiking Trails, New Hampshire Division of Parks and Recreation
Information: Monadnock State Park, Route 124, Jaffrey, NH 03452; 603-271-3556; or New Hampshire Division of Parks and Recreation; 603-532-8862; *www.nhparks.state .nh.us/ParksPages*

Getting there: From Jaffrey, travel 4 miles west on Route 124. The park is located off the north side of Route 124. Turn on Dublin Road and follow park signs. The park is about 2 miles from the highway along Dublin Road.

It's almost the law in New England: at some point in time, you must hike Mount Monadnock. In fact, Monadnock is said to be the second most frequently hiked mountain in the world, after Japan's Mount Fiji. What's the draw? This barren peak in southern New Hampshire may not be as lofty as others farther north, but the views from its top are nothing short of stunning. Hit this peak on a clear day, and you'll have jaw-dropping views into all six New England states. Some are convinced that you can even see into New York.

Of course, Monadnock's popularity leads to a near carnival-like atmosphere in the summer and fall months. That's why we don't even go near it until the snow begins to fly. It's not an easy hike. The White Cross Trail to the summit makes a near straight shot up the mountain, a steady, unrelenting pull that's guaranteed to get your heart pumping and adrenaline flowing. In some ways, a winter snowshoe trek up Monadnock is easier than its summer counterpart. The trail in summer can be a rock-and-root-strewn menace, a twisted ankle waiting to happen. A good snow cover can smooth out the ruts and cover the rocks. But—and it's a big but—the top stretches can get pretty icy. Ask about snow conditions. You can consult with a staff person, usually available on weekends throughout the winter or call the state park office. Better yet, chat with other hikers, especially the die-hard campers, who pitch a tent at the on-site campground (open year-round) and spend the days hiking,

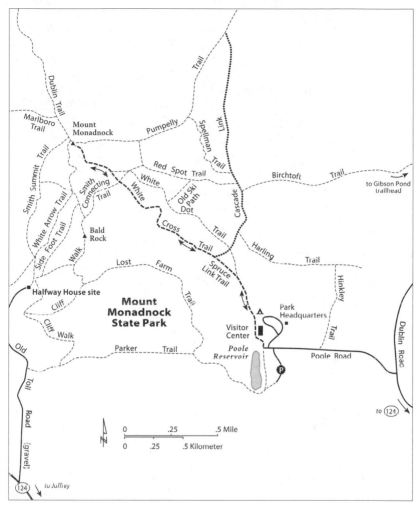

climbing, skiing, and generally honing their outdoor skills. Not a bad way to go. Bring your camping gear, pick the best day to hike Monadnock, and spend the rest of the time hiking some of the more than 40 miles of trails that criss-cross through the park.

Monadnock State Park covers 5000 acres of protected land. The word, now a standard geological term for any singular mountain, came from the Abenaki Native American word for "mountain that stands alone." Indeed, Mount Monadnock, rising 3165 feet, is the lone peak in an expansive forest.

Begin near the visitor center, where you'll pick up the Spruce Link Trail. The trail starts to climb almost immediately, gaining 500 feet or so in elevation in the first 0.6 mile before it veers to the left. Keep to the right on the now-combined White Cross/White Dot Trail. You'll pass a spur path on your right leading to Falcon Spring and a major junction with the Cascade Link Trail. Stay to the left and follow the White Cross Trail, marked (surprise!) with a white cross. There is little rest for the weary on this trail. You'll continue at a steady rise, climbing up the southeast slope of the mountain, past the Smith Connecting Trail, and on to the upper junction with the White Dot Trail at 1.8 miles. You're almost there! But the most challenging, the final pull up the cone, is steep and tough. "Are you sure you read the map right? It's got to be more than a third of a mile!" is our standard joke when we reach this point.

The final 0.3 mile is a scramble and can be dangerous in icy conditions. Watch your step and, as always, be prepared to turn around if bad weather—especially high wind—kicks up. But if it's clear, keep going. The final thigh-burning climb over the bare and exposed rock faces is worth it. Grab a seat and take a look: Mount Ascutney, Mount Sunapee, Mount Greylock, Mount Wachusett, Boston, the Whites...a 360-degree postcard-pretty view.

--7--

Hamlin Recreation and Conservation Area

Rating:	Easy to more difficult
Round trip:	5.5 miles
Hiking time:	5 hours
Elevation gain:	300 feet
High point:	900 feet
Map:	Town of Meredith, Hamlin Recreation and Conservation Area base map
Information:	Town of Meredith Conservation Commission Steward, Town Hall, 41 Main Street, Meredith, NH 03253; 603-279-4538; *www.meredithnh.org*

Getting there: From Route 104 in Meredith, head out of town, south toward Hampton. Turn left onto Meredith Center Road, then right on Chemung Road. From here, follow the signs to the Hamlin area parking lot.

Psst . . . Looking for the perfect day hike? The Hamlin Recreation and Conservation Area, a little-known gem tucked in the Hampshire Lakes Region, offers three diverse trails, meandering through hemlock and hardwood forests, around ponds and beaver-made meadows, and up to open ledges with mountain and lake vistas. Depending on the energy and skill levels in your group, you can pick the short route, longer, or longest, ranging from 1.6 miles to 5.5 miles. The short Four

Ponds Loop Trail covers 1.6 miles and is perfect for those short on time or energy. The flat trail, the easiest in the preserve, skirts a beaver pond and small brook with pleasant views along the way. The 2.7-mile Crocketts Ledge Loop Trail, blazed in yellow, climbs to a lofty overlook. The Lakes to Ledges Loop Trail, our favorite in the preserve, combines Crocketts Ledge with an upper trail, adding an additional 2.3 miles for a total of 5.5 miles round trip. The extra miles are well worth the effort—you'll be rewarded with sweeping views of several of New Hampshire's major mountain ranges, before descending to the shoreline of Lake Wicwas.

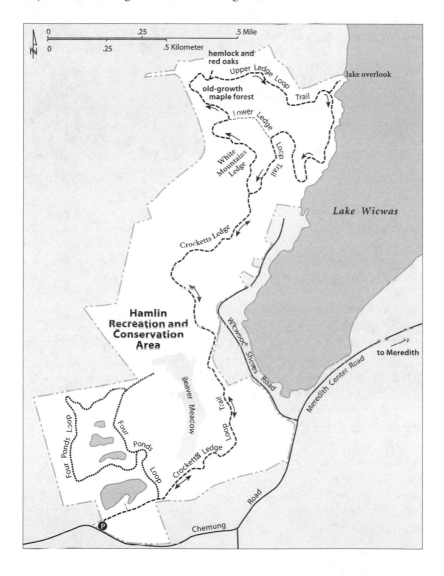

Woods, water, and views at the Hamlin Recreation and Conservation Area

The trails all begin at a small parking lot; you can pick up a map of the conservation area with trail descriptions at the small kiosk, at the base of the parking lot.

The Crocketts Ledge Loop Trail meanders around a small beaver pond and open meadow, before entering sparse woods dotted with large glacier-dropped boulders. You'll wind around the boulders, following a gentle, up-and-down path. About a half a mile in, you'll see an attractive, old stone wall lining both sides of the trail. Look for remnants of the mid-1800s Stanton cemetery around the next bend. The Crocketts Ledge Loop Trail continues to climb gently through a large clearing, overlooking an open beaver meadow, before descending into sparse, light-filtered woods and ending on a wide logging road. You'll walk the wide path for a short distance. You do not want to follow this to the end of the road; instead, look for the trail sign and large paint blotch that marks the trail, heading into the woods on your left.

From here, the trail begins to climb more steeply, heading north about 1.3 miles to Crocketts Ledge. The view from the ledges, of Lake Wicwas and Lake Winnisquam and the Gunstock-Belknap Mountain Range in the distance, demands that you stay awhile. Grab a seat on the rocks and enjoy your bird's-eye view. When you're rested, it's time to take in the rest of this lakes-to-mountains hike.

The trail descends from the ledges, then meets up with the Upper and Lower Ledge Loops. We like the Upper Ledge way, heading northwest (left). The next part of the trail is our favorite—a short, steep climb to open ledges with far-reaching views. You'll want to step slowly through here, stopping several times along the way; it's tough to walk and gawk at the same time. From the ledges, you'll see the Waterville and Sandwich Mountains. Look to the left for a glimpse at the high peaks of the Franconia Ridge.

The trail splits again when it meets the Lower Ledge Loop. Head left, to the west, and enter an old maple grove. A short spur path leads to an ancient red oak, the largest on the preserve. The going gets easy from here, as you descend to the Lake Wicwas shoreline (a marked side trail leads to a waterfront viewpoint). You'll snake along the shoreline, before heading back into the boulder-strewn forest (take a moment to appreciate the old growth hemlock grove). Retrace your steps across Crocketts Ledge and back to the parking area. And, tell only your best friends about this hidden gem.

-- 8 --
Mount Cardigan

Rating: More difficult
Round trip: 3 miles
Hiking time: 3 hours
Elevation gain: 1121 feet
High point: 3121 feet
Map: Mount Cardigan State Park, West Side Hiking Trails
Information: Cardigan State Park and Forest, off Route 118, Orange, NH 03741; 603-927-4096; *www.nhstateparks.org /ParksPages/Cardigan*

Getting there: Take I-93 to Route 104 west (exit 23, New Hampton). Follow Route 104 west, to Route 118 north. Follow signs to the park.

If you were a kid growing up in New Hampshire, it's likely you hiked this up-and-back route to the top of Mount Cardigan. This bare, fire-scourged mount in the Lakes Region is a magnet for school groups, hiking clubs, families—and just about anyone and everyone who wants quick gratification for minimal effort. The pain-to-gain ratio on this climb can't be beat! There are bigger, higher mountains to the north, but this peak boasts equally beautiful vistas. Of course, summer brings hordes, but winter—ahhh, winter—the crowds thin and the surrounding mountains, valleys, and forests take on a new look, covered in a blanket of white. One word of caution: The Mount Cardigan summit is completely exposed and though not super-high, it can be dangerous if high winds and storms move in. Check forecasts and conditions before you begin this hike, and stay alert to weather fronts that might be moving in.

Mount Cardigan sits in the 5000-acre Cardigan State Park. The park is open year-round, but there are few facilities. Most people come to hike the trails, then leave. There is no camping in the park, but if you'd like to stay longer to explore the park and surrounding Lakes Region area, consider a stay at the nearby Appalachian Mountain Club Cardigan Lodge. The former (and newly renovated) ski lodge has thirteen bunkrooms and two private rooms. It operates on a self-service basis during the winter months, which means you'll need to bring your own food, sleeping bags, and towels. Guests can use the kitchen facilities. The state park and West Ridge trailhead are nearby, but if you stay here you'll also have more than 50 miles of backcountry trails to explore on 1200 acres of AMC-owned woods bordering Cardigan State Park.

Several trails lead to the open summit of Mount Cardigan, but the easiest is the West Ridge Trail. Depending on winter weather conditions, the road to the trailhead parking lot may be open. If not, you'll need to walk a mile or so from the park entrance down the road to the West Ridge trailhead.

The trail starts out level, then loops to the right to begin the moderate climb up the west side of the mountain. You'll walk a relatively straight shot through dense forest. It's a steady grade, climbing about 100 feet every 0.4

Snow gathers on boulders along the West Ridge Trail, Mount Cardigan.

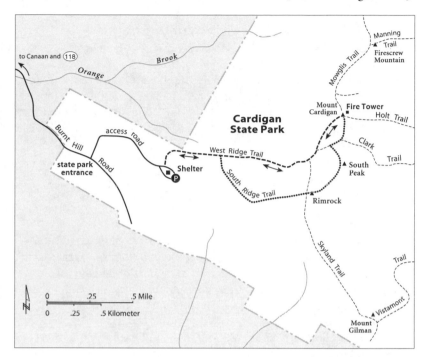

mile. In about 0.5 mile, you'll reach the junction with South Ridge Trail. Continuing on the West Ridge Trail, you'll work your way up the slope and look for a frozen waterfall, about 1 mile into the hike. Just past here, you'll break through the trees, and begin to climb the steeper, open ledges.

The last haul, about 0.5 mile, is the toughest, with steep pitches that can be slippery in the winter. You'll be glad you have crampons to help maneuver this final climb to the top. You'll be glad you toughed it out, too, when you see the expansive, eye popping views.

The summit fire tower was built in 1924, several years after an 1855 forest fire destroyed all the vegetation on Mount Cardigan's peak. Today, visitors to the bare summit have views of the White Mountains to the northeast, the Green Mountains of Vermont to the west, and Mount Monadnock to the southwest. Weather permitting, stay awhile and take it all in.

You can retrace your steps following the West Ridge Trail back to the parking lot. Or, follow signs to South Peak, heading southeast, then descend on the South Ridge Trail. You'll cross the junction with the Skyland Trail, then descend the ridgeline, meeting up with the West Ridge Trail about 0.4 mile from the parking lot. This alternate route down from the Mount Cardigan peak will add about 0.5 mile to the trip.

GUIDED HIKES IN NEW HAMPSHIRE

The following resorts, outfitters, and ski centers offer guided snowshoe hikes and special programs:

The **Appalachian Mountain Club Highland Center** in Crawford Notch (603-466-2727, *www.outdoors.org*) offers daily, step-on (no reservations necessary) guided hikes in the White Mountains, as well as backcountry techniques and skill-building programs, winter camping, and overnight winter hikes.

Take a guided nature walk through the woods at the **Gunstock Cross Country Ski and Snowshoe Center** (800-gunstock, *www.gunstock.com*). Tours—perfect for beginners—are offered Saturday mornings at 11:30. The ski resort also offers guided backcountry tours, ridgeline tours, and moonlight walks.

The **Mountain View Grand Resort and Spa** in Plainfield (603-837-2100, *www.mountainviewgrand.com*) offers guided walks on 400 acres of wilderness and through the adjacent White Mountain National Forest.

Outdoor Escapes (603-528-0136, *www.outdoorescapesnewhampshire.com*) offers guided animal tracking, orienteering, multi-day, and winter camping snowshoe trips.

The **EMS Climbing School** (800-310-4504, *www.emsclimb.com*) also offers snowshoe lessons, excursions, and programs for beginner through advanced hikers.

WHITE MOUNTAINS—
PINKHAM NOTCH/CRAWFORD NOTCH

--9--
Peaked Mountain

Rating:	Easy/moderate
Round trip:	4.2 miles
Hiking time:	4 hours
Elevation gain:	1189 feet
High point:	1739 feet
Map:	*AMC White Mountain Guide*, Map 5:I11
Information:	Green Hills Preserve/Northern NH Program, P.O. Box 310, 2760 White Mountain Highway, North Conway, NH 03860; 603-356-8833; log onto *www.nature.org* and search for "Green Hills Preserve"

Getting there: On NH Route 16, travel 0.5 mile south of North Conway village. Turn left onto Artist Falls Road. Go 0.3 mile and bear right onto Thompson Road. Drive 0.4 mile to the parking area for Pudding Pond and the Green Hills (just before the powerlines). Hike parallel to the powerlines for 0.2 mile until you reach an information kiosk.

If you're looking for a great family-friendly day hike and a chance to see lofty mountain views, check out the Peaked Mountain Trail. As day hikes go, this one is near perfect. It's close, off Route 16 just south of North Conway. It's short, 4.2 miles, up and back. And, the reward-to-effort ratio is delightfully disproportionate. The trail climbs gradually 1100 feet to the bare summit of Peaked Mountain for open views of mountains and valleys. On clear days, you might catch a glimpse of the top of Mount Washington.

Peaked Mountain, along with Middle Mountain, Black Cap, and Cranmore, are within the 5022-acre Green Hills Preserve, managed by The Nature Conservancy. A variety of well-marked and interconnected trails crisscross the forest and climb the major peaks.

The trail starts out easy on an old road, a broad snowy path leading through sparse woods. Pick a sunny day, and warm rays will filter through the open stands of red pines. Giant granite boulders, covered in moss and lichen,

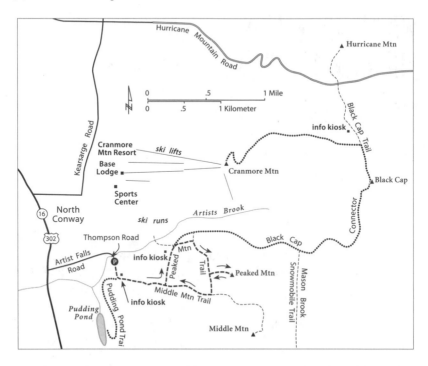

dot the woods. In minutes, you'll come to a narrow brook, cold, gurgling waters snaking through the woods. From here, the trail begins to ascend gently through the forest until it reaches the intersection with Pudding Pond Trail. The Pudding Pond Trail is a decent side trip, especially if you have young kids in tow. The easy, 2-mile walk leads to a pond with beaver dams and lodges. It's a favorite with local families seeking a bit of exercise and fresh air.

We nearly always make the short loop to Pudding Pond before continuing up Peaked Mountain. Look for a narrow, snowy path under the powerlines, next to a snow fence. Here, you'll enter the woods and begin the gradual ascent up to Peaked Mountain.

At 0.7 mile you'll come to the junction with Middle Mountain Trail. Middle Mountain Trail continues straight ahead; you'll turn left and follow the rolling terrain a half mile to an information kiosk. The Black Cap Connector Trail forges straight ahead, while the Peaked Mountain Trail heads to the right.

The climb becomes a bit steeper at this point, but you'll begin to get views to the west of the Presidential Mountain range. Climb further to open ledges and the summit of Peaked Mountain. Did you pack a lunch? This is the spot to stop for a snack, and rest on the snowy, sun-warmed granite slabs. (Be careful, as the granite can be icy and slippery in spots.) From the open ledges, you'll have views of a nearby ski hill, the Presidentials, the snow-dusted summit of Mount Washington, and the expansive White Mountain Valley in the distance.

In the summer, the open mountainside is carpeted with red-tinged blueberry bushes—a favorite with the local black bear population. In fact, Green Hills Preserve, rich in berries and nuts, is considered one of the top places in the East to view black bears—low-growing brush and sparse woods make it easier for folks like us to see the bears. Once, on a late summer hike, we sat at the top of Peaked Mountain. A hundred yards or so from us, a big black bear walked into the open meadow. We watched as it dug in the dirt and clawed at bushes and trees, looking for food. This bear was oblivious to us, intent on fattening up before the long winter rest. We watched for several minutes as it lumbered around the woods, then headed out of sight.

The bears, of course, are out of sight in the winter. But the season brings its own pleasures and opportunities. A little exercise, fresh air, and fine views . . . what more could we ask for in a day snowshoe hike? Try it out.

Views from atop Peaked Mountain

There are several other choices of good hikes in the Preserve. The Peaked Mountain Trail also connects with the Middle Mountain Trail. This 2-mile hike climbs 1200 feet to the summit, through steep, open forestland. There are several cascades along the way and the open summit has fine mountain views. The Black Cap Trail is an easy climb to the bare, 2000-foot summit of Black Cap, the highest peak in the Green Hills Preserve. The trail travels through old-growth spruce forest and hardwoods before reaching open ledges, with mountain and valley views. The Cranmore Trail to the summit of Cranmore Mountain leaves the Black Cap Trail, climbs over a steep knoll, and follows a ski area service road, before reaching the summit.

--*10*--
Mount Willard

Rating:	Easy to more difficult
Round trip:	3.2 miles
Hiking time:	2–3 hours
Elevation gain:	900 feet
High point:	2800 feet
Maps:	Crawford Notch State Park Hiking Trails and Summits, NH Division of Parks and Recreation; *AMC White Mountain Guide*, Map 2:G8
Information:	New Hampshire Division of Parks and Recreation Crawford Notch State Park, Route 302, Harts Location, NH 03812; 603-374-2272; *www.nhstateparks.org*; AMC Highland Center, Route 302, Bretton Woods, NH 03574; 603-466-2727; *www.outdoors.org*

Getting there: From points south, take I-93 north to Route 3 to Route 302 south. Trailhead parking is located at the Appalachian Mountain Club Crawford Depot information center or the Appalachian Mountain Club Highland House center, both on the west side of Route 302 in Crawford Notch.

This popular hike in Crawford Notch State Park offers top-of-the-ridge views of the notch and surrounding mountain ranges for minimal effort. Some consider it the "best little hike in the Whites." We won't argue. The path to open ledges is broad and easygoing, with gradual ascents and short distances. The trail is widely popular in the summer with day hikers and tourists; it's also within short walking distance from the Appalachian Mountain Club's new Highland House lodge and information center. Mount Willard is a frequent destination of Highland House guests and small-group guided tours. But, the good news is that come winter, much of the hiking horde has disappeared, leaving this lovely mountain trail to savvy winter walkers and snowshoers.

Stop in at the Highland House for a look around, updates on trail conditions, and prepared trail lunches and snacks. You'll find the staff knowledgeable and friendly and, if you like, you can hop on one of their guided snowshoe hikes, offered several times a day. In any case, don't miss a trek on this little gem of a trail—guided or not.

The trail begins at the historic Crawford Depot site, off Route 302. The AMC operates an information center at the site, with a small photo exhibit detailing some of the history of Crawford Notch. You can park at the Crawford Depot or the AMC Highland House.

During the summer, trains offering scenic trips through the Notch still stop at the depot. The construction of the railroad, in the mid-1800s, was considered an impressive accomplishment. The tracks ran from Portland, Maine, through the Notch to Fabyans Station, where Ethan Allen once operated a small inn. According to park statistics, the railroad tracks rise 1623 feet in elevation in the 30 miles between North Conway and Fabyans. There is an average rise of 116 feet per mile for the 9 miles between Bemis Station at the south end of the Notch and Crawford Depot. The Frankenstein trestle (you

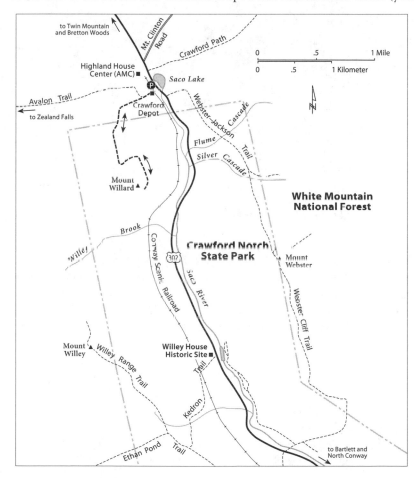

Frosty views along the Mount Willard trail.

can see this as you travel Route 302 through the Notch) is 80 feet high and 500 feet long; the Willey Brook Bridge is 100 feet high and 400 feet long.

From Crawford Depot, you'll cross over the tracks and begin a slow ascent through the woods. The trail follows an old carriage path for a short distance before reaching Centennial Pool about 0.5 from the trailhead. Take the short spur path overlooking the picturesque, snow-covered mountain pool, with bubbling cascades moving under thin sheets of ice and snow.

The main trail veers left and begins to climb at a slightly steeper, steady incline. At 1.5 miles, another side trail heads to the left; this short 0.2-mile path leads to a view of Hitchcock Flume.

Back on the main trail, you'll reach the open ledges of Mount Willard in no time (it's 0.1 mile from here). Get out your cameras; from the lofty perch, you'll be rewarded with grand views of Crawford Notch, and Mount Webster (3910 feet) and Mount Willey (4302 feet) to the south.

--11--
Mount Washington

Rating: Most difficult/backcountry
Round trip: 17 miles
Hiking time: 12 hours
Elevation gain: 4368 feet
High point: 6288 feet
Map: *AMC White Mountain Guide*, Map 1 G8–F9
Information: White Mountain National Forest, Androscoggin Ranger Station, 80 Gorham Road, Gorham, NH 03581; 603-466-2713; *www.fs.fed.usr9/white*

Getting there: From points south, take I-93 north to Route 3 to Route 302 south. The trailhead is located off Route 302 in Crawford Notch, at the Crawford Depot (see hike 10). Winter trailhead parking is located at the Appalachian Mountain Club Crawford Depot information center, on the west side of Route 302 in Crawford Notch. (The summer trailhead is located off Mount Clinton Road, and a spur path is used to reach Crawford Path; Mount Clinton Road is closed in the winter, however.)

The first time we attempted a winter ascent of Mount Washington, we didn't make it. We remember it well: The climb was excruciating, the weather dismal. We stepped and rested, stepped and rested. We dug our crampons in and climbed the steep, snowy path, through a nasty brew of stinging ice and blinding snow. A biting wind chased us up the mountain, howling in our ears and blowing us off balance. We scrambled for footholds. And finally—rightly—we gave up and headed back down, several miles from the summit.

Attempting a winter climb to the summit of Mount Washington is not for the meek and weak. It's long (17 miles round trip); it's steep (more than 4000 feet elevation gain); and it travels through a region known to have the "worst weather in the world." Even summer attempts can be dangerous; in winter, extreme caution should be taken and you should be prepared to turn back if the weather turns nasty (as it so often does). Many lives have been lost on Mount Washington. That said, this classic climb to the top of New England's highest peak is at the top of the list for avid outdoor enthusiasts. And the rewards are plentiful.

Our second attempt was successful. We trudged up the ever-increasingly steep path, above treeline, and up the bare, exposed summit cone. Clouds swirled above and the wind whipped, but the weather held. Finally, we broke through the clouds and onto the peak. It was like Mother Earth held her breath for a moment. The wind died and the sun appeared in a deep blue sky. We were the only ones up there, looking across a wild winter-scape.

The Crawford Path, on Mount Washington's western slopes, is considered the oldest continuously maintained footpath in the country. A section of it, from just north of Mount Pierce to the summit of Mount Washington, is part of the Appalachian Trail; much of it, north of the Eisenhower–Franklin col, is above treeline and exposed to the mountain's fierce and fickle weather.

The trail is a teaser, starting out gently and leading you into a false sense of ease and security. About a half-mile in, there's a short side path to Gibbs Falls, for a view of frozen cascades—if you don't mind taking a few extra steps on an already long journey. All too soon, about 1.5 miles from the trailhead, you'll leave the brook and begin an easy, steady climb up the valley ridges. You'll pass the Mizpah Cutoff trail at just under 2 miles, leading to the Appalachian Mountain Club Mizpah mountain hut (closed in winter). Keep on trudging through the snow, up to the junction with the Webster Cliff Trail, leading to the Mount Pierce summit at 4312 feet.

The path now leads through sparse woods from Mount Pierce to Mount Eisenhower. Look around! You'll have fabulous, open views of the Presidential Range. Be careful in this section. Open, snow-covered ledges can be slippery and tough to navigate. It's easy to lose the path, so pay attention and look ahead for the cairns that mark the way. If you're feeling hardy, you can take the Eisenhower Loop Trail to Mount Eisenhower's 4760-foot summit, adding 0.2 mile to the trip

Views of the Presidentials and Mount Washington's summit

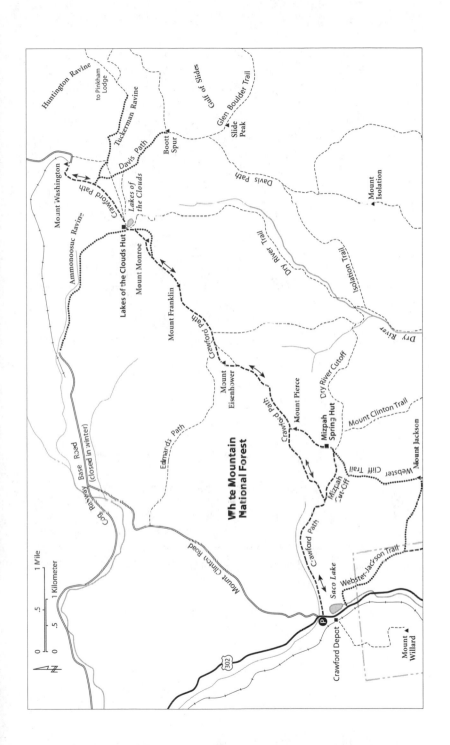

and an additional 300 feet or so of elevation. Consider it only in decent weather.

At Mount Eisenhower you're more than halfway to the summit, and the trail evens out a bit as it makes its way toward Mount Franklin. It's a huff and puff up the ridges of Mount Franklin, but you'll have good views. At a little over 6 miles into the hike (whew!), a side trail leads to the twin summits of Mount Monroe. Take it for the views, if the sky is clear enough to see anything; in iffy weather, stay the course on the less exposed Crawford Path.

Now, you'll have a short reprieve as the trail descends slightly to the Lakes of the Clouds mountain hut (closed in winter). This is a great place to stop for a well-deserved rest, along the snowy banks of two pretty mountain ponds. Several paths cross the trail in this area: the Ammonoosuc Ravine and Dry River Trails enter near the hut, and in a short distance the Davis Path to Boott Spur and Tuckerman Crossover Trail take off from the right.

From the lakes, you'll climb the southeast ridge of Mount Washington, passing junctions with Davis Path and the Westside Trail before you begin the final, very steep climb up to the summit of Mount Washington. At 8.3 miles, you'll converge with the ridgeline Gulfside Trail and then make the final pull up to the summit. If you're lucky, the clouds will part and you'll have unparalleled views of the Presidential Range, Tuckerman Ravine, and the great Gulf Wilderness.

MOUNT WASHINGTON OBSERVATORY

The top of Mount Washington is a wild place. It's said to have some of the worst weather on the planet and still boasts the world record for wind speed at 231 miles per hour. What better place for a permanent weather observatory?

Typically, the observatory is closed to visitors in winter, but you can join a unique education trip. You'll travel to the summit in a snow tractor and stay overnight at the observatory, studying topics ranging from meteorology and mountain photography to avalanche and snow safety. You may not have to hike to the top, but don't discount the effort this will take. According to the trip requirements, "participants need to be in excellent physical condition for mountaintop explorations, possess the appropriate equipment (winter hiking clothing, sleeping bags, crampons, and ice axe), and be able to hike during high winds and severe weather."

Programs run from mid-December through mid-April and are open to members of the Mount Washington Observatory. You must become a member ($40 for an individual membership) in order to participate. The trip costs about $400. For more information, call 603-356-2137, or visit *www.mountwashington.org*.

--*12*--
Pinkham Notch

Rating:	Easy/more difficult
Round trip:	2.6 miles
Hiking time:	3 hours
Elevation gain:	543 feet
High point:	2575 feet
Map:	*AMC White Mountain Guide,* Map 1:F9–F10
Information:	Appalachian Mountain Club, Pinkham Notch Visitor Center, Route 16, Gorham, NH 03581; 603-466-2725; *www.outdoors.org*

Getting there: Take Route 16 to the AMC Pinkham Notch Visitor Center, 18 miles north of North Conway and 10 miles south of Gorham. The trailhead leaves from the back of the visitor center.

Icy streams, giant boulders, high bluffs, open ledges, and pretty woods make this half-day trip on Liebeskind's Loop a winner. An added benefit is that the hike leaves from the AMC Pinkham Notch Visitor Center, where you can warm up, pick up supplies, check on trail conditions, and grab a hot chocolate on your way out. And if you're left with energy and motivation after completing the

Chuck Ward stops along a frozen stream on the Liebeskind's Loop trail.

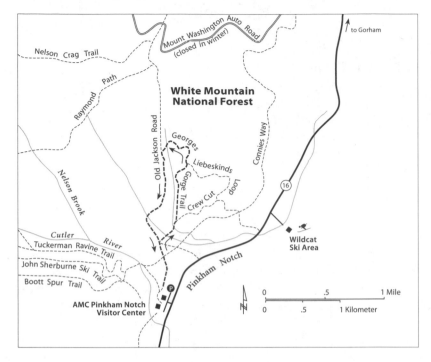

loop, there are plenty more trails in the area, leading into the White Mountain National Forest and Mount Washington mountain range.

The short loop, with an elevation gain of about 600 feet, is completed by combining four trails: Old Jackson Road, George's Gorge, Liebeskind's Loop, and Crew Cut. Pick up the Old Jackson Road first, from the Pinkham Notch Visitor Center.

The wide, flat path is part of the Appalachian Trail, providing popular access to a number of other trails in the area. You're likely to encounter a few claw-footed climbers on their way up to Mount Washington, and cross-country skiers; there are several marked ski trails in this area.

At about 0.4 mile from the visitor center, you'll cross a bridge and take a right on Crew Cut Trail. There are a couple of small stream crossings before reaching the left-hand turn off onto George's Gorge Trail. It starts to get interesting here, as George's Gorge Trail becomes steeper, climbing up the snowy banks of a mountain brook. This trail can get slippery in spots, depending on the snow cover. But your crampons should help get you up the trail, even in icy conditions.

Continue the ascent for about half a mile. Just as you start to doubt whether you're on the right trail, going in the right direction, you'll reach the

Liebeskind's Loop trail sign, on the right. There's a brief reprieve, with a short descent, before the loop trail begins the gradual climb to Brad's Bluff. It's time for a rest—and this is a great place for it. Grab a seat in the snow and take in the sights. You'll have unobstructed views of Pinkham Notch and the eastern slope of Mount Washington.

When you're ready, follow the trail to the left (as you look off the bluff). There are giant boulders, rock walls, and caves along the trail as it skirts the edge of the cliff. The trail dips into a couple of ravines before climbing again to the ridgeline. Look for the spur trail (there's a small sign) leading to Lila's Ledge. It's a short, 0.1-mile jaunt to the open ledge, with more rewarding mountain views.

Back on the main trail, you'll work your way down the ridge. The tight trail can get tricky in spots, especially if it's icy. More than a few hikers have opted to scoot down the steeper, boulder-strewn spots on their butts! But in a short time, the path levels out. One more river crossing (you may want to scout upriver for the easiest crossing spot), a few more steps, and you're back at the beginning, with the visitor center in sight.

--*23*--
Arethusa Falls

Rating: Easy/more difficult
Round trip: 2.6 miles
Hiking time: 3 hours
Elevation gain: 760 feet
High point: 2000 feet
Map: *AMC White Mountain Guide*, Map 2:H8
Information: New Hampshire Division of Parks and Recreation, Crawford Notch State Park, Route 302, Harts Location, NH 03812; 603-374-2272; *www.nhstateparks.org*

Getting there: From points south, take I-93 north to Route 3 to Route 302 south. The trail leads from a parking lot off Route 302, 0.5 mile south of the Dry River Campground.

Yes, this little jaunt in the Notch gets a fair amount of traffic; tons of tourists clamor up its path in the summer. Even during the harsh winter months, you probably won't have the trail to yourself. But there are good reasons why this trip is so popular—and why it should be on your winter must-do list. For starters, it's a relatively short hike, easily doable in half a day. It's located in the popular and scenic Crawford Notch State Park. And, did we mention that it leads to the Granite State's tallest waterfall?

Besides a view of frozen falls and crystal cascades, you may see another spectacle: ice climbers working their way up the icy walls. Arethusa Falls, and nearby Ripley Falls and soaring Frankenstein Cliff, are hot spots for New Hampshire's cold-climate climbers. Also, if you're looking to expand your snowshoe trip, there are plenty of options with several connecting trails leading to Ripley Falls, Frankenstein Cliff, and beyond.

Hop on the trail, and almost immediately you'll begin a steady climb through the woods, at a manageable but heart-pumping rate. Though deep dumps of snow may slow you down, it's usually easier to hike this trail in winter than spring or summer, when slippery rocks and roots are in the way.

You'll climb above Bemis Brook, overlooking a narrow gully. At a little over a mile, you'll cross a wooden bridge spanning the narrow, serpentine stream. Continue the more gradual up-and-down hike for another 0.5 mile or so, to the base of Arethusa Falls. The nearly 200-foot-tall waterfall is named

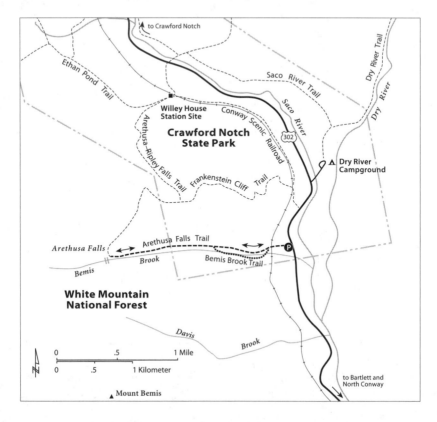

Ice climber on Arethusa Falls

after a Greek mythology character that transformed into a fountain to escape an undesirable lover. It is a sight to see. Layers of frozen cascades form thick walls of ice that hang from steep, open ledges. You'll want to linger here for awhile, taking photos of the massive, frozen waterfall, and watching the ice climbers that are often seen hanging off the walls. When you've had your fill of the scenery, backtrack to the parking lot.

Feeling adventurous? Have more time? You can easily expand this snowshoe hike into a 6-mile loop, taking in some of the finest views in the 5775-acre state park. At the falls, turn right on the Arethusa–Ripley Falls Trail, climbing to the junction with Frankenstein Cliff Trail. Turn right and continue along the ridgeline. The sweeping mountain and valley views from the soaring, open bluffs are stunning. The trail continues, descending steeply, to the Dry River Campground. A short trail leads back to the Arethusa Falls parking area. This loop will add 3.4 miles to your trip.

--*14*--
Carter Notch

Rating: More difficult
Round trip: 7.6 miles
Hiking time: 8 hours
Elevation gain: 1813 feet
High point: 3300 feet
Map: *AMC White Mountain Guide,* Map 5:F10
Information: White Mountain National Forest, Androscoggin Ranger Station, 80 Gorham Road, Gorham, NH 03581; 603-466-2713; *www.fs.fed.us/r9/white*

Getting there: From points south, take I-95 to Route 16 north. Follow Route 16 to Pinkham Notch. Carter Notch is just east of Pinkham Notch. The trail is located off Route 16, about a mile north of the Mount Washington Auto Road.

This hike follows the Nineteen-Mile Brook Trail through Carter Notch, but don't let the name of this trail scare you off. The moderately steep trail climbs only 3.8 miles to the Appalachian Mountain Club Carter Notch Hut, passing

Along the Nineteen-Mile Brook Trail through Carter Notch

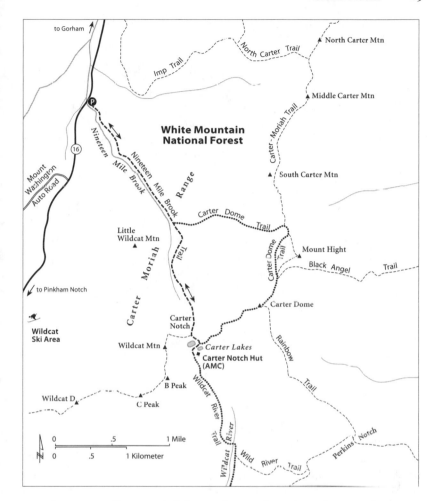

cascades, two small mountain lakes, and open views along the way. It's a popular route, both summer and winter, offering plenty of scenic outlooks as it winds through the picturesque notch, wedged in between the ridges of Wildcat Mountain and Carter Dome.

It's a long day trip, but doable for intermediate hikers. Another option is to reserve a space at the backcountry stone hut, the oldest in the AMC White Mountain hut system. The shelter sleeps forty in two unheated bunkhouses (bring a winter-weight sleeping bag), and guests have access to kitchen facilities. Be sure to make reservations in advance, as the hut fills up fast. In fact, winter, we're told, is the busiest season for the Carter Notch hut. It's a favorite among backcountry winter hikers, who use it as a base for day hikes to Carter Dome and the summit of Wildcat Mountain (steep and tough climbs, but the views are awesome!).

The AMC Pinkham Notch Visitor Center is just down the road, and a good place to check on trail conditions and fuel up on a hearty, hot breakfast before heading out.

You can expect the trail to be well traveled and packed. It begins at a moderate grade, along an old road. At about the halfway point, you'll pass a dam and reach the junction with the Carter Dome Trail. Continue your push, as you cross a footbridge, then pass a pretty set of icy cascades. At about 2 miles, you'll cross a second footbridge, and more cascades. Now it gets a bit steeper and tougher on the lungs. You'll also have to be careful at this section of the trail, as it can get icy along the edges. This is when your crampons come in handy.

The final 0.7 mile of the trail always seems longer than it is. We're typically anxious to reach the hut and take a rest, and the trail grows steeper as it makes its final push up the lip of the ridge. By now, we're thankful for the crowds who have gone before us, clearing the way. Huff and puff your way up the last steep pitch, and you'll reach the height-of-land and the treetops at 3.6 miles. Ahh . . .

It's downhill from here, though steeply downhill. Descend a mere 0.2 mile and you'll reach the first, and largest, of the Carter Lakes. The trail snakes between the lakes on its way to the Carter Notch hut. But, if the weather's been cold enough (as it usually is), the lakes will be frozen and you can shortcut your way across them to the hut. As always, be cautious traveling on ice. (Check out the ice safety tips in the Introduction.) Grab a seat near the woodstove, prop up your feet, and relax before heading back down the way you came.

If you're staying overnight at the Carter Notch hut, consider a 2.4-mile up-and-back side trip, the next day, to Carter Dome, where you'll have open views of Mount Hight and South Carter to the north and Wildcat Mountain to the west.

HAPPY HAUNTING GROUNDS

Strange things are said to happen at the Appalachian Mountain Carter Notch hut. This cabin overlooking spectacular Carter Notch, the oldest building in the AMC hut system, is said to be haunted. The story goes that the ghost of "Red Mac" MacGregor, hut manager in the 1920s, likes to play pranks on the hut crew. Check it out for yourself—if you dare! The hut, which sleeps forty in two unheated bunkhouses, is open year-round. Call the AMC at 603-466-2725 for reservations.

--25--
Tuckerman Ravine

Rating: Most difficult/backcountry
Round trip: 4.8 miles to base of the ravine, with options to continue
Hiking time: 6 hours
Elevation gain: 1843 feet
High point: 3875 feet
Map: *AMC White Mountain Guide,* Map 1:F9
Information: White Mountain National Forest, Androscoggin
Ranger Station, 80 Gorham Road, Gorham, NH 03581;
603-466-2713; *www.fs.fed.us/r9/white*

Getting there: From points south, take I-95 to Route 16 north. Follow
Route 16 to Pinkham Notch. The Tuckerman Ravine Trail begins at the
Appalachian Mountain Club Pinkham Notch Visitor Center on Route 16.

In southern New England, the crocuses are up. The robins are back. The sidewalk vendors are hawking bouquets of tulips and daffodils. And hundreds of people are ascending the slippery ridges of granite, with slopes as steep as 55 degrees, above the vast Tuckerman Ravine—an enormous cirque on the southeast side of Mount Washington.

Every spring, when avalanche danger subsides and the sun crests the edge of the bowl and softens the ice, this wild and challenging region in northern New Hampshire opens to daredevil skiers. On this White Mountain hike, you'll get a great workout, fine mountain views, and have the added bonus of seeing the backcountry powderhounds take on "Tucks." In April and May, and some years into June, crowds (sometimes more than 2000 people on a spring weekend!) gather at Picnic Rocks, a jumble of giant boulders at the base of the ravine. They come to enjoy the surrounding winter splendor and to ooh and ahh as skiers successfully maneuver the mountain—or to gasp and groan as others slip, slide, tumble, and turn into fast-moving, human snowballs.

Snowshoers can also connect with the Lion Head Trail leading to the summit of Mount Washington, New England's highest peak—a classic, must-do trek for in-shape winter hikers (see also hike 11).

If you're up for a show, do this hike in spring; otherwise, hit it early in the season. No matter when you go, you won't be alone on the trail; this is one of the most popular routes in the White Mountains. In winter, the headwall is impassable to all but the most experienced technical climbers; this 4.8-mile round trip will take you to the base of the headwall. If you plan to continue to the summit of Mount Washington (adding another 3.6 miles and 2413 feet of elevation to the trip), take the Lion Head Trail, which bypasses the headwall and can be accessed off the Tuckerman Ravine Trail. In any case, you'll have fabulous views of a seemingly endless expanse of white-capped mountains, jagged spires, rugged gardens of craggy granite, and in the distance, rolling valleys, icy ponds, and pine forests.

The trail is well marked, and the AMC staff at the visitor center can point you in the right direction, as well as provide up-to-the-minute information on trail conditions and avalanche danger. If you'd like to camp overnight, you can stay at the Hermit Ranger Station, two-thirds of the way up. It's first-come, first-served accommodations at a rustic lean-to. A giant snow wall often closes in the front of the shelter, in which case you'll have to crouch your way in the small opening at one end of the wall, and grab a spot for your sleeping bag. It's very cozy accommodations! The lean-to just might have the best occupancy rate in northern New England during spring mud season. It's often filled to capacity. Campers not only get first tracks, but they awake to the crystalline splendor of the mountains, an incredible expanse of

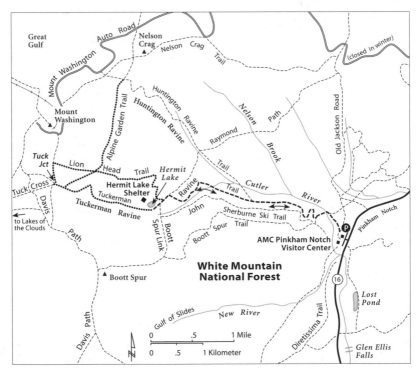

View of Mount Washington along Tuckerman Ravine trail

white powder and shimmering ice. (If you elect to camp out, you'll need to purchase a ticket at the Pinkham Notch Visitor Center.)

The well-traveled trail is often hard-packed, but don't underestimate the challenge and energy it'll take to complete it. The craggy, untamed wilderness of Mount Washington's granite ridges is known for its severe, fickle weather, record-breaking winds, and snow depths of 75 feet or more. Be prepared for the worst, and be willing to turn back.

The trail begins at a moderate but steady grade. In less than a half-mile, you'll pass a side trail to view Crystal Cascade. The trail crosses several rivers and tributaries over footbridges as it continues its relentless, huff-and-puff climb up the steep southeast slopes of Mount Washington. At 1.7 miles, you'll reach the junction with Huntington Ravine Fire Road. If you plan to climb to the summit of Mount Washington, you'll need to travel this road 0.1 mile to the junction with Lion Head Trail. This is the safest winter route to the summit.

The main trail continues its climb, reaching the base of the ravine at 2.4 miles. Here, you'll see the side trail leading to the Hermit Lake shelter. Grab a seat and take in the sights. You'll have great views of the headwall, the Lion Head cliffs, and the Hanging Cliffs of Boott Spur. Did you bring your skis? If so, join the crowds as they ascend single file up the headwall, and pick their spot to begin the plunge down. Or, sit back and watch the show.

WHITE MOUNTAINS—FRANCONIA NOTCH

--16--
The Flume

Rating: Easy
Round trip: Varied trails, all less than 2 miles
Hiking time: 1–2 hours
Elevation gain: 200 feet
High point: 500 feet
Maps: Franconia Notch State Park Hiking Trails, NH Division of Parks and Recreation; *White Mountains Map Book*, Map Adventures, Franconia Notch
Information: Flume Gorge and Visitor Center New Hampshire Division of Parks and Recreation, Franconia, NH; 603-745-8391; *www.flumegorge.com*

Getting there: From points south, follow I-93 to the Franconia Notch Parkway. Take exit 34A to the Flume Visitor Center exit.

They looked like colorful spiders, arms and legs clinging to the ice, slowly crawling up a frozen waterfall. Swift chops of an axe sent pieces of ice tumbling off the wall. Each worked a route up the cold blue ice, digging spiked crampons into slippery toeholds, stretching to find the perfect spot to land ice axes. "Look for a sweet spot," the guide instructed. "Someplace where there's snow or an indentation to set your tool in."

They crept higher up the wall . . . alpine spidermen and -women, slipping, finding a hold, slipping, until they reached the top, or gave up, legs quivering and arms screaming.

We were watching ice climbers navigate the frozen waterfalls at The Flume in Franconia Notch State Park, a favorite spot for winter climbers. But even if the climbers are not there to put on a show, the short, meandering trails in the area, leading to a series of soaring, blue-tinged waterfalls, make for a great winter's walk. While in the summer The Flume is a popular tourist destination, with hordes of visitors strolling the boardwalks through the notch and to the waterfalls, come winter the crowds disappear and it's free! Though some of the boardwalks are removed, snowshoers can explore much of the area.

The Flume is a natural 800-foot-long gorge, carved thousands of years ago by the rushing waters of the Pemigewasset River. The walls in the narrow chasm rise as high as 70 to 90 feet; sparkling cascades and foaming waterfalls tumble down smooth granite slabs. In the winter, it is especially beautiful when the gorge is sparkling with ice and the frozen spray of the falls. In the middle of a cold winter, the falls themselves freeze into giant layers of blue ice.

We like to start with an easy stroll on the Roaring River Nature Trail, which begins at the lower, southern parking lot at the Flume Visitor Center. This is especially pleasant with young children in tow. The broad, level trail winds through a deciduous and pine forest; trees, plants, and other points of interest are marked along the way. You'll pass Little Stream. A gazebo in the woods is the perfect spot to stop and take in the surrounding mountain views, including Mount Liberty (4459 feet) and Mount Flume (4328 feet) at the southern end of the Franconia Range. In all, the mile-or-so-long trail should take you less than an hour to complete.

Now head to the back of the visitor center (opposite the parking area), where you'll find a wide trail leading north. This trail is unmarked but easy to locate and follow—it's the main trail heading into The Flume. In about a third of a mile, you'll turn right on a well-trodden trail heading east into The Flume. You'll pass through the often-photographed red covered bridge over the bubbling Pemigewasset River. The Flume Covered Bridge was erected in the 1800s and is one of the oldest in the state. Stop for a photo, then continue

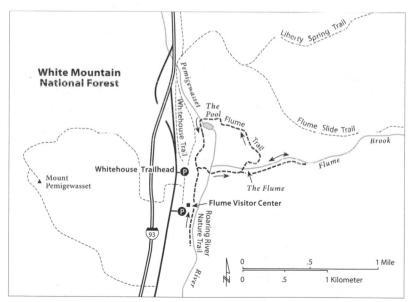

on the trail for the gradual ascent into the chasm. Avalanche Falls is located at the head of the Flume; the impressive waterfall is created by Flume Brook as it plunges down smooth granite slabs over the lip of the gorge. In the dead of winter, the frozen spray of the falls surrounds the tumbling waters.

The trail loops around to pretty Liberty Gorge Cascade, perched over a deep ravine. Here, frozen cascades decorate the granite walls of the chasm. Continue on the trail, as it meanders another half-mile or so to The Pool, a huge 150-foot-wide, 40-foot-deep basin. It sits at the floor of towering granite walls, surrounded by icy cascades. From here, it's a short walk back to the parking lot and visitor center.

--17--
Bald Mountain and Artists Bluff

Rating:	Easy
Round trip:	1.5 miles
Hiking time:	1–2 hours
Elevation gain:	340 feet
High point:	2340 feet
Maps:	*AMC White Mountain Guide,* Map 4:G4; Franconia Notch State Park hiking map
Information:	Franconia Notch State Park, New Hampshire Division of Parks and Recreation, Franconia, NH; 603-745-8391; *www.franconiastatepark.com*

Getting there: From points south, follow I-93 to the Franconia Notch Parkway. Take the Cannon Mountain Peabody Slopes exit off the parkway, north of Echo Lake. Park in the upper parking lot for the ski area. The trailhead is located at the northern edge of the upper parking lot for the ski area.

We've classified this hike up Bald Mountain and around Artists Bluff in Franconia Notch State Park as easy. The distance is short, and the elevation gain of 340 feet is gradual and easy to manage. Best of all, the views are great for small effort and limited time. There is a bit of scrambling over the rocky ledges near the top (these can be slippery) and open cliffs. However, with a bit of caution, even families with small children in tow can do this short winter outing.

We often make this trip with our downhill skiing friends. They ski Cannon Mountain 'til they drop; we cut out early and walk over to the trailhead for the

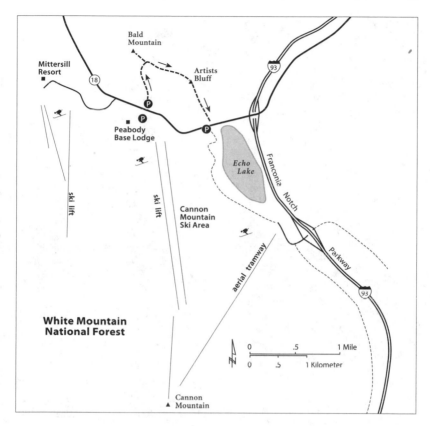

quick jaunt up the bare summit cone of Bald Mountain. While they're in the lodge sipping toddies, we're sitting on open mountain ledges gulping Gatorade (okay, sometimes we guzzle from the wineskin!). Even if you don't take in Cannon Mountain skiing, you'll enjoy this quick snowshoe excursion.

The Bald Mountain Trail, leaving from the northern edge of the upper parking lot, begins at a slow-moving, easy pace along an old carriage road. You'll hear the snow guns, the snow machines, the general noise of the ski resort, and the drone of traffic along the highway. It quiets down fast as you enter the snowy, hushed winter woods. At 0.3 mile you'll reach the top of the small ridge and the junction with the path leading to the summit of Bald Mountain. Turn left on this spur path and clamber up 0.1 mile to the top. To the south, you'll have great views of the maze of ski trails snaking down the mountain, Echo Lake, and the Cannon–Kinsman Ridge beyond. To the east, you'll see the Franconia Range.

When you're done soaking up the views, backtrack to the main trail. Continue through the woods at an easy grade to a wooded cliff. From here,

View of Cannon Mountain Ski Area from Artists Bluff

you'll drop down into a narrow valley. Look for a spur path that leads to Artists Bluff, an open cliff on the southeast side of Bald Mountain, where you'll have more fine views. The main trail continues to descend down the valley to Route 18. You'll have to walk a short distance along the road back to the parking lot.

If you have time and inclination, you might consider a snowshoe walk around pretty Echo Lake. You can't miss the lake; a short walk from the parking area will get you to the snow-banked shoreline. A well-worn path circles the lake, in the shadows of the Cannon–Kinsman Range and Franconia Ridge. There are a handful of picnic tables and rustic benches along the way, and plenty of scenic views. Following the unmarked but easily seen trail around the lake is a favorite outing for families, dog walkers, and folks needing a bit of fresh air and exercise.

--*18*--
Lonesome Lake

Rating: Easy to more difficult
Round trip: 2.4 miles
Hiking time: 3 hours
Elevation gain: 970 feet
High point: 2740 feet
Map: *AMC White Mountain Guide,* Map 4:H4
Information: Appalachian Mountain Club, Pinkham Notch Visitor Center, Route 16, Gorham, NH 03581; 603-466-2721 (general information) or 603-466-2725 (White Mountain trail conditions); *www.outdoors.org*

Getting there: From points south, follow I-93 to the Franconia Notch Parkway. Take the parkway to the Lafayette Campground exit and park in the lot located on the west side of the highway.

Who can resist its name? In fact, the Lonesome Lake Trail leads to an isolated low mountain pond that attracts a fair amount of traffic year-round. The lake sits at 2740 feet, tucked in a valley, just south of the high ridge of the Cannon–Kinsman Range. You'll have nice views of surrounding mountains, including the Franconia and Cannon mountain ranges. It's a pretty walk in the woods, a steady but gentle climb that's perfect for a short day's outing.

Or, pack your sleeping bag and stay overnight at the Lonesome Lake Hut, operated by the Appalachian Mountain Club. The facility sits on the southwest shore of the lake and sleeps forty-eight people in two bunkhouses. You'll have access to kitchen facilities, mattresses, and pillows. The Lonesome Lake Hut is the most easily accessible hut in the White Mountains, making it a great choice for families and less-experienced hikers. If you've ever wanted to spend the night in the winter woods, awakening to fresh snow and pristine landscape, this is a nice option. For those hikers looking for a more extended trip, the Lonesome Lake Trail connects with a network of trails crisscrossing the Cannon–Kinsman Range.

The trail is well marked, often hard packed, and easygoing. You'll gain about 1000 feet in elevation, over moderate grades and gentle switchbacks. Begin by crossing over the Pemigewasset River on a footbridge. Even in the dead of winter, we can often hear the fast-moving water rumbling beneath the sheets of ice. The trail travels through sparse hardwoods and pines, crossing

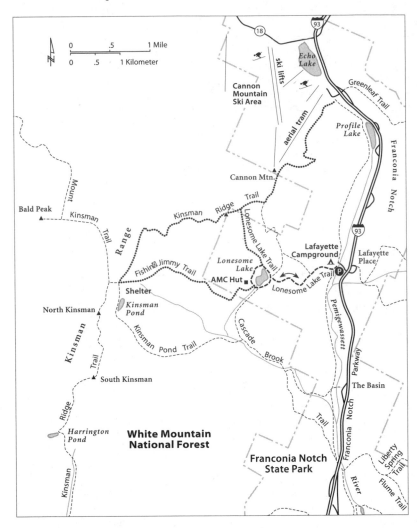

a couple more small brooks. In summer, the cool brook waters are welcome spots to dunk toes; come winter, the brooks disappear under ice and snow.

At about a half-mile in, the trail begins a series of long switchbacks, gaining elevation until it reaches a plateau and descends to the shores of Lonesome Lake at 1.2 miles. We like to ramble around the lake for a while. The main trail continues along the north shore, hooking up with several others (including Cascade Brook, Fishin' Jimmy, and Around-Lonesome-Lake Trails) to form a circuit around the lake. You won't get lost; just follow the footpath or walk the banks of the lake. You'll have nice mountain views, as you hike the perimeter, across snowy beaches and bogs. Look

Lonesome Lake is a popular destination for hikers.

for deer and moose tracks in the bogs, and listen for the rat-tat-tat of woodpeckers hunting for a winter meal. You'll also spot the AMC hut along the way.

If you like, continue northwest on the Lonesome Lake Trail as it climbs to meet the Kinsman Ridge Trail in about 1 mile. Now, you have the entire Kinsman and Cannon mountain ranges at your feet.

--19--
Falling Waters

Rating:	More difficult
Round trip:	5.6 miles to Shining Rock
Hiking time:	5 hours
Elevation gain:	570 feet
High point:	2350 feet to Shining Rock
Map:	*AMC White Mountain Guide,* Map 2:H4–H5
Information:	Appalachian Mountain Club, Pinkham Notch Visitor Center, Route 16, Gorham, NH 03581; 603-466-2721 (general information) or 603-466-2725 (White Mountain trail conditions); *www.outdoors.org*

Getting there: From points south, follow I-93 to the Franconia Notch Parkway. Take the Lafayette Campground exit and park on either side of the highway. There are parking lots on both sides (an under-the-road pathway travels between them).

This up-and-back hike, in the shadows of the Franconia Range, features a series of spectacular waterfalls and frothy cascades. The frozen falls, reaching 60 to 80 feet, are a sight to see against the surrounding granite backdrop and snowy ridges. Take this trail, even in the coldest of winters, and you'll walk to the sound of gurgling water moving beneath sheets of ice and snow. It's one of our favorites in New Hampshire's White Mountains.

The entire trail stretches 3.2 miles (one way) to the top of Franconia Ridge. However, we don't recommend that you go much farther than Shining Rock, an impressive granite ledge. Most folks, in fact, end their hike at the last of the three major waterfalls, cutting the trip to less than 3 miles round trip and avoiding the steepest sections of the trail. Those who travel up and around the waterfalls, continuing to Shining Rock and farther to Franconia Ridge, will be rewarded with open mountain and valley views. But the trail can be dangerously icy and lung-burstingly steep. In any case, don't feel guilty about opting for the short trip—it's a fine one, with plenty of its own rewards.

Though the trail is well traveled even in winter, you'll want snowshoes with a good set of claws. The path, especially near the falls and river edges, can get slippery. It's also narrow and steep in some places, even at the lower sections.

The trail begins from the east parking lot and follows an easygoing incline through an open field, crossing the Old Bridle Path junction, before crossing Walker Brook and heading into the woods. At 0.7 mile you'll cross Dry Brook, then follow the banks up a rising slope. It won't take long before you're rewarded with your first view of the icy cascades known as Stair Falls. We like to linger here, looking for tracks of animals that may have come for a drink or watching the fast-moving water bubble up in the holes in the ice. The trail continues climbing above Stair Falls, passing underneath impressive Sawteeth

Waterfalls along Falling Waters trail

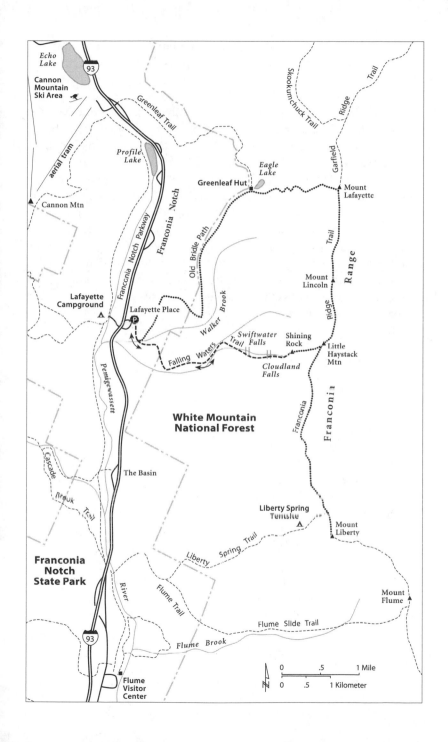

Echo
Lake

Cannon
Mountain
Ski Area

93

aerial tram

Greenleaf Trail

Profile
Lake

Eagle
Lake

Greenleaf Hut

Cannon Mtn

Franconia Notch

Old Bridle Path

Mount
Lafayette

Greenleaf Trail

Skookumchuck Trail

Garfield Ridge Trail

Garfield Trail

Mount
Lincoln

Ridge

Range

Franconia Notch Parkway

Lafayette
Campground

Lafayette Place

Walker Brook

Swiftwater
Falls

Shining
Rock

Little
Haystack
Mtn

Falling Waters
Trail

Cloudland
Falls

Pemigewasset

Franconia

Franconia

White Mountain
National Forest

Cascade

Brook

Trail

The Basin

Liberty Spring
Tentsite

Mount
Liberty

Franconia
Notch
State Park

River

Flume Trail

Liberty Spring Trail

Mount
Flume

Flume Slide Trail

93

Flume Brook

Flume
Visitor
Center

N

| 0 | .5 | 1 Mile |

| 0 | .5 | 1 Kilometer |

Ledges, before crossing the brook once more to the north bank. The trail becomes a bit narrower and steeper in this section as it approaches Swiftwater Falls. This swath of frozen ice and misty water rises 60 feet. Keep going; there's more!

We love this section of the trail, surrounded by water everywhere—frozen, icy, snow-covered, gurgling below, bubbling beneath our feet. The trail climbs the north bank, more steeply now, with a series of switchbacks, leaving Swiftwater Falls behind. There's a bit of stair-stepping and climbing in this section as you work your way up the narrow trail. (We've been known to sit and scoot our way down on this section of the trail on the return.) But the tallest waterfall looms ahead, 80-foot tall Cloudland Falls (at 1.5 miles), and its view keeps us happily moving forward and up. Go ahead, stand next to the waterfall; just be careful of soft spots in the river and, of course, slippery ice.

Decision time: you can (carefully!) climb above the falls for a mountain and valley vista, and then continue on for the steep climb to Shining Rock at 2.8 miles and up to Franconia Ridge (for experienced winter hikers only) at 3.2 miles. Or, take some photos of the awesome waterfalls, savor a trail snack, and head back down the way you came.

--*20*--
Zealand Falls

Rating: Easy
Round trip: 14.6 miles
Hiking time: 8–10 hours
Elevation gain: 630 feet
High point: 2630 feet
Map: *AMC White Mountain Guide*, Map 2:G7
Information: White Mountain National Forest, Gorham Ranger Station, 80 Gorham Road, Gorham, NH 03581; 603-466-2713; *www.fs.fed.us/r9/white*

Getting there: From points south, follow Route 16 north to Route 302 north toward Twin Mountain. The trailhead is located at the end of Zealand Road. From about mid-November to mid-May, you'll have to park on Route 302, in a small lot 0.2 mile east of Zealand Road, then hike down the road to the trailhead.

This gentle trail, through snow-covered woods, open meadows, and along-side beaver ponds, ends at pretty Zealand Falls and the Appalachian Mountain Club shelter. At trail's end, you'll be rewarded with stunning views of sur-

The Zealand Trail skirts a bubbling brook.

rounding mountain peaks and Zealand Valley. It's very popular with cross country skiers, too, and makes for a fine family outing.

You could do it up and back in a day, but the distance is long. That's because the trail is located off Zealand Road, which is closed in the winter. You'll have to snowshoe down the road an extra 4 miles (one way) to the trailhead. But it's a pretty trek along a hardwood and pine forest, and the going is easy. We'd suggest breaking the trip up into two days and spending the night at the Zealand Falls hut. This is one of the AMC's most popular shelters, housing thirty-six people in two coed bunkrooms. The nineteenth-century hut sits at nearly 2700 feet, with great views. You'll also have access to kitchen facilities, water, and a network of trails that crisscross the White Mountains and Pemigewasset Wilderness at your doorstep.

The trail is well marked and follows an old railroad bed much of the way. You'll enter a forest of mixed hardwoods and hemlock, a gentle meander on a nearly flat grade. At a little under a mile, you may begin to hear the sound of gurgling water. Though snow-banked and icy, the Zealand River often flows in the winter as it tumbles over granite ledges. The trail leaves the railroad bed and follows the west bank of the river as it oh-so-gently climbs toward Zealand Notch. You'll follow the river most of the way.

At about a mile and a half, the views begin to open up, as you enter open meadows, bogs, and beaver ponds. Take a moment to check out the beaver activity in the area. The big buck-toothed rodents (they're North America's largest native rodent) have been busy building dams and lodges in this area for years. In winter, beavers remain active, feeding on branches and twigs at the bottom of the ponds, beneath the winter ice.

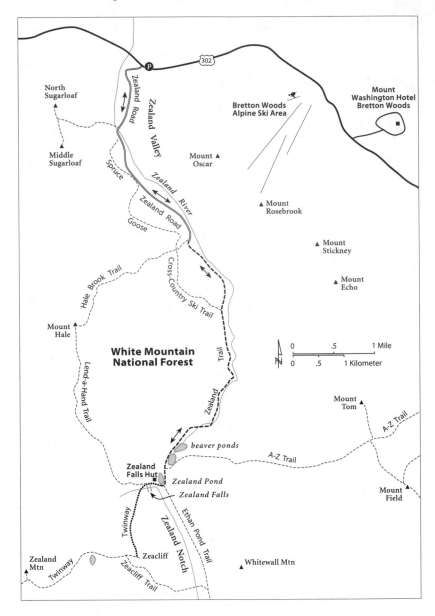

The trail continues at a gentle pitch, meandering across a small tributary brook and along Zealand Pond. The trail ends at the junction with the Ethan Pond Trail and the Twinway Trail, at 2.5 miles. Take the Twinway for another 0.3 mile to reach Zealand Falls and the AMC hut. The last leg of this trip to the falls is the toughest. It's a steep climb, on a series of stone steps (which may or may not be packed down in the winter). Push on; the extra effort is well worth it. As you sit by the side of the sparkling, icy waterfall, you'll have views of Carrigan Notch, Mount Anderson, Mount Lowell, Whitewall, Vose Spur, and Zealand Valley.

If you stay overnight at the hut, plan to get up early the next morning to explore the surrounding area. The easy Ethan Pond Trail leads to open bogs and meadows, and is prime moose-watching territory. The tougher, steeper Twinway Trail climbs toward Zealand Ridge. At 1.4 miles, you'll reach the Zeacliff spur path, which will take you to an outlook with spectacular, open views.

AMC WINTER HUTS

The Appalachian Mountain Club operates a network of eight high-country huts throughout the White Mountains. Three of the huts, open on a self-service basis in the winter, are located in New Hampshire. Guests can use the kitchen facilities at the huts and should bring food, sleeping bags, and towels.

Lonesome Lake Hut (see hike 18) sits at 2760 feet, overlooking a glacier pond and the Franconia mountain range. The hut sleeps forty-eight in two bunkhouses.

The **Zealand Falls Hut** (see hike 20) is tucked into Zealand Notch, at the base of a waterfall. It sits at 2700 feet and sleeps thirty-six in two bunkhouses.

Carter Notch Lodge (see hike 14) is a favorite with snowshoers and cross-country skiers looking for access to backcountry terrain. It sits at 3288 feet, overlooking the dramatic notch. There's space for forty in two unheated bunkhouses.

Cardigan Lodge (see hike 8) is surrounded by the 5000-acre Cardigan State Park, offering an extensive trail network for snowshoers. It has thirteen bunkrooms and two private rooms. The AMC also rents a rustic backcountry **High Cabin** in the Cardigan Mountain region, with a woodstove, composting toilet, and twelve bunks.

In Maine, the AMC rents full-service camps on **Little Lyford Pond** in the Greenville region year-round, with seven cabins and one bunkhouse (see hike 35). An additional self-service cabin is also available on nearby Long Pond.

Reservations are required at all huts and cabins. Contact the Appalachian Mountain Club, P.O. Box 290, Gorham, NH 03581-0298, 603-466-2727.

WHITE MOUNTAINS—KANCAMAGUS HIGHWAY

--21--
Lincoln Woods

Rating: Easy
Round trip: 5.8 miles
Hiking time: 4 hours
Elevation gain: 293 feet
High point: 1450 feet
Maps: White Mountain National Forest, Lincoln Woods X-C Ski Trails; *AMC White Mountain Guide,* Map 2:I5-H7
Information: White Mountain National Forest, Pemigewasset Ranger Station, Kancamagus Highway, Lincoln, NH 03264; 603-536-1315; *www.fs.fed.us/r9/white-mountain*

Getting there: Take I-93 to Route 112/Lincoln exit. Travel east on Route 112 for about 4 miles to the Lincoln Woods Visitor Center.

This flat, easy hike off the scenic Kancamagus Highway is one of the most popular trails in the White Mountain National Forest. We avoid it in fall and summer, when the route is clogged with tourists and day hikers, and offers little of the peace and serenity we expect to find in the mountains and woods. But when the mercury drops, fair-weather visitors leave the area and hiking the trail becomes bearable again. Even in the dead of winter, you won't have the path to yourself; it's a popular cross-country route, too. But it's a fine walk in the woods, along the roaring East Branch of the Pemigewasset River, to icy ponds and frozen waterfalls.

The trail also provides access to a spiderweb of other trails leading into the Pemigewasset Wilderness, one of the largest roadless areas in the eastern United States. Want to try your hand at winter camping? Easy-to-access, low-elevation sites along the Wilderness Trail (the Lincoln Trail turns into the Wilderness Trail as it enters the Pemigewasset Wilderness) are some of the finest spots for first-time and veteran winter campers.

You'll need to purchase a day-use parking permit at the outdoor kiosk. Stop in and say hi to the friendly rangers at the visitor center who love to chat about weather, trail conditions, and recent hikes. There's usually a fire going in the stove, perfect for warming hands and feet before and after heading into the woods.

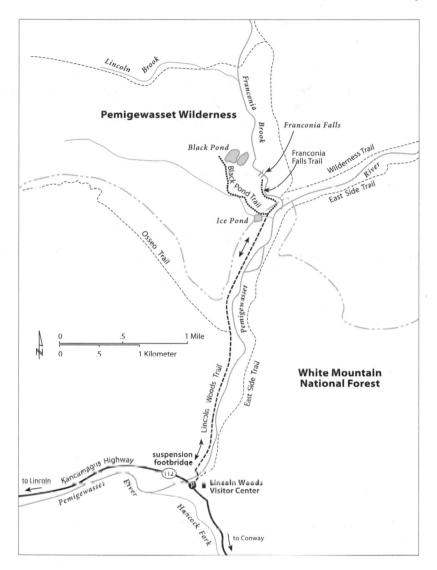

As you leave the visitor center, cross the suspension bridge over the river to pick up the Lincoln Woods Trail, then turn right into the woods. You'll be heading north, following an old railroad route. It's all easygoing, a perfect snowshoe hike for families with young children. Be aware, however, that you share the trail with cross-country skiers. Snowshoers are asked to stay off their tracks, keeping to the middle of the trail.

Along the way, you'll have a few glimpses of the frosty, fast-moving river, and a good view of it and the surrounding mountains from a clearing at around 1.7 miles. A little less than a mile farther, you'll reach the Ice Pond, and the Black Pond Trail. It's an easy 0.7 mile to the snow-covered, frozen mountain pond. We've been here on a quiet midweek afternoon, when soft snowflakes fluttered down, creating a fairyland setting.

Back on the main trail, you'll pass a stone wall and the side trail leading to Franconia Falls. The pretty cascade, framed in icicles, snow, and frost, is a great destination for this simple snowshoe hike.

If you like, you can continue by crossing the bridge over Franconia Falls. The Lincoln Woods Trail ends here and becomes the Wilderness Trail. Another alternative is to take the service road that leaves the visitor center and travels the east side of the Pemigewasset River. The level, woodsy path offers plenty of river views and fewer crowds. The downside is that you may not be able to cross the Pemigewasset River to view Franconia Falls.

--22--
Champney Falls

Rating: Easy to more difficult
Round trip: 2.8 miles
Hiking time: 3 hours
Elevation gain: 520 feet
High point: 1780 feet
Map: *AMC White Mountain Guide*, Map 3:J9
Information: White Mountain National Forest, Pemigewasset Ranger Station, Kancamagus Highway; 603-536-1315; *www.fs.fed.us/r9/white*

Getting there: From points south, take Route 16 to Conway. From Conway, travel west on Route 112 (the Kancamagus Highway) for 11.5 miles, through the Rocky Gorge scenic area. The Champney Falls Trail leaves the Kancamagus Highway on the south side of the road.

This is about as near perfect of a short, half-day hike as you can get. You'll walk a well-marked, easy-to-follow footpath, traveling through pretty snowy woods, up a gentle incline to a series of cascades and waterfalls. The spot is a popular summer hiking destination and swimming hole; come winter, the waterfalls take on a more stark seasonal beauty: a wall of frozen froth and ice, glimmering in filtered sunlight. The round trip will take about three hours or so to complete, plus time to linger along the way and at the falls. You'll likely share the trail with other hikers, backcountry skiers, and ice climbers.

If you're looking for a longer hike and a bit of a challenge, continue on to the connecting Piper Trail, leading to the top of 3500-foot Mount Chocorua. The extra jaunt adds 4.8 miles and some steep huff-and-puff pulls, gaining an additional 1700 feet or so in elevation. But the sweeping mountain and valley views from the top are spectacular.

There's a good-sized parking area at the trailhead. Parking tickets ($3 per day) are available at the self-help ticket kiosk at the trailhead.

Pack your camera and snacks, and hit the trail! You'll cross a small brook over a footbridge, then turn right and head into the woods. Just a few steps into the hike, you'll pass the junction with the Bolles Trail, on your right. The Bolles Trail leads south into the Sandwich Range Wilderness area and connects with a network of hiking paths. Stay straight on Champney Falls Trail.

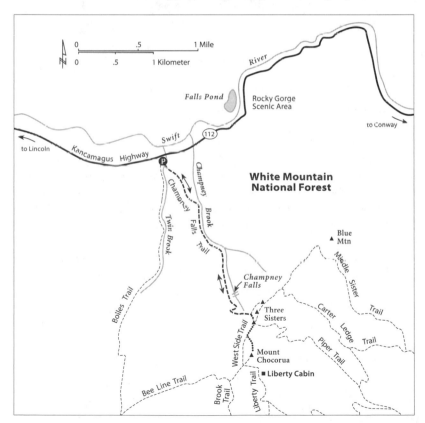

Angela Mangini enjoys the winter hike on the Champney Falls trail.

You'll travel due south, following the contour line and marching up at a gradual pace. The trail reaches the frozen banks of Champney Brook and weaves to the right. From here, you'll start a slightly steeper ascent up the small ridgeline, with views into a woodsy gully. The trail moves away from the brook, into the woods, and at 1.4 miles reaches the junction with the falls loop path. Turn left here and make your way to Pitcher Falls and Champney Falls.

During the summer, there are several fine toe-dunking holes and rock seats in front of the falls to sit on. In the dead of winter, you can walk the frozen stream to the base of the falls. The easy, close-up access to the frozen falls is a real plus for ice climbers. If it's been a good, cold winter, you're likely to see climbers on the face of Champney. In any case, the falls are a sight to see. Grab a seat in the snow and stay a while.

You can stay on the spur trail, climbing the snow-covered stone steps and looping around the back of the falls. The trail connects back with the main trail in about 0.5 mile. But, this spur path is steep and the ledges surrounding the falls can be slippery, so take caution. You might want to poke around the falls for a while, but retrace your steps back to the main trail instead of climbing up and around the falls on the loop trail.

Now, you can decide what you want to do from here. You can follow your tracks back down the trail to the parking lot. Or, head up to Mount Chorcorua for a real workout! Or, pack up your snowshoes and head into nearby North Conway for dining and shopping. . . .

TWO HIKES IN THE NORTH COUNTRY

New Hampshire's rugged North Country, a near-empty expanse of dense forests, bogs, lakes, and mountain peaks, is a paradise for outdoor enthusiasts. The locals here may strap on a pair of snowshoes or hop on a snowmobile just to get to the corner store! The Cohos Trail runs through much of the region. New Hampshire's longest single through-trail system stretches 159 miles through the state's wildest and most remote country. Kim Robert Nilsen, founder of the Cohos Trail Association and author of *The Cohos Trail Guidebook to New Hampshire's Great Unknown*, recommends these two snowshoe treks in the North Country.

Coleman State Park to Tumble Dick Notch: Park in Coleman State Park lot near Little Diamond Pond. Try walking on the frozen surface of the pond (see the ice safety tips in the Introduction), or take the narrow pathway that circumnavigates the pond just off the shore in the woods. Or trek out of the park and southbound on the Cohos Trail (a snowmobile trail in the winter), watching for yellow blazes on the wide trail. Trek a long mile south on the Cohos Trail, staying level at first but then climbing gradually off the plateau and up the flank of Sugar Hill (2995 feet). Eventually, the trail reaches the height of land between Sugar Hill and Tumble Dick Mountain, then drops a short distance to a doughnut-shaped area. Walk to the south edge of the doughnut to a clearing in the trees. You'll have a fine view south and east over endless blue 3000-foot ridges.

Second Connecticut Lake: This trek is a lake walk, across one of the premier undeveloped bodies of water in the state of New Hampshire. It is easy to reach by driving Route 3 to the top of the state. Motor north of Pittsburg Village nearly 20 miles until you see a sign for the state boat launch. Turn right onto the access road and drive 1000 feet to the pull-off on the right. Descend to a parking area at the edge of the lake.

Put on your snowshoes and spend the day exploring the numerous islands and peninsulas that jut into the 1200-acre lake. Be sure to wait until January or February to trek out onto the lake, when the lake is sure to be solid over its entire length. Stay clear of the dam and areas where streams enter the lake, as the ice will be thinnest here (see Safety on Ice in the Introduction).

Second Connecticut Lake is a big lake full of features to explore. The views are stunning, particularly of big Rump Mountain to the east, Diamond Ridge and Mount Magalloway to the south, and Mount Salmon, Mount Kent, and Mount D'Urban to the north, along the Canadian border.

--23--
Greeley Ponds

Rating: Easy
Round trip: 4.4 miles
Hiking time: 3 hours
Elevation gain: 240 feet
High point: 2180 feet
Map: *AMC White Mountain Guide,* Map 3:J6–I6
Information: White Mountain National Forest, Pemigewasset
Ranger Station, Kancamagus Highway; 603-536-1315;
www.fs.fed.us/r9/white

Getting there: From points south, follow I-93 north to Route 112 east
(Lincoln exit). The trailhead is located on the Kancamagus Highway
(Route 112) about 8.5 miles east of I-93.

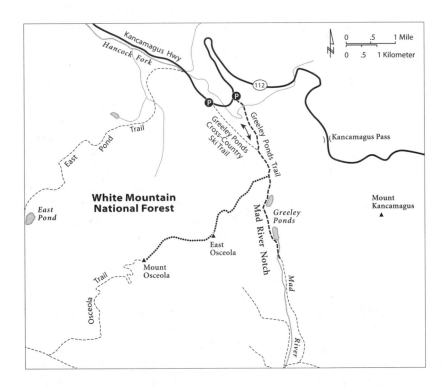

Along the Greeley Ponds trail

This pleasant, relatively flat trail, through Mad River Notch, was the first snow-shoe hike we ever completed. We began on the Kancamagus Highway side, meandering through sun-dappled woods until we reached the set of gorgeous mountain ponds. We had views of Mount Osceola and Mount Kancamagus, and of the steep-side cliffs of Mad River Notch. In less than three hours, we were back in nearby Lincoln, nibbling on Elvio's famous white pizza. What's not to like about this sport, we thought?

It remains one of our favorite, easy treks, perfect for visiting relatives and our more timid friends. For little effort, you get a touch of mountain wilderness and pristine winter scenery. In Lincoln, a popular tourist town, you'll find a variety of shops, restaurants, and lodgings. There are also a handful of outdoor guide and gear outfits, where you can sign up for a guided trip into the woods, rent snowshoes, pick up maps, and get trail information. If you have downhill ski enthusiasts in your group, there are several alpine ski resorts in the area.

The entire Greeley Ponds Trail runs from the Kancamagus Highway to Livermore Road, near the Waterville Valley Ski area, covering 10.2 miles round trip. But we suggest an up-and-back 4.4-mile-hike from the Kancamagus Highway to the ponds, as described here. There's a small parking area that also accesses a cross-country ski trail that parallels and sometimes crosses the hiking trail.

The trail begins—and remains—at an easy grade as it enters the woods, crosses the South Fork Brook, and climbs gently into Mad River Notch. You're likely to see cross-country skiers to your right, as they glide through the woods on a blue-blazed ski trail. At 1.3 miles, the Osceola Trail enters on your right. If you're looking for a challenge, go ahead and take it. From this junction, the trail climbs 2.5 miles to the summit of 4340-foot Mount Osceola, with great views from open ledges.

Back on the main trail, you'll enter the steep-sided notch, tucked between East Osceola and Mount Kancamagus. At 1.7 miles, you'll reach the upper pond; walk another half mile, and you'll be on the snowy banks of the lower pond. From the south end of the upper pond, you'll have an impressive view of the ragged cliffs of East Osceola. We like to poke around the Greeley Ponds, venturing out along the banks, and taking pictures of the surrounding mountain views. It's an amazingly quiet and pristine place, nestled at the foot of the notch, covered in a blanket of snow.

SNOWSHOE-FRIENDLY INNS IN NEW HAMPSHIRE

Knowledgeable innkeepers and easy access to snowshoe trails make these country inns in New Hampshire great getaway destinations. Most also offer cozy fires to warm up to at the end of the day, good dining, and great locations for all outdoor activities.

The historic grand **Mount Washington Hotel and Resort** in Bretton Woods (800-314-1752, *www.mtwashington.com*) sits at the base of mighty Mount Washington, with acres of forests and mountains at its doorstep. Guided snowshoe hikes, maps, and rentals are available on-site.

The secluded **Snowvillage Inn**, with staggering views of the Presidentials, offers snowshoeing and cross-country skiing on its private grounds.

The Balsams in Dixville Notch (603-255-3400, *www.thebalsams.com*) offers 15,000 acres of private forest and mountain preserve to explore. Guided hikes, rentals, nature tours, and more are offered at this grand resort hotel.

The eighteenth-century **Nestlebrook Farm on the River** in Jackson (603-383-9443, *www.lmgnh.com*) has rolling meadows and riverside trails to explore. Sleigh rides, nature walks, and more are also available.

Snowshoers on the trail to Lost Pond have views of Mount Katahdin.

MAINE

SOUTHERN MAINE

--24--
Scarborough Marsh

Rating: Easy
Round trip: 4 miles, with options
Hiking time: 1½–2 hours
Elevation gain: 100 feet
High point: 100 feet
Maps: Eastern Trail Road Guide, Eastern Trail Alliance, Figure 12, Old Orchard Beach and Scarborough; Scarborough Marsh Audubon Center trail map
Information: Scarborough Marsh Audubon Center, Route 9/Pine Point Road, Scarborough, ME 04074; 207-781-2330; *www.maineaudubon.org*

Getting there: From Route 1 in West Scarborough, turn on Route 9 (Pine Point Road). The Scarborough Marsh Nature Center (and trailheads) will be 2 miles east on your left.

Sometimes, just a small change in scenery can put you in the extraordinary. Snowshoeing the trails in this protected marsh area in southern Maine, just minutes from the busy Route 1 highway, transports you to another world. Here, narrow channels and tidal rivers snake through frost-tinged salt marshes; wintering birds feed in the rich, still-moving waters; and the briny smell of low tide fills the air, even in the dead of cold season. It's an easy walk, with lots of options. Keep your eyes peeled for bald eagles and for a rare glimpse of a snowy owl.

Scarborough Marsh is the largest salt marsh in the state of Maine and considered one of the most important and productive on the New England coast. It includes more than 3000 acres of tidal marsh, salt creeks, fresh marsh, and uplands and is a resting, breeding, and feeding ground for an array of wildlife, particularly birds. "The salt marsh is one of our great treasures," Thomas Urquhart told us on a recent trek through the marsh. Urquhart, past executive director of the Maine Audubon Society, has been involved in conservation organizations for more than twenty-five years. Best places in Maine for birdwatching? "This [Scarborough Marsh] would be one of them," he said.

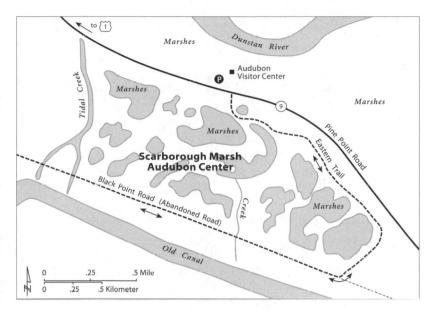

Waterfowl, egrets, herons, glossy ibises, and many species of shorebirds feed in the rich estuary, rest here during migration, and use the watery preserve as nesting habitat. In fact, the marsh provides habitat for twenty-seven endangered, threatened, rare, or declining bird species. The marsh also plays a key role in the recovery of peregrine falcons and bald eagles, which come to the marsh to forage and rest. Muskrat, mink, otter, and deer are also visitors to the marsh. Spring, of course, is prime time for birdwatching. But you're likely to see plenty of wading birds and ducks on your snowshoe walk through the preserve.

The Eastern Trail traverses the center of the marsh, traveling a scenic route through sparse woods and along an old canal and picturesque salt pannes. The long-distance, off-road hiking and biking path will eventually travel from Portsmouth, New Hampshire, to Casco Bay in South Portland. The completed path through the marsh is arguably one of the trail's prettiest stretches.

Pick up the trail just south of the Audubon visitor center (the center is closed in the winter but a small area is plowed for parking). Cross the footbridge through the marsh, or cross Pine Point Road and go toward Old Orchard Beach and Saco. The narrow gravel road makes for an easy snowshoe trek.

You'll meander along a mass of frosty sea grasses and fuzzy cattails, laced with ribbons of icy streams and tidal rivers. As you follow the path, you'll have views of frozen salt pannes and tidal waters. Look for wintering birds and waterfowl that forage in the marshes and open waters. An old tidal canal

Deer tracks are a common sight in New England's winter woods.

snakes through the marsh, its banks frozen and snow-covered in the winter, but its flowing salt water a magnet for wintering wildlife. The trail continues into a stand of thin woods, near its end on Black Point Road, where you'll need to turn around and retrace your steps back to the car.

If you have time, consider a visit to nearby Pine Point Beach, a great place to wander the bank of a tidal river where it meets the Atlantic Ocean. Then head into Scarborough for a warm mug of hot cocoa.

--*25*--
Gilsland Farm

Rating: Easy
Round trip: 1.5 miles
Hiking time: 1 hour
Elevation gain: 0 feet
High point: 0 feet
Map: Gilsland Farm brochure map
Information: Maine Audubon Society, Gilsland Farm, 20 Gilsland Farm Road, Falmouth, ME 04105; 207-781-2330; *www.MaineAudubon.org*

Getting there: From Portland, take I-295 to exit 10 and then left on Bucknam Road. At the light, turn right onto Route 1 and continue south for 1 mile. After the blinking light at the intersection of Routes 1 and 88, Gilsland Farm Road is on the right at the light blue sign.

This pristine 65-acre sanctuary on the Presumpscot River estuary is headquarters for the Maine Audubon Society—and a great place for a winter
stroll. You can hike more than 2 miles of trails that weave through open
fields, meadows, and woodlands, and along tidal shoreline and salt marshes.
As you might guess, this is a bird-lover's paradise. On your winter walk,
you're likely to hear—and see—flocks of Canada geese and a variety of
waterfowl. Join one of the center's guided night walks and listen for the *hoot-
hoot* of an owl.

The environmental center is a good place to hang out; there are exhibits,
a library, and a children's discovery area, along with hot drinks and snacks.
The center rents snowshoes and hosts a variety of programs and guided hikes
throughout the winter.

The land was once home to the Wabanakis, who fished and hunted the
rich tidal flats and waters of Casco Bay. Later, the land was farmed by settlers.
Portland lawyer, David Moulton, bought the farm in 1911 and spent the next
forty years raising Jersey cattle on the land. He also planted it with extensive
gardens, including more than 400 species of peonies. Come here in June,

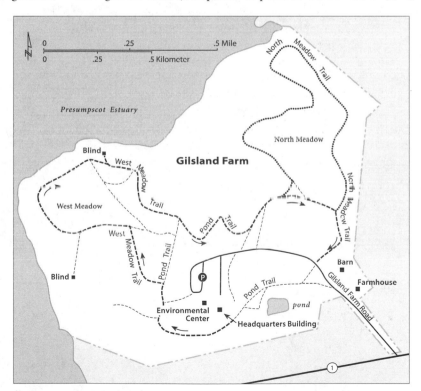

and you'll still see remnants of the garden—peonies in bloom. Moulton's daughters inherited the property and between 1974 and 1984 donated the land to the Maine Audubon Society. The "green-design" environmental center opened in 1996.

The main trailhead is located just outside the environmental center at the end of the driveway. You can access all the trails from here. Start with the 0.7-mile West Meadow Trail as it circles the winter-frosted field. You'll walk through the frozen wetland out into the field, overlooking the Presumpscot River estuary. The cluster of buildings you see in the distance is the Portland city skyline. If you'd like to observe winter waterfowl, take one of the two spur trails to an observation blind that overlooks the mudflats.

Back at the main trail, pick up the Pond Trail for a loop through a century-old red oak and hemlock forest. Paper birch trees decorate the forest, creating ghostly images. Look above the forest, and you'll see gnarled-branched apple trees in the snow-covered orchard. Continue on the trail to the edge of the frozen inlet. We've stood here during a soft snowstorm, when flakes as big as quarters settled on our winter parkas and drifted to the ground. A magical scene! Walk the road back to the parking lot. The Pond Trail loop is only 0.6 miles long and will take less than a half-hour, not counting your pause at the shores of the pond.

If you still have time, take the North Meadow Trail, a 1.2-mile walk through more forests and fields. Stay right along the base of the parking lot, then head into the forest of oaks and hemlocks and out to North Meadow. The trail will take you on a wide loop around the picturesque field, once filled with farm crops and Jersey cows. This is a favorite hangout for wintering Canada geese and a hunting ground for hawks and eagles. If you come early in the season, you may spot some lingering birds of prey.

--26--
Harris Farm Cross-Country Ski Center

Rating: Easy
Round trip: 3 miles, Bobcat Loop
Hiking time: 2 hours
Elevation gain: 80 feet
High point: 200 feet
Map: Harris Farm Trail Map
Information: Harris Farm Cross-Country Ski Center, Buzzell Road,
Dayton, ME 04005; 207-499-2678; *www.harrisfarm.com*

Getting there: From the Maine Turnpike, head north on Route 35, 11.5 miles through Goodwin Mills to the intersection of Buzzell Road. Turn right onto Buzzell Road and travel 1 mile east.

This family-owned, 500-acre plot is home to a dairy farm, a tree farm, a maple sugaring business, a vegetable farm stand, and, in the not-so-off-season, a cross-country ski center. If you have Nordic skiers in your crowd, small children, or just want to tromp around in the quiet woods and snow-covered fields, this off-the-beaten-path property is a fine destination. Located about a half-hour from the resort town of Kennebunk, the farm is a serene haven, with warming huts, equipment rentals, a sledding hill for the kids, and a helpful, friendly staff. If you've never snowshoed, this would be a great place to give it a try. If you're an old hand, you'll appreciate the pastoral setting, solitude, and elbowroom. Besides, where else can you spend a few good hours

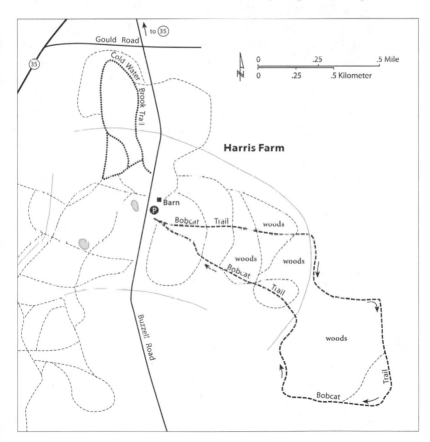

Over the hill and through the woods!

snowshoeing, then go home with a bottle of fresh bottled milk (regular, chocolate, even blueberry-flavored)?

The trails access more than 1000 acres of private land, including neighboring acreage and forest. There are 65 kilometers (40.3 miles) of groomed, designated trails, but snowshoers can also make their own tracks through sheltered forests and open fields. Trails range from gentle beginners' loops to rolling terrain with some lively ups and downs. And, thankfully, the only snowmobile you'll see around here belongs to the Harrises; snow machines are forbidden on these pristine acres. "We tried to set aside some trails for snowmobilers awhile back," says Keith Harris, "but it didn't really work." We're glad it didn't.

Start out at the ski center barn where you can pick up maps, rent snowshoes, and gather general information. Most people, especially beginning cross-country skiers, head for 5-mile Joe Buzzell Lane. It's an easy meander, but snowshoers would do best to avoid it. If you'd like a warm-up before you take the more challenging, 3-mile Bobcat Loop, head first to the Cold Water Brook area, where you can walk through woods and over bridge crossings. The terrain offers a pleasing variety, with tree-lined curves giving way to glistening snowfields.

For the Bobcat Loop, head out from the lodge, cross Trail #2 (the Maternity Loop), and turn right onto the Bobcat Loop, Trail #7. You'll walk alongside snowy woods, up a short, gentle hill. Follow the trail through a couple of pretty maple groves (you'll see where the trees have been tapped for the Harrises' maple sugar business) and a spruce and hemlock forest, dotted with white birch trees.

The trail climbs gently up two small hills, crosses a bridge over a frozen stream, and turns right. You'll loop through the quiet forest on gradual up-and-down terrain, before descending more abruptly. You'll cross over the stream once more before heading back to the lodge.

End your excursion with a tall glass of milk—fresh from the Harris Farm!

WESTERN MOUNTAINS

--27--
Caribou Mountain

Rating:	More difficult
Round trip:	5.4 miles
Hiking time:	6 hours
Elevation gain:	1990 feet
High point:	2850 feet
Map:	*AMC Maine Mountain Guide,* Map 5:E13–E14
Information:	White Mountain National Forest, Evans Notch Region, 18 Mayville Road, Bethel, ME 04217-4400; 207-824-2134; *www.fs.fed.us/r9/white*

Getting there: Take Bog Road, off Route 2, 1.3 miles west of the West Bethel post office. Drive to the end, where there's a small, plowed-out parking area. You'll need to walk the rest of the way down the road, about a quarter-mile, to the trailhead.

This trail leads to the open summit of 2850-foot Caribou Mountain in the Evans Notch region, straddling the Maine–New Hampshire border. It's a long, steady climb, with nearly 2000-foot elevation gain. But the hike through

The Caribou Mountain trail leads to lofty views.

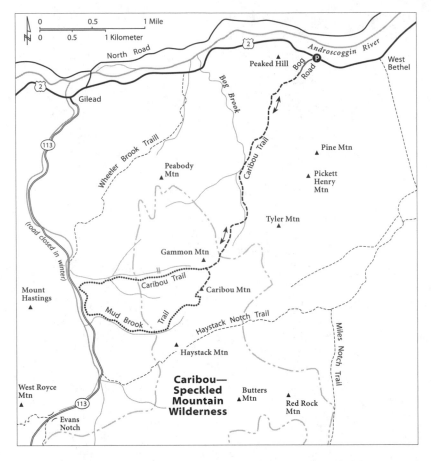

the dense pine forests of the Caribou–Speckled Mountain Wilderness and the sweeping views from the top of Mount Caribou make the effort worthwhile. While popular with summer hikers, few complete the snowshoe hike to the top, but you're likely to find the tracks of some hardy locals who appreciate the exercise and the scenery.

First, stop by Bethel's Best diner on Route 2, a couple of miles east of the trailhead, to stock up on body fuel. They open for breakfast at 7:00 AM, but you'll also want to pick up one of their bulky sandwiches or wraps for the trail. We usually opt for the overflowing "lobstah" roll, arguably one of the best in the state.

Be sure to start at the east trailhead, off Bog Road. The west trailhead, located off Route 113 (and the route that is typically featured in hiking books), is more difficult to access and will add several miles onto your trip, as Route 113 is closed to motor vehicles in the winter.

You ease into this trip slowly, with a level walk through open woods and fields. This part of the trail is often used by cross-country skiers and local families, but most turn back before the trail begins its steady climb. The trail is well marked most of the way (look for faded yellow splotches on the trees), but it can get tricky as you near the top. Stay alert to trail markings.

The trail enters the forest and begins its steady pull up the mountain, with occasional steep pitches. While there are no hands and knees spots or scrambles up rock faces, you will be huffing and puffing at the continual ascent—especially if you're trekking through dumps of deep, virgin snow. The trail continues its uphill battle, entering the Caribou–Speckled Mountain Wilderness. The protected area spreads over 12,000 acres in the White Mountain National Forest and is one of only two wilderness areas in Maine. Caribou Mountain is the preserve's second highest peak; Speckled Mountain is the highest point at 2906 feet.

About 2 miles into the hike, you'll come to the well-marked junction with the west branch of the Caribou Trail. Be sure to head south (left) on the Mud Brook Trail from here to reach the summit of Caribou Mountain. (If you continue straight on the Caribou Trail, you'll end up on Route 113, a long way from your car.) From here, it's a breeze as the trail levels out, winding through dense evergreens, before breaking out onto the open summit. What a view! The mountaintop is dotted with stunted pines, dusted with snow and ice. In the distance, you'll have views across the Caribou–Speckled Mountain Wilderness into the White Mountains of New Hampshire. On clear days, you'll see the snow-covered summit of Mount Washington and the Presidential peaks. Brush the snow off a flat granite slab, take a seat, and unwrap that "lobstah" roll.

--28--
Carter's Cross-Country Ski Center

Rating: Easy
Round trip: 4.08 miles
Hiking time: 3 hours
Elevation gain: 500 feet (approximate)
High point: 1000 feet (approximate)
Map: Carter's Cross-Country Ski Center/Bethel Center Trail Map
Information: Carter's Cross-Country Ski Center, Intervale Road, Bethel, ME; 207-824-3880; *www.cartersxcski.com*

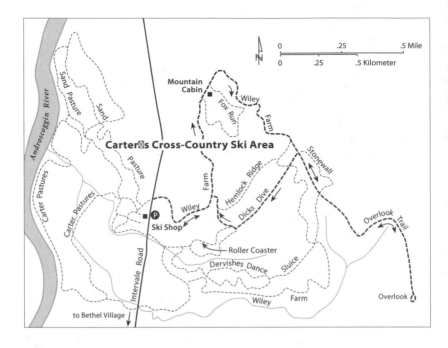

Getting there: Take I-95 north to the Maine Turnpike. Take exit 11 (Gray) and follow Route 26 for 52 miles. Take a right on Intervale Road, go 3.5 miles. The center is on the left.

"It's a bit swamp Yankee, don't ya' think?" said one of our hiking companions of this down-home ski center. We'll admit, if you're looking for Aspen chic and oh-so-refined atmosphere, don't bother to come here. The place is a bit rough around the edges, with hand-scrawled signs on the trails and tattered sofas in the lodge. But turn your back on the accoutrements and feast your eyes instead on the surroundings. You can't beat the scenery, 1000 or more acres sprawled along the Androscoggin River, surrounded by snowy peaks.

Trails crisscross old farmlands, skirt the river, and skitter up hillsides for open views. Most trails are used by Nordic skiers, but there's a handful of woodsy snowshoe-only paths. Big-foot hikers can join the skiers on most of the trails, but remember to be considerate by staying off the machine-groomed tracks. Snowshoers will also find plenty of area to explore on their own, if they don't mind seeking out unmarked, ungroomed territory.

For a short, half-day walk with rewarding views, head to the Overlook Trail. Stop in the lodge to purchase a trail pass (about $12 for adults, kids under five are free) and pick up a map. Likely, owner Dave Carter will be around to chat about the property, the thrill and serenity of skiing and back-woods living, and the old days. Equipment rentals and repairs, snacks, and the warmth of a wood-burning stove are also offered.

From the ski shop, you'll walk the easy, flat Sand Pasture Trail a short distance before heading across the road into a large, open farm field. Follow the Wiley Farm Trail, through open pasture and sparse woods. You'll pass a rustic mountain cabin (the cabin, without electricity and running water, rents for about $85 a night), then wind through the woods on an easy grade.

If you'd like to do a bit of bushwhacking, you can jump off the tracked path here and head up through the woods, making your own way to the Overlook Trail. The quarter-mile or so stretch through the woods is a pleasant, gradual climb in often untracked snow. The Overlook Trail meanders along a ridgeline, in a gentle up-and-down cadence. You'll pass a few homes tucked away in the woods, signs of the increasing development that's occurring on the edges of the Carter property.

After a short, easy climb, the view opens up. Some say the overlook is one of the best views in the Bethel area. From here you'll have a panoramic view of the Mahoosuc and Presidential mountain ranges. The downhill ski trails of the Sunday River Ski Resort snake down the mountainside to the east.

Shelter along the trail is a welcome sight at Carter's Cross-Country Ski Center.

When you're done gawking at the view, retrace your tracks back down to the stone wall where Dick's Dive takes a left, and head down. This snowshoe-only path descends through a pretty hemlock forest, where a canopy of flat boughs drape dramatically over the trail. Keep an eye out for evidence of wildlife that lives in the area: tracks and scat of deer, moose, rabbits, fox, and the neighboring dogs. The trail dumps back into pasture and farmland across the street from the ski shop.

--29--
Sunday River Cross-Country Ski Center

Rating: Easy to more difficult
Round trip: 3 miles
Hiking time: 3 hours
Elevation gain: 1063 feet
High point: 1763 feet
Map: Snowshoe Trail Map, Sunday River Cross-Country Ski Center
Information: Sunday River Cross-Country Ski Center, 23 Skiway Road, Newry, ME 04261; 207-824-2410; *www.sundayriverinn.com*

Getting there: Take the Maine Turnpike to exit 11 at Gray. Follow Route 26 north from Gray to Bethel, then take Route 2 east 3 miles to Sunday River Access Road. Turn left on Sunday River Access Road and travel 2 miles to the center, in Newry.

Bring the kids, bring the dog, bring Grandma . . . This fun, family-friendly center is a great place to spend a day, offering snowshoe-only paths, cross-country ski trails, a children's play area, warming shelters, a groomed dog trail, a downhill practice area, and instruction. A full-service ski shop, outdoor seating area, and restaurant are also on-site. Just up the street is the popular Sunday River Ski Resort (no affiliation with the cross-country center). On Friday evenings, from 7:00 PM to 9:00 PM, there are guided snowshoe hikes, ending with a marshmallow roast over an open bonfire. On Thursday and Saturday evenings, the center offers a guided hike to a prime hillside spot to view the fireworks at the Sunday River Ski Resort.

There are gentle, short walks around streams and brooks and through pine and hardwood forests. Or you can take a hike (alongside a downhill ski

Snow mounds create a fluffy meringue.

trail) to the Summit Hotel and Moonstruck Café. Looking for something more challenging to get the heart rate up? You'll find it here, too, along the Raven Ridge Trail, which climbs steeply to open cliffs. You can also access the Locke Mountain Trail from here, an unmarked backcountry trail leading to the open 1924-foot mountain summit. (A handful of Sunday River's downhill ski trails crisscross Locke Mountain.)

Pick up a trail map and a cup of hot chocolate at the ski center before heading out. Day use trail fee for snowshoers is $7; there are equipment rentals available, too. You can meander around the farm land, passing the Chicken Coop warming hut, a farmhouse and cottage, and skirting around a small pond, before picking up the Raven Ridge Trail.

The trip starts out gently, through open fields and sparse woods. At about 0.5 mile, the trail meets up with the snowmobile route. Alas, you'll have to share part of Raven Ridge Trail with the snowmobilers. The trail begins to climb gradually, then more steeply in spots as it gains purchase up the ridge. You'll gain about 500 to 600 feet in elevation before reaching the top section of the trail. This is a good time to take a break before tackling the rest of the trail.

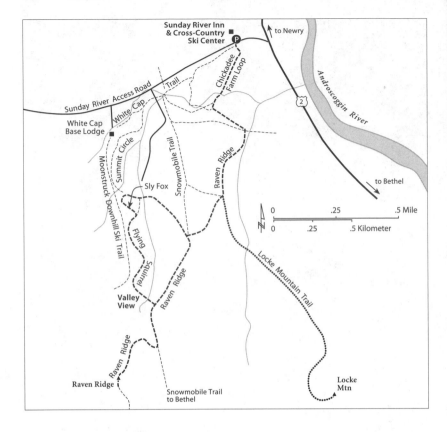

The upper section of Raven Ridge Trail is narrow and steep, but the distance is short (less than 0.5 mile) and the views from the top are rewarding. You'll gain about another 400 feet in elevation before reaching the summit overlook. And, what views! The Presidentials, the Mahoosuc Range, and the peaks and valleys beyond . . .

Backtrack your way down the upper Raven Ridge Trail to the Valley View Trail junction. Take a left onto the Valley View Trail and follow it along the ridgeline to Flying Squirrel Trail. Head down the Flying Squirrel Trail, dropping into the valley, then retrace your tracks along the lower section of the Raven Ridge Trail back to the ski shop.

Looking for an overnight backcountry experience? The center rents Camp Ella, a "Real Maine Camp," located on the 30 secluded acres of riverfront, woods, and beaver ponds. Amenities include kerosene lamps, gas appliances, a woodstove, hand-pumped water, and deluxe outhouse.

--*30*--
Table Rock

Rating: Moderate
Round trip: 2.8 miles (with options to continue)
Hiking time: 3 hours
Elevation gain: 900 feet
High point: 2400 feet
Map: *AMC Maine Mountain Guide,* Map 6
Information: Grafton Notch State Park, 1941 Bear River Road, Newry, ME 04261; 207-624-6080; *www.state.me.us/doc/parks*

Getting there: From Bethel, take Route 2 east to Route 26 north (Bear River Road). Turn left on Route 26 and travel to Grafton Notch State Park. The parking lot for the AT and the Table Rock Trail is on the left side of the road, about 12.5 miles from the junction of Routes 2 and 26.

If you're looking for sweeping mountain views with a short burst of effort, you can't beat this trail in Maine's picturesque Grafton Notch State Park. The 3112-acre park, located in western Maine, is a favorite destination among outdoor

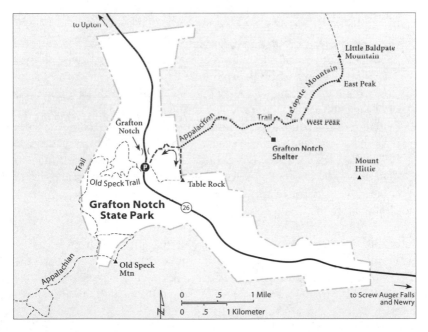

lovers. Hiking trails, including the Appalachian Trail (AT), crisscross the woods, dotted with lakes, ponds, and rivers. The park is also home to Old Speck; at 4180 feet, it's Maine's third-highest peak (ranked behind Katahdin and Sugarloaf). Snowshoeing up Old Speck should be left to the experienced—and very hardy. But this moderate, short jaunt up to Table Rock will reward you with similar mountain views. Table Rock is a huge, open ledge overlooking Grafton Notch, Old Speck, and the surrounding valleys and peaks of western Maine.

The trail to Table Rock begins at the Grafton Notch State Park parking lot off Route 26. Cross the highway, then follow the white-blazed trail into the woods. We always take a moment to consider the AT thru-hikers that have gone before us, nearing the end of their epic 2100-mile-plus journey. You'll follow in their footsteps as you make your way up to Table Rock.

The trail begins a gradual ascent through the woods, passing a few small brooks and tiny frozen streams along the way. If it's early in the season, or the weather has been mild, be cautious as you cross the marshy areas and streams. We've gotten a fair share of soakers on this trip! The barren birch trees and towering pines are winter homes for woodpeckers, chickadees, and nuthatches. You'll likely see the small birds flying about the branches. We've heard woodpeckers hard at work in the trees and seen remnants of their efforts—wood shavings scattered in the snow. But for the most part, this is a peaceful walk in the snow.

The trail continues the steady ascent up the west slope of Baldpate Mountain. At 0.9 mile, it reaches the junction with Table Rock Trail, to the right. Follow the blue-blazed trail about 0.5 to Table Rock. The open ledge is perched 900 feet above the floor of the notch, the perfect place to stop and rest, and take in the panoramic mountain and valley views. You'll find several caves, beneath the overhanging granite slabs, to explore. Be careful; the caves are deep, and the area around them is slippery. A fall into one of them could be serious.

We suggest backtracking from here, following the same AT route down to the trailhead and parking lot. Another option would be to follow the blue-blazed Table Rock trail. But this is a fairly steep and often slippery descent.

If you have the energy, consider continuing on the AT another 2 miles to the 3680-foot West Peak of Baldpate Mountain. The trail is steep and rough in some areas, but you'll be rewarded with 360-degree vistas from the summit. A side trail leads to the Grafton Notch shelter along the way.

Be sure to save time to explore two nearby waterfalls. Pretty Screw Auger Falls, about 5 miles to the east of Grafton Notch, is just steps from a parking area off Route 26. Icy granite boulders and snow-banked pools surround the falls. Mother Walker Falls and Moose Cave, a skinny, deep gorge, is just a mile or so north of Screw Auger Falls, also off scenic Route 26. Both are easy to access and worth the stop.

RANGELEY/SUGARLOAF

--31--
Piazza Rock

Rating: Easy/more difficult
Round trip: 3 miles to Piazza Rock, 3.6 miles to Saddleback summit
Hiking time: 3 hours
Elevation gain: 500 feet
High point: 2500 feet
Maps: *Maine Appalachian Trail Club (MATC) Appalachian Trail Guide to Maine,* Map 6; *AMC Maine Mountain Guide,* Map 2
Information: Maine Appalachian Trail Club, *www.matc.org;* National Park Service, Appalachian National Scenic Trail, Harpers Ferry Center, Harpers Ferry, WV 25425; 304-535-6331; *www.nps.gov/appa*

Getting there: From Rangeley, travel Route 4 south for approximately 9 miles. The AT trail is well marked; parking is on the west side of the road, opposite the trailhead.

Big boulders, a giant hanging rock, and secret caves make this short jaunt a must-do in the Rangeley Lakes region of western Maine. The up-and-back hike follows the famed Appalachian Trail and is a fun one to do with children. The walk is relatively short and gentle (perfect for short attention spans and little legs), and kids love to see the massive rock that seems to be magically suspended in air. Nearby, they can explore a series of boulder caves.

We also like the options you have to lengthen this hike. Travel a bit farther, and you'll come to the shores of a scenic mountain pond. Opt in for the long haul, and continue on the trail to the windblown, arctic-like summit of 4120-foot Saddleback Mountain—a classic, though strenuous, hike on the AT on its way across Maine. (The final leg of the long-distance Appalachian Trail, from Georgia to Maine, is the "Hundred Mile Wilderness" between Monson and Mount Katahdin.)

Saddleback Mountain range boasts several high peaks, extending east–west across the western lakes region. Two of the peaks, the Saddleback summit and The Horn (4023 feet), rise above 4000 feet and are connected by a

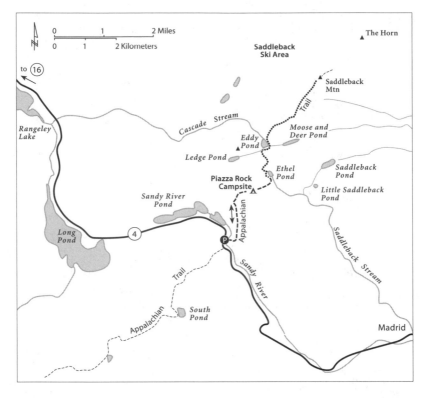

1.6-mile ridge. This hike takes you up the southwestern side of the mountain. The downhill ski runs of the Saddleback Mountain resort dominate the northwestern slope.

We like to pack a picnic lunch to be enjoyed at the Piazza Rock lean-to, maintained by the Maine Appalachian Trail Club. If you'd like to try your hand at winter camping, this sheltered destination is a good option. Camping here can also break up the long 10.2-mile summit trip. Though the trail to Piazza Rock is gradual, more often than not you'll be hiking through deep powder. The area is known for its long, snowy winters, with frequent, heavy snowfalls. Several times, we've arrived at the trailhead early to make fresh tracks in virgin snow, sometimes sinking up to our calves. Wind-sculpted snowdrifts, some several feet high, form odd shapes, and we imagine them as eerie animals and giant people. In a good season (read: snowy), snowbanks crowd the edges of the trail, and you'll walk in a white, hushed tunnel, pine boughs carpeted with snow hanging overhead.

The parking lot on the west side of Route 4 is usually plowed; if not, you'll have to find a spot farther down on the side of the road and walk back. The trail begins on the east side of the road, descending a short distance to the Sandy River. The trail begins to climb out of the valley at a gentle incline. Listen for pileated woodpeckers that feed in the trees. They're easily spotted if you look and listen carefully.

At 1.4 miles, you'll reach the Piazza Rock lean-to. Drop your bags and go explore! A side path leads to the top of Piazza Rock, a giant granite slab jutting impossibly out from the cliffs and hanging some 30 feet above the valley. Back on the AT, walk another few yards up to the side trail leading to The Cliffs. Take your time exploring the boulder caves and tiny, narrow passageways.

Keep an eye out for pileated woodpeckers in New England's winter woods.

You can continue on the AT another (steep) mile to the western shores of Ethel Pond, with mountain and valley views. Saddleback summit lies another tough 2.6 miles from the pond, up the steep, krummholz-covered slope and out across open—and very exposed—slabs. The far-reaching views of Maine's western mountains, pine forests, and lakes are stunning. One note of caution: Saddleback summit, and much of the trail leading up to it, is exposed, and prone to high winds and sudden storms.

--32--
Burnt Mountain

Rating:	More difficult/most difficult
Round trip:	7 miles
Hiking time:	6 hours
Elevation gain:	2209 feet
High point:	3609 feet
Map:	Sugarloaf/USA Outdoor Center Trail Map
Information:	Sugarloaf/USA, 5092 Access Road, Carrabassett Valley, ME 04947; 800-THE-LOAF; *www.sugarloaf.com*

Getting there: Take I-95 north to Augusta, exit 112B (formerly 31B). Follow Route 27 north through Farmington and Kingfield. The Outdoor Center is located 1 mile south of the Sugarloaf/USA ski resort access road; you'll see the sign on the south side of Route 27.

Solitude, commanding views, and a touch of wilderness mark this little-used route up the round-domed Burnt Mountain. This peak in Maine's Carrabasset Valley sits in the shadows of Sugarloaf Mountain, minutes from the popular ski resort. The hiking trail is best accessed through the resort's cross-country and snowshoe Outdoor Center. The added bonus is that anyone in your group who doesn't want to make the long, more challenging trek up Burnt Mountain can play around on the network of trails that wind through the pretty woods and bogs at the base of the center.

In fact, that's exactly what we did the first time we visited the center. We snowshoed through a winter wonderland, walking on 5-foot-deep snow paths, flanked by towering emerald pines and barren white birch trees. We skirted frozen Moose Bog, blanketed with the season's deep dumps of snow. This area is known for its heavy snowfall, and the season tends to last longer here than in many parts of New England. Then, gently, one foot at a time, we followed the trail as it circled through the woods, and less than an hour later, ended back at the Sugarloaf/USA Outdoor Center. In our small group, we had a novice (her first time on snowshoes), a five-year-old, and a nine-month-old in a backpack child carrier. It was the perfect little jaunt, but the next time we returned, we wanted more. We found it in this hike up Burnt Mountain.

Start at the Outdoor Center lodge, where you can pick up trail maps and get information on conditions. The center also has a giant fireplace, deck, and food at the local favorite Bull Moose Bakery and Cafe, serving freshly made soups, stews, and sandwiches. There's an Olympic-sized outdoor skating rink, too, if you have the energy left after this hike!

Follow the Route 1 West Trail a few yards to the Upper Blue (snowshoe) Trail. The snowshoe-only trail crosses #29, #2, and #7 cross-country ski trails, and continues to climb past the Orange (snowshoe) Trail, #22 ski trail, and #51 ski trail. It's a steady push up, gaining 600 feet in elevation before reaching the intersection with the Burnt Mountain Hiking Trail about 1.5 miles from the lodge. The #50 Burnt Mountain Loop Trail intersects here, too.

Turn right onto the Burnt Mountain Hiking Trail, heading south, and begin the moderate ascent through a towering stand of spruce. In less than 0.5 mile you'll reach the junction with the expert-rated ski trail #51. You'll follow the same path for a few yards before the ski trail veers to the left and you stay straight. You'll intersect the ski trail once more, before you leave all civilization behind to make the final mile-or-so push to the top of the mountain.

The trail travels through a fragrant balsam fir forest before breaking out into the open for views of the Bigelow Mountain range. You'll walk across a blissfully flat, broad plateau for the last quarter-mile. Chances are that you'll be alone to appreciate the 360-degree vista—towering 4237-foot Sugarloaf to the west with a

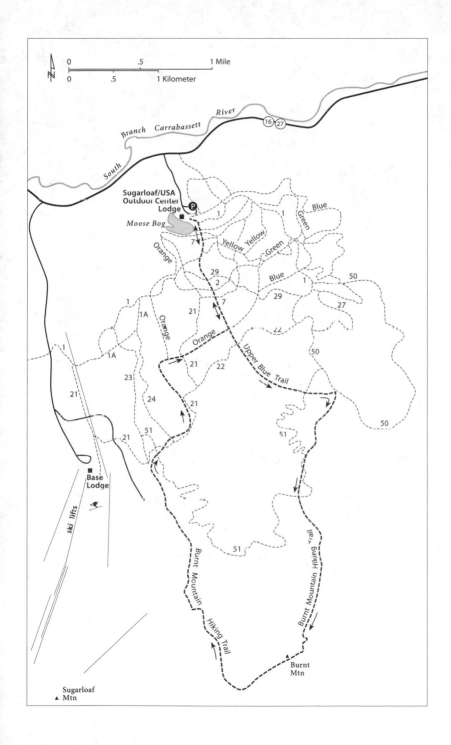

The path beckons!

spiderweb of downhill ski trails carved on its face, the Bigelow Mountain range to the north, Spaulding Mountain and Mount Abraham to the south, and more.

To return, you can retrace your steps for the easy descent down. Or, if you'd like to make a loop, find the Burnt Mountain Trail as it continues, heading southwest off the mountain. Follow this as it loops around to the north. The trail is underused and a bit overgrown, so it can be tricky to follow. But it generally heads north, following West Branch Brackett Brook and paralleling the Sugarloaf downhill ski trails. The Burnt Mountain Trail merges with the Blue Trail snowshoe route. Follow this to the Orange Trail, turn right, and follow this to the Route 1 Trail back to the lodge.

GUIDED HIKES IN MAINE

There are several places to take a guided hike or snowshoeing excursion in the Pine Tree State.

The **L.L. Bean Outdoor Discovery School** (888-552-3261, *www.llbean .com*) offers a variety of snowshoeing programs, including guided nature walks, animal tracking, backcountry hikes, and winter overnight trips.

At the **Sunday River Cross-Country Center** (207-824-2410, *www .sundayriverinn.com)* you can join an evening, full-moon walk through the woods, culminating with a fireworks show.

The **Sugarloaf/USA Outdoor Center** (800-THE-LOAF, *www.sugarloaf .com*) offers a variety of guided hikes, including beginner walks to the bog, moonlight walks, and a weekly "Shoe and Stew" lunch hike.

The Birches resort (800-825-9453, *www.birches.com*) sits on 11,000 private acres of northern Maine woods, on the edge of Moosehead Lake. Join their guided, overnight trip to a backcountry hut.

MOOSEHEAD REGION

-- 🜛🜛 --
Mount Kineo

Rating:	Moderate to more difficult
Round trip:	4.4–4.6 miles
Hiking time:	3–5 hours
Elevation gain:	760 feet
High point:	1789 feet
Maps:	Mount Kineo, Maine Bureau of Parks and Lands; Moosehead Lake Map and Guide, DeLorme Mapping Company
Information:	Maine Bureau of Parks and Lands, 106 Hogan Road, Bangor, ME 04401; 207-941-4014; *www.state.me.us /doc/prkslands*

Getting there: From Greenville, follow Route 15 north for 20 miles to Rockwood. In the center of town, turn onto Village Road to the town dock parking lot.

Mount Kineo, with its steep and exposed cliffs, rises some 800 feet from the waters of Moosehead Lake. The sheer-sided mountain sits on a tiny peninsula in the center of the lake and is a magnet for summer hikers, who take a boat or ferry from the public launch in Rockwood and shuttle the short 0.8-mile distance to the foot of the rocky mountain. However, in the winter, you can park at the town dock lot (on Village Road, off Route 15) and cross the frozen lake on foot. The lake's ice conditions vary, of course, with the season. The Moosehead Lake Chamber of Commerce will have up-to-date information on conditions. (Read the ice safety information in the safety section of the Introduction.)

(Note: Try to avoid snowshoeing here on the weekends when snowmobile traffic can be heavy. In any case, take caution to stay clear of the snowmobile markers on the lake.)

There are three trails that lead from the Carriage Trail to the top of Kineo; the Indian Trail is the steepest and most difficult but also the trail with the most dramatic views along the way. Care should be taken in all conditions, but don't attempt it at all if the trail is icy or the weather dicey. Opt instead for a hike to the summit via the gentler Bridle Trail or North Trail, which climbs

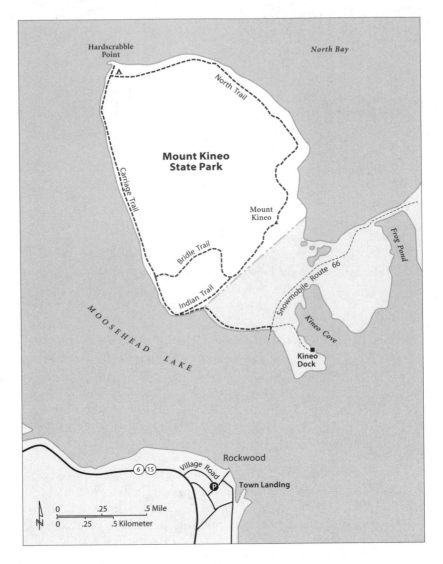

the northeast slope of Kineo. No matter which trail you choose, you won't be disappointed. The views from the top of 1789-foot Mount Kineo, of Moosehead Lake and surrounding northern Maine forests, are splendid.

Mount Kineo has an interesting past. Henry David Thoreau once camped along the shores of the peninsula. You'll be following in his footsteps when you hike to the summit; he, too, made the climb during his 1857 trip to Maine (though not on snowshoes). From the late 1860s to the 1930s, the peninsula was home to the Mount Kineo House hotel, which at one time was the largest inland water hotel in the country. In 1990, the State of Maine purchased 800 acres of Kineo, including all of the property from the cliff face north.

The first time we tried to find the start of the Carriage Trail and Bridle Trail, we had noticed a flock of snowmobiles congregating on a steep hill at the base of Kineo and assumed this was where the trail started. We later realized that we were walking on Route 66. To help you avoid making the same mistake, here's a tip: When you look across to this steep hill (which is very easy to spot even from clear across the other side of the lake), focus on walking up to the left of this area—up the bank a little. The Carriage Trail is clearly marked with a sign and is for hikers only. All trails branch off from the Carriage Trail.

In about 0.5 mile, you'll reach the first junction with the Indian Trail, a steep and nearly direct climb to the summit. If you're up for a huff-and-puff hike, take a right here onto the Indian Trail. The trail follows the edge of the cliff, with several open ledges and narrow passes.

The Bridle Trail, leaving the Carriage Trail about 0.25 mile beyond the Indian Trail junction, is a more moderate, gradual climb to the summit and observation tower (1.1 miles).

If you prefer a gentle lakeside hike, consider staying on the Carriage Trail. The well-traveled path runs 2.2 miles along the west shore of the peninsula out to Hardscrabble Point. There are three primitive campsites on the point. From Hardscrabble Point, you can pick up the North Trail. It is a longer loop, but an opportunity to see more of the peninsula. The path meanders the west shore, before climbing 1.9 miles to the summit. You can descend via Indian or Bridle Trail before walking back across the frozen water to Rockwood.

-- 34 --

Lily Bay State Park

Rating: Easy
Round trip: 2–4.6 miles
Hiking time: 2–4 hours
Elevation gain: 100 feet
High point: 1060 feet
Maps: Lily Bay State Park map; Moosehead Lake Map and Guide, DeLorme Mapping Co.
Information: Maine Dept. of Conservation, Bureau of Parks and Lands, 106 Hogan Road, Bangor, ME 04401; 207-941-4014; *www.state.me.us/doc/prkslands*

Getting there: From Greenville, go 9 miles northeast on Lily Bay Road (also called Kokadjo Road) to park entrance.

This little jewel of a park sits on the eastern shore of Moosehead Lake, boasting 925 acres and 8 miles of hiking trails. In the summer, it's a buzz of activity, with the noisy excitement of campers, swimmers, and boaters filling the air by day, and bonfire chats and loon calls during the evening. Come winter, alas, the buzz you hear is most likely the revving of snow machine engines. No matter, the trails are fun to explore, with rewarding views of sheltered coves, distant mountains, and expansive Moosehead Lake.

The 116-square-foot lake is the largest in New England and famous for its cold, deep, pristine waters, surrounding dense forests and mountain wilderness, and its large population of moose. By the way, Moosehead Lake gets its name from its shape, not for its most famous wildlife residents. Nonetheless, you'll find moose tracks everywhere throughout the park. Explore the park quietly at dusk or dawn, and you may even get a first-hand look at one. The trails are very sheltered, so they're ideal for spotting wildlife. Look for moose, of course, but also deer, fox, coyote, eagles, rabbits, and a host of small mammals. While the area has become more discovered and there's serious talk of major development, it still remains relatively quiet, spacious, and untrammeled.

One of the fun parts of visiting Lily Bay is that you can pretty much explore any area you like, poking around the shoreline, climbing up and around campsites, meandering woodsy, snow-covered roads, and walking lakeside paths. The

Sparse winter woods sometimes allow pretty distant vistas.

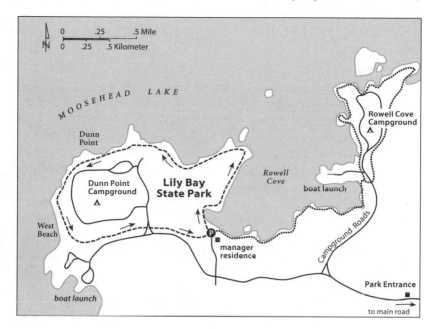

paths and snow-covered roads are usually well-packed, mostly flat and gentle—making Lily Bay a great place for families, or anyone looking for an easy outdoor snowshoeing excursion. Bring a snack or picnic lunch; the campground picnic tables remain on each site and make great places to sit, rest, relax, and munch—and, of course, take in the sweeping Moosehead Lake views.

A small parking lot is plowed at the main entrance to the park, off Lily Bay Road. From here, walk up the main road, then head north (past the campground manager's residence) down to the lakeshore and Rowell Cove. You can pick up the hiking trail that leads in both directions, skirting around the shoreline. Head to the left (as you look at the lake), and you'll walk along the west shore of sheltered Rowell Cove. You'll have mountain and open lake views, as you make your way out to scenic Dunn Point. Continue around the west side of the campground to West Beach before reaching the main campground road leading back out to the parking area.

At Rowell Cove, if you take the trail in the opposite direction (heading east), you'll skirt the shoreline, dipping in and out of tiny coves, past the Rowell Cove camping area before looping back down the road and out to your car. Or simply just meander as you please—following tracks in the woods and along the frosty shoreline.

(Note: Be sure the lake is safely frozen before venturing out onto the ice. See the ice safety section in the Introduction.)

-- 35 --
Gulf Hagas

Rating: Most difficult/backcountry
Round trip: 21 miles
Hiking time: 6–8 hours a day over three days
Elevation gain: 200 feet
High point: 1200 feet
Map: Maine Appalachian Trail Club (MATC) Appalachian Trail Guide in Maine, Map 2
Information: Appalachian Mountain Club, Pinkham Notch Visitor Center, Route 16, Gorham, NH 03581; 603-466-2721; *www.outdoors.org*. Note: A stay at the AMC-operated Little Lyford Pond Camps is required to do this multi-day hike.

Getting there: Little Lyford Pond is located 15 miles east of Greenville, and 20 miles northwest of Brownville. Access to Little Lyford Pond Camps is via logging roads. Lyford Pond staff will meet you in Greenville and give specific directions to the winter parking lot (location varies depending on weather conditions.) A four-wheel-drive vehicle is required to reach the lot. Staff will transport gear and personal items to the camps (fee). If you prefer, they will also arrange for transportation to the winter parking lot from Greenville.

Stand—carefully—on the rim of Gulf Hagas, and you'll know why it's called the "Grand Canyon of the East." Steep, sheer slate walls plunge to the riverbed, creating a deep, narrow chasm. The walls shine like crystal in the winter, coated with layers of ice. Impossibly long icicles hang from jagged rocks. On the way to the rim, you'll pass a series of impressive waterfalls, frozen in mid-air on their tumble down the river basin. Thick layers of icy cascades hang on snow-covered rocks. The colors are amazing: a rainbow of deep blue, green, black, and white.

Many make the trek in summer to visit this spectacular area, now a Registered National Landmark; few make it in winter. If you're looking for a multi-day trek into ruggedly beautiful country, and don't mind a little logistical hassle, look no further. An added benefit to this trip is the opportunity to stay in one of the cabins at heated, full-service Little Lyford Pond Camps, operated by the Appalachian Mountain Club. There are seven cabins, each sleeping one

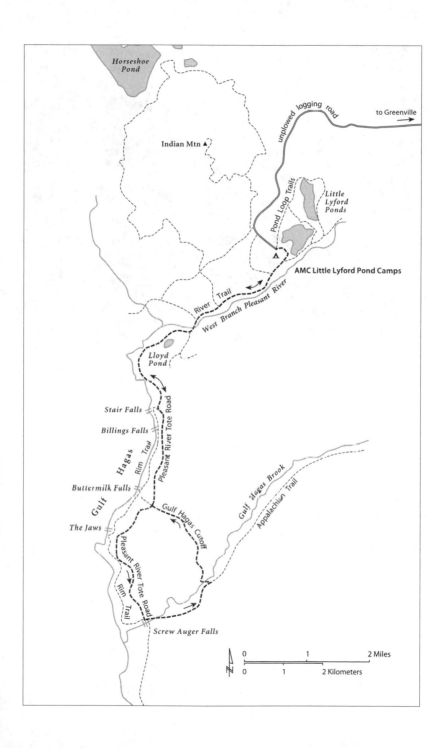

Horseshoe
Pond

unplowed logging road

to Greenville

Indian Mtn ▲

Little
Lyford
Ponds

Pond Loop Trails

△

AMC Little Lyford Pond Camps

River   Trail

West Branch Pleasant River

Lloyd
Pond

Stair Falls

Billings Falls

Pleasant River Tote Road

Hagas   Rim Trail

Gulf

Buttermilk Falls

Gulf Hagas Cutoff

The Jaws

Gulf Hagas Brook

Appalachian Trail

Pleasant River Tote Road

Rim   Trail

Screw Auger Falls

0   1   2 Miles

0   1   2 Kilometers

N

Snow-capped boulders decorate winter woods.

to six people. Each cabin has a woodstove and gas and kerosene lamps. There's also a coed bunkhouse with twelve bunks. Common areas include a lodge with a dining room (staff prepare meals year-round), activities center, and small library. It's rustic, but a lot easier than winter camping.

Planning this trip takes a bit of time. You'll need to reserve a space at the camp and arrange transportation to the winter parking lot (see Getting there above). From the parking lot, you'll have a 6.5-mile or more hike into the camp. Much of this is a straight, even shot on a wide, gently rolling logging road. Many choose to cross-country ski into the camp and don snowshoes for the hike to Gulf Hagas. But you can snowshoe it in about five hours.

By the time you travel from Greenville to the winter parking lot and hike into the camp, much of the first day will be over. Settle into your cabin and take in the views. The camp is located on the West Branch of the Pleasant River, surrounded by mountain peaks. You could spend days here exploring the Maine woods and mountains, with access to more than 400,000 acres of land at your doorstep. But Gulf Hagas is on the agenda for this trip. Rest up and drink plenty of fluids for the next day's 8-mile trek to the Gulf.

The trail leaves the lodge and enters the woods before climbing steeply to the banks of the West Branch of the Pleasant River. Follow the Little Lyford Pond Camps trail signs to the junction with the Appalachian Trail, about 2 miles from the camp. Follow the AT for a half-mile or so to the Gulf Hagas Rim Trail, on your right. You'll descend a short distance to the start of the Gulf.

The West Branch of the Pleasant River runs 4 miles through the Gulf, dropping some 400 feet. You'll enter a winter wonderland of frozen waterfalls, glistening cascades, ice, and snow. The Rim Trail travels along the edge of the canyon with awesome views. There are a number of side trails that take you to overlooks and falls. Footing can be precarious, so be cautious (you'll be thankful for those crampons!). Often there are ice climbers picking their way up the frozen ice walls to add to the show. The further you travel into the canyon, the narrower it becomes, until you reach the aptly named Jaws.

When you're done gawking, double back on the Rim Trail and retrace your steps back to the camp. Or, continue around the rim, looping back to the main trail. The next day, hike back out the logging road to the parking lot.

SNOWSHOE-FRIENDLY INNS IN MAINE

Looking for a weekend—or longer—getaway that combines great snowshoeing with a stay at a cozy country inn? Check out these snowshoe-friendly inns in Maine.

The Sunday River Inn in Newry (207-824-2410, *www.sundayriverinn.com*) offers casual, family-friendly lodging at the base of their cross-country and snowshowing center.

The rustically elegant **Lodge at Moosehead Lake** in Greenville (800-825-6977, *www.lodgeatmooseheadlake.com*) knows how to cater to outdoor enthusiasts, especially winter hikers and snowshoers. Explore the wilderness surrounding Moosehead Lake, then come back to the lodge for gourmet dining and ultra comfy, plush rooms.

The **5 Lakes Lodge** in Millinocket (207-723-5045, *www.5lakeslodge.com*) sits at the doorstep of Baxter State Park. With its sweeping views of Mount Katahdin, homemade cedar log furniture, whirlpool baths and a large, always-roaring fireplace, the lodge is one of the finest places for winter hikers to stay in Maine's north country.

Not much stays open in the Acadia National Park/Bar Harbor area in the winter. But you can count on a comfortable stay and knowledgeable, friendly staff at the **Atlantic Oakes By-The-Sea** in Bar Harbor (800-336-2463, *www.barharbor.com*). The family-owned, motel-style resort stays open year-round and is a convenient jumping-off spot for winter activities in the park.

BAXTER STATE PARK

--36--
Lost Pond

Rating: Moderate
Round trip: 8.6 miles
Hiking time: 5 hours
Elevation gain: 400 feet
High point: 1200 feet
Maps: Baxter State Park/Katahdin Map and Guide, DeLorme Mapping Company; Baxter State Park winter trails map
Information: Baxter State Park, 64 Balsam Drive, Millinocket, ME 04462; 207-723-5140; *www.baxterstateparkauthority.com*

Getting there: From Millinocket Lake, take GNP Golden Road 10 miles to Abol Bridge. The parking area is on the left, just before the bridge and a small general store and campground (not open in the winter) on the right. Please note that very few roads in the park are plowed for winter use; access is limited. Check with the Baxter State Park Authority, located on the main road in Millinocket, to ask about road and trail conditions.

You'll walk in the shadows of Mount Katahdin on this North Woods excursion in Baxter State Park. Katahdin, the Abenaki name for "greatest mountain," holds a special place in the hearts of New Englanders. Its cloud-shrouded 5267-foot summit is the terminus of the long-distance Appalachian Trail. And while it's not New England's tallest mountain (6288-foot Mount Washington is), it is perhaps the most wild. The mountain is a jumble of cliffs, ridges, serrated peaks, and glacial cirques, rising steeply from the northern Maine forest. It looms even larger and more dramatic in the winter, when the leaves have fallen from the trees, leaving nearly unobstructed views.

This lowland route to a chain of ponds is one of the easier (and accessible) winter hikes in Baxter State Park. But don't underestimate it; it is still backcountry terrain, with few nearby services. The trail is likely to be well tracked—but don't count on it. After a fresh, hefty snowfall, it'll take a lot longer to hike and require a lot more work. Lost Pond, an 8.6-mile up-and-back hike, is a nice destination for the day. You can continue to Daicey Pond and on to Katahdin Stream Campground to spend the night. (You need

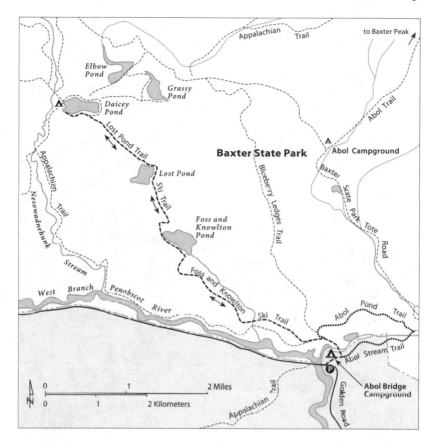

advance reservations for winter camping in Baxter.) The Foss and Knowlton Ski Trail begins directly across from the parking lot. Walk up a portion of the often busy (be careful!) snowmobile road. You'll notice a large gravel pit on the left before approaching the trailhead. You will then notice a sign for the Abol Stream Trail and various other possible trails. Cross over the small footbridge. Next, you'll come to a Baxter State Park sign detailing park rules. Now you're on the trail!

At roughly 0.5 mile, you'll come to a small kiosk at the junction with the Abol Pond Trail to the right. All skiers and snowshoe hikers must sign in and mark their intended trail and duration of stay. This is a good place to get situated or munch an energy bar before continuing.

From here, the trail is clearly marked with blue blazes—and Mount Katahdin is in full view to your right. "It feels as if I can reach out and touch Katahdin," a hiking companion once exclaimed.

Snowshoers on the trail to Lost Pond have views of Mount Katahdin's craggy peak.

The gentle up-and-down trail brings you to Foss and Knowlton Pond, 3.2 miles from the trailhead at Abol Bridge. This is a great spot, and even if you only have time to make it to this point, it's very rewarding. Stop here for a snack and cup of hot chocolate and take in the golden views of Katahdin. There are plenty of rocks to sit on and pretty sheltered areas under the pine trees. You'll also spot some small rowing boats and two canoes that are used in the warmer months to carry gear across the pond. If (as is likely in snow deep enough for snowshoeing) the pond is frozen solid and safe to walk on, you can venture across the pond in your snowshoes to connect to the trail again; otherwise, follow the full trail around the outer left perimeter of the pond. If the latter, you'll find the trail still clearly marked, but you'll have to pick your way through lots of brush and bumpy terrain.

Continue on the trail heading toward Lost Pond. This portion of the trail is a bit steeper than the last part, but more sheltered. In a half mile or so, you'll reach the frosty banks of Lost Pond. You can continue to Daicey Pond or turn around to retrace your steps. But remember, it gets dark early in Maine's northern, wintry woods.

CLASSIC SNOWSHOES

If you've ever said to yourself, "Gee, they don't make things like they used to," you've never met Bob Howe. Howe, a Registered Maine Guide, makes his own line of Maine Guide Snowshoes. He cuts the trees himself (white ash makes the best snowshoes, he says) and creates the shoes by hand in his workshop in Pleasant Ridge, Maine.

Each pair—beautifully varnished and hand-laced with neoprene—takes about two weeks to make. Neoprene is strong, waterproof, and won't stretch or sag, Howe says, but he'll use rawhide (made from the best cow hides) in the classic style if a customer requests it. Maine Guide Snowshoes are available in six styles, including the classic Bear Paw ("Rabbit hunters love these, since they're great in heavy brush," Howe says) and the skinny Alaskan, perfect for deep snow and long-distance snowshoeing. Prices range from $125 to $165. Howe sells about 300 pairs each year. Howe is his own best advertisement: He guides nearly every day of the year, and he's been at it for thirty years. "My father showed me how to walk in the woods, to fish, to hunt, and how to think like an animal, and how we're all linked," Howe says. Of course, he's in big demand with the hunting-and-fishing crowd, but he also guides trips that have nothing to do with "harvesting" animals. He guides snowshoe photo safaris ("I can take you places where you'll see 150 deer—my special spot," Howe says), moonlight snowshoe treks, and, March and April, trips into the woods to look for moose shed—antlers that the moose have rubbed off during the winter.

Howe and his wife Andrea also run Pine Grove Lodge, where the stuffed mounts in the parlor will make you a believer: This guy knows his stuff. His secret: He'd rather make snowshoes than hunt animals. "I don't shoot anything," Howe confesses. "I haven't shot anything in five years." For more information about Howe's guided snowshoe trips and Maine Guide Snowshoes, call 207-672-4011 or visit *www.pinegrovelodge.com*.

--*37*--

Chimney Pond

Rating: More difficult/backcountry
Round trip: 27 miles or more
Hiking time: 4 days or more
Elevation gain: 2470 feet
High point: 2930 feet
Maps: Baxter State Park/Katahdin Map and Guide, DeLorme Mapping Company; Baxter State Park winter trails map
Information: Baxter State Park, 64 Balsam Drive, Millinocket, ME 04462; 207-723-5140; *www.baxterstateparkauthority.com*

Getting there: From Millinocket Lake, take GNP Golden Road 10 miles to Abol Bridge. The parking area is on the left, just before the bridge and a small general store (on the right). Please note that very few roads in the park are plowed for winter use; access is limited and conditions may vary. Check with the Baxter State Park Authority, located on the main road in Millinocket, to ask about road and trail conditions.

Wild, rugged, remote, and dramatically beautiful . . . Chimney Pond, nestled in a semi-circular glacial bowl at the foot of towering, 1000-foot cliffs on the northeast side of Mount Katahdin, is arguably one of the prettiest hike-in spots in New England. Backcountry hikers, skiers, winter climbers, and snowshoers book months in advance for the privilege of staying in the bunkhouse or lean-tos clustered around the pond. It is one of Baxter State Park's most sought-after destinations, and for good reason. Make the long, two-day trek into Chimney Pond, and you'll have unparalleled views of Katahdin's South Basin and surrounding wilderness.

The path, though well trodden, should not be taken lightly. The four-day, up-and-back hike is long, sometimes strenuous, and, like all backcountry winter travel, requires planning and preparation. You'll need advance reservations to camp the first night at Roaring Brook and the second at Chimney Pond. Winter road access into Baxter State Park is very limited and often sketchy. This hike requires a 10-mile or more walk down an unplowed perimeter park road before reaching the steep Chimney Pond Trail. But if you're looking for a backwoods adventure, this is at the top of the list.

The 204,733-acre Baxter State Park boasts forty-six mountain peaks; eighteen are over 3500 feet. The land was donated to the state by former Governor

Percival Baxter, on the condition that it "shall forever be left in the natural wild state." Maine has done its darnedest to comply. There are few trappings of civilization in the park—even during its kinder, gentler summer months. In winter, once off the few roads that snow machines are allowed, you'll have plenty of peace and quiet and elbowroom.

Chimney Pond is surrounded by the twin peaks of Katahdin and the summits of Pamola and Chimney Peak. Winter mountaineers use the site as a base to

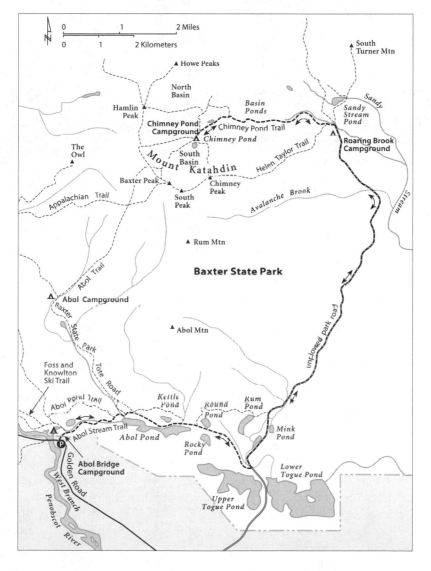

Views of Mount Katahdin in Baxter State Park

launch an ascent of Katahdin and to climb nearby ice cliffs. But once we're settled into the bunkhouse or one of the nine, four-person lean-tos, we're blessedly
content to soak in the wild views while others scramble up Pamola's icy shelves.

You'll begin this hike at the Abol Bridge crossing. Follow the ski trail that
skirts Abol Stream to the Perimeter Road. Walk the unplowed road to the
Togue Pond Gate, where you'll begin your long walk in to Roaring Brook
Campground. You'll follow the relatively flat, wide road (recreational snowmobiles are not allowed on the road) for 8 miles. Depending on recent weather
conditions and foot traffic, the snow might be heavy and tough going, making for a very long day. In any case, you'll be happy to see the campground at
day's end. There are eight lean-tos, ten tent sites, and one eight- to ten-person
bunkhouse at Roaring Brook Campground. No open fires are allowed, but
you'll find a very welcoming woodstove in the bunkhouse. Rest up; the next
day's hike to Chimney Pond is short but steep.

Sleep in—the day's hike should only take two to three hours. Follow the Basin Ponds tote road as it skirts the frozen banks of Roaring Brook. At a little more than 0.5 mile, you'll push away from the brook and begin to climb more steeply. The trail zigzags left and right, continuing to ascend at a steady, steep pull.

At 2.0 miles, you'll cross a clearing as Lower Basin Pond comes into view. Skirt the southwest shore of the pond before entering into sparse woods. Stay on Chimney Pond Trail (ignore the North Basin Cutoff) as it dips into aptly named Dry Pond.

Keep climbing; at 3.3 miles, you'll reach Chimney Pond Campground, sitting at 2930 feet under towering Katahdin. Drop your pack and take out your camera!

When you're ready, simply retrace your steps back.

BAXTER STATE PARK WINTER RULES

If you plan on day-hiking in Baxter State Park, below treeline, no special permission is required. But be sure to check in and out at the self-registration boxes, or at park headquarters.

Any winter overnight use or any winter above-treeline travel requires a permit. Camping is permitted by reservation only in authorized sites. Parties must register with the ranger at Chimney Pond, or self-register at unstaffed ranger stations, upon arrival at any campsite. Winter parties must have confirmed camping reservations (including all paperwork and full payment submitted) at least ten working days prior to the actual start of the trip. The park office begins accepting and processing winter reservations for the upcoming season on the first business day in November each year.

Other regulations, including a required list of clothing and equipment for winter hikers, are available from Baxter State Park, 64 Balsam Drive, Millinocket, ME 04462; 207-723-5140; *www.baxterstateparkauthority.com*.

ACADIA NATIONAL PARK

-- 38 --
Cadillac Mountain

Rating: More difficult
Round trip: 5 miles
Hiking time: 5 hours
Elevation gain: 1126 feet
High point: 1532 feet
Map: Mount Desert Island and Acadia National Park Complete Hiking Trail and Carriage Road Map, Friends of Acadia, Parkman Publications
Information: Acadia National Park, P.O. Box 177, Eagle Lake Road, Bar Harbor, ME 04609-0177; 207-288-3338; *www.nps .gov/acad*

Getting there: From Bar Harbor, take Route 233 west about 1.5 miles to the intersection with the Park Loop Road on your left. Look for a plowed area for parking a few yards along the Park Loop Road.

To outdoor enthusiasts who appreciate mountain-to-sea scenery and solitude, a winter visit to Mount Desert Island, home to Acadia National Park, is hard to beat. The snow doesn't always last long on this windy seacoast, but hit it right and you'll find paradise. The scenic carriage roads that wind through park woodlands and mountains will be carpeted in layers of snow; 45 miles are open for cross-country skiing and snowshoeing. Another 41 miles of unplowed park roads lead to backcountry lakes and ponds, and mountaintop vistas.

Winter hikers have even more choices; there are 120 miles of trails, ranging from flat oceanside walks to more adventurous mountain and cliff climbs. In summer, you're likely to follow a line of bikers cruising carriage paths or hikers walking the more popular trails. Come winter, you'll have them all to yourself. "I'm feeling like royalty," our traveling companion remarked one afternoon, as we gazed out at mountains and sea. And with a sweep of his arm, "We have all this to ourselves!"

The North Ridge Trail up Cadillac Mountain and the descent down a dramatic, narrow gorge is one of our all-time favorite hikes. Cadillac is the tallest

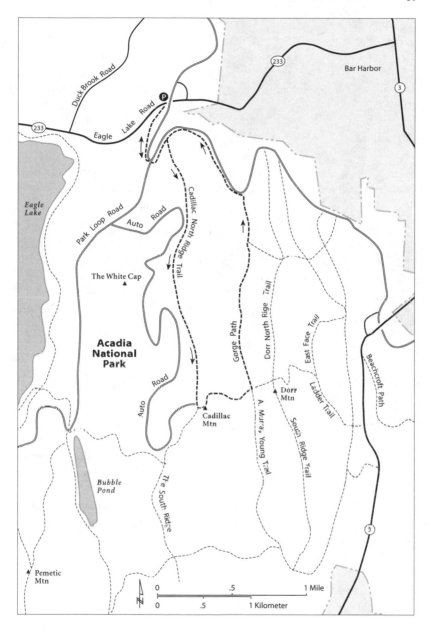

mountain on the Atlantic coast (north of Brazil). From its 1532-foot summit, you'll have inspiring views of Mount Desert Island's mountains, Frenchman Bay, and the open Atlantic Ocean, dotted with pine-studded islands.

Gorge Path waterfalls, Cadillac Mountain North Ridge

From the plowed parking lot on Route 233, take a left on the Park Loop Road. Several yards up, you'll find the Cadillac North Ridge trailhead on the right. Begin the gradual ascent up the side of the mountain, walking through sparse woods and open fields. Cairns and blue splotches on the rocks mark the trail. You'll get immediate rewards with views of frozen Eagle Lake to the west and ice-banked Frenchman Bay. As you climb farther, Dorr Mountain and the broad ledges of Cadillac Mountain come into view.

The trail comes close to the auto road two or three times along the way; the first encounter is a little less than a mile into the hike. In the summer, this is a drawback; the noise and fumes from the cars can be intrusive. In winter, the only sound you're likely to hear is the crunch, crunch of your snowshoes on the trail and the occasional buzz of a snowmobile engine. (The auto road is open to snowmobile traffic.)

The trail can be difficult to follow as you near the summit, especially in deep snow when cairns and trail markings can disappear entirely. But you'll see the top, so just head up, traveling around the scattered boulders and climbing the ledges. You'll reach the summit at 2.2 miles from the trailhead—a broad, ledgy cone, overlooking forests, mountains, Frenchman Bay, and the rocky Maine coastline.

Climbing down the mountain to find the connecting path to Gorge Path can be a bit tricky. Look for the Dorr Mountain Connector Trail from the summit. You'll need to be very cautious as you work your way down the icy cliff to the Gorge Path trailhead.

The Gorge Path leads through the deep gorge separating Cadillac and Dorr Mountains. Granite walls draped with icicles and frozen waterfalls tower 30 to 40 feet above snow-carpeted woods. Listen to the sounds of moving water, bubbling below the surface ice of the stream that snakes through the bottom of the gorge. The going can be a bit rough in areas as you maneuver over and around slippery boulders and thin ice. But the scenery is worth it.

The further you descend into the gorge, the narrower and narrower it becomes, the icy rock walls pushing closer together. Then the trail drops abruptly into a sparse forest, ending at the Park Loop Road just a short distance from where you started the North Ridge Trail. This is a hike you're bound to remember for a long time.

--39--
Eagle Lake

Rating: Easy/more difficult
Round trip: 6.7 miles
Hiking time: 5 hours
Elevation gain: 330 feet
High point: 588 feet
Maps: Acadia National Park Carriage Road User's Map; Mount Desert Island and Acadia National Park Complete Hiking Trail and Carriage Road Map, Friends of Acadia, Parkman Publications
Information: Acadia National Park, P.O. Box 177, Eagle Lake Road, Bar Harbor, ME 04609 0177; 207 288 3338; www.nps.gov/acad

Getting there: From Bar Harbor, take Route 233 west about 3 miles to the Eagle Lake Carriage Road, #6. (Note: Numbered carriage road locations, usually junctions, are marked on both the trail and on maps.) Parking is on the north side of Route 233.

This long loop hike combines an easy stroll on one of Acadia National Park's famed carriage roads around picturesque Eagle Lake with a short scramble up Connors Nubble. Fine vistas greet you nearly every step of the way, and the view from the top of the nubble is nothing short of spectacular. Though the hike along the Eagle Lake carriage road is relatively easy, it is long. Families with young ones in tow may elect to backtrack from Connors Nubble, cutting the trip by more than 4 miles.

This is a popular route for cross-country skiers, too. When the snow is deep enough (at least four inches), park volunteers lay ski tracks on the west

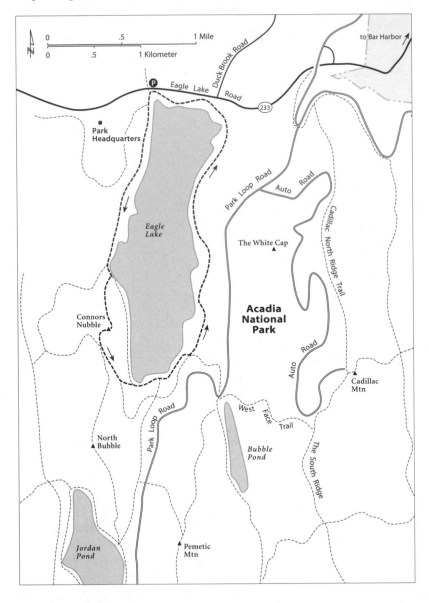

The Eagle Lake loop

side of the lake. Be sure to stay to the sides and out of the tracks. From the Route 233 entrance, you'll walk the wide, flat carriage road, taking in views of the quiet winter woods. There are 45 miles of carriage roads weaving through the park, offering hikers (and bikers in the summer) a look at the less-visited interior park landscape. The carriage road system, including sixteen stone bridges, was a gift of John D. Rockefeller, Jr. and remains one of the finest examples of hand cut stone roads left in America.

Look for snowshoe hare and deer tracks that crisscross the snow-carpeted woods. You'll also have nice views of the lake and the ice-fishing shanties that decorate the frozen expanse.

In a little more than a mile, you'll reach the Eagle Lake Trail on your left, heading to the shoreline of Eagle Lake. Follow this hiking trail for 15 yards to reach the junction with Connors Nubble Trail. Turn right onto the trail, heading away from the shoreline to climb the north side of Connors Nubble. The climb is a bit of a thigh-burner, but blessedly short. In 0.4 mile, you'll reach the top. You'll see Acadia's most prominent mountain peaks: Cadillac to the east, The Bubbles to the south, and Penobscot and Sargent Mountains to the west. Below is a wide-angle view of Eagle Lake; at 425 acres, it's the largest freshwater lake in the park.

To continue around the lake, turn your back on Eagle Lake and head down the southwest side of Connors Nubble. It's a short, steep scramble, but in less than a quarter mile you'll reach the Eagle Lake carriage road. Turn left and follow the broad road as it loops around the south end of the lake, then turns north. The way back is an easy, day-dreaming shuffle, with gentle grades and views of pine woods and the snow-banked, icy lake. You'll walk a little over a mile to the Eagle Lake Shoreline Trail and Bubble Pond carriage road junction (#7). Follow the carriage road north as it skirts the eastern shoreline for another 2 miles or so back to where you started. Whew! You've earned a "lobstah" dinner—good in any season!

--*40*--
Gorham Mountain

Rating: More difficult
Round trip: 4 miles
Hiking time: 3 hours
Elevation gain: 525 feet
High point: 525 feet
Maps: Acadia National Park Carriage Road User's Map; Mount Desert Island and Acadia National Park Complete Hiking Trail and Carriage Road Map, Friends of Acadia, Parkman Publications
Information: Acadia National Park, P.O. Box 177, Eagle Lake Road, Bar Harbor, ME 04609-0177; 207-288-3338; *www.nps .gov/acad*

Getting there: From Bar Harbor, take the Park Loop Road to the Sand Beach parking area. (This portion of the Park Loop Road remains open in the winter.)

Easy accessibility, quick climb, no backtracking, and mountains-to-sea views . . . what more could you ask for? This hike up 525-foot Gorham Mountain is the perfect half-day jaunt. It's not rail-trail flat, but the elevation gain is gradual and the rewards far outweigh the effort. Combine this hike with a walk along Sand Beach, then return to Bar Harbor for a cup of steaming chowder, and you have the makings for a fine winter day.

Take the Park Loop Road to the Sand Beach parking lot, then walk the Ocean Path about 1 mile to the Gorham Mountain trailhead.

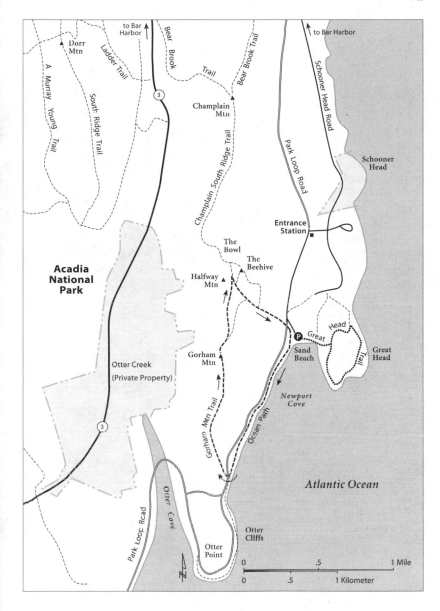

You'll climb easily through spruce forest. Shortly into the hike, you'll pass a plaque honoring Waldron Bates–Pathmaker. Bates was an early trailblazer in Acadia and is credited to be the first to use stone stairways and iron rung ladders to help hikers ascend steep cliffs and slippery slopes.

Hanging plants, toppled trees, and cliffs decorate the Gorham Mountain trail.

Soon the trail splits and a spur path leads right to Cadillac Cliffs. The 0.5-mile side loop is well worth it. You'll walk under hanging rocks and ledges to a series of steep cliffs and an ancient sea cave. Be cautious; the ledges and rocks around the cliffs are often ice-covered and slippery. But the site is impressive and a nice break from all those pretty ocean views!

The spur trail wraps around to meet the main trail heading up to Gorham Mountain. Views begin to open up, and already you've made it to the top—but not quite. The spot is known as Gorham's false summit. The area was cleared by the famous 1947 fire that devastated much of Mount Desert Island. Real summit or not, you'll have pretty views of Otter Cliffs, Baker Island, and the Cranberry Islands to the south. To the north, you'll see Frenchman Bay. Follow the cairns to the true summit, where the vistas only get better.

You could retrace your steps from here, but we suggest you continue on, dropping down the northeast side of the mountain as you head toward The Beehive, a 546-foot mount overlooking Sand Beach. The Beehive is a strenuous hike if you are looking for an additional challenge. Otherwise, stay right as the trail splits and descend to its junction with the easygoing Bowl Trail. Walk the gentle, woodsy trail back to the Park Loop Road, just a short distance from the Sand Beach parking lot. Did you pack a picnic lunch? Sand Beach's oceanfront venue is a great place for one. Or if you have the time, consider a walk along the 1.3-mile Great Head Trail that begins at Sand Beach and circles around the western landmass jutting out into Newport Cove. Then return to Sand Beach and the parking lot.

--42--
Day Mountain

Rating:	Easy/more difficult
Round trip:	1.5 miles
Hiking time:	2 hours
Elevation gain:	333 feet
High point:	583 feet
Maps:	Acadia National Park Carriage Road User's Map; Mount Desert Island and Acadia National Park Complete Hiking Trail and Carriage Road Map, Friends of Acadia, Parkman Publications
Information:	Acadia National Park, P.O Box 177, Eagle Lake Road, Bar Harbor, ME 04609-0177; 207-288-3338; *www.nps .gov/acad*

Getting there: From Bar Harbor, take Route 3 south toward Seal Harbor. Look for the Champlain monument. Trailhead parking is across from the monument on the south (left) side of the road.

Day Mountain, elevation gain 583 feet, round trip 1.5 miles . . . At first glance, it's easy to discount this little hike up a little mountain. But you'd be wrong to do so. A short walk on this trail through winter-white woods will take you to an eagle's-eye perch looking across the rocky Maine coast and the wildly cold

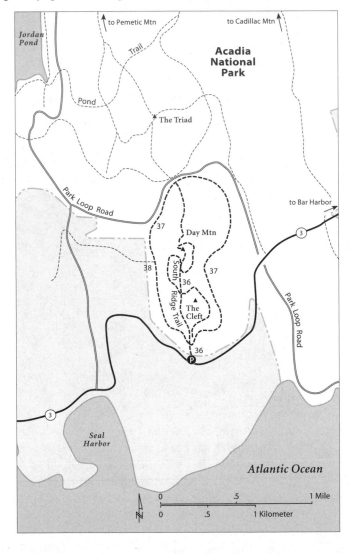

Boats in Seal Harbor

blue waters of the Atlantic. It's no wonder John D. Rockefeller, Jr. carved a carriage road to the mountain peak. And no surprise why summer visitors travel the road in horse-drawn wagons, hikers and bikers clamber up its slopes, and winter skiers and snowshoers track their way to the top.

You have lots of options, too. There's a hiking trail that runs up the south side and down the north, hooking up with a carriage road to complete a loop. There's a carriage road—popular with cross-country skiers—that runs up and back down from Day Mountain's scenic summit. And there's a carriage road that circles the perimeter. We like to take the hiking trail up and carriage road back down (or vice versa), leaving us plenty of time to poke around the Seal Harbor General Store. Better idea: stop at the store first to stock up on gourmet picnic items, including fresh-made sandwiches, cookies, and fruit to take with you on your hike. We nearly always make another stop here on our return, to browse the general store's expansive wine section—offering one of the best selections on the island.

The trail starts across the road from the parking area and climbs a short distance, about 0.2 mile, before it meets the first junction with carriage road # 36. Here, you're likely to encounter several cross-country skiers. Local volunteers carve tracks along one side of the carriage road, and the twisty ski up and back is one of the more popular winter ski trips on the island. A second carriage road, # 37 circling the foot of the mountain, also intersects here. You'll want to stay to the left of the carriage roads; look for a post designating the Day Mountain Trail.

It's an uneven climb to the top of this mountain. You'll gain some 300 feet of elevation in the 0.7 mile or so to the summit, but it comes in fits and starts. You'll climb a hump, then the trail evens out a bit providing a short rest, then it climbs and evens again. But in quick time, less than an hour, you'll be standing in front of a postcard-pretty, panoramic view. You'll see pretty Seal Harbor and, beyond, the white surf of the Atlantic pounding the rocky Maine coastline to your south; The Triad and Pemetic Mountain rise above the dense forests in the north.

After you've noshed on your picnic goodies and soaked in the views, head back down the way you came, or take the slightly longer, meandering carriage road. The road swings left and right, up and down before it loops to the left. You'll get a glimpse of The Cleft, an impressive cliff on the steep, southeast slope of Day Mountain, before the final 0.5-mile walk to the parking area. If you have time and energy, poke around the village, stroll the harbor, visit the Town Wharf, and pick up a cookie for the ride home at the Seal Harbor General Store.

WINTER IN ACADIA NATIONAL PARK

Surrounded by the cold, pounding Atlantic waters, 47,000-acre Acadia National Park is blessed with scenic riches. Rugged granite cliffs and glacier-carved mountain jut from the sea and deep lakes and icy ponds dot the inland valleys, forest, and marshlands. It's true that snow conditions can vary in the park; snowfalls are sporadic and the powder quickly melts. But hit it right, and you'll find a quiet winter dreamland.

The park welcomes nearly two million visitors a year—most during the high summer season. As expected, December, January, and February are the slowest months. In winter, the park becomes a quiet haven for snowshoers and cross-country skiers. (Note: Snowmobiles are allowed on the 27-mile Park Loop Road and most fire roads. But only 2 miles of the 45 miles of carriage roads are open to snowmobilers as connector trails.)

There is no winter camping allowed in the park, but you'll find a handful of inns and motels in Bar Harbor that remain open. The Winter Visitor Center and Park Headquarters is located 3 miles west of Bar Harbor on Route 233. The center is open November 1 to mid-April, 8:00 AM to 4:30 PM, daily, except Thanksgiving Day, December 24 and 25, and January 1.

Following Thoreau's footsteps along the shore of Walden Pond

MASSACHUSETTS

THE BERKSHIRES

--42--
Hoosic River/Ashuwillticook Trail

Rating: Easy
Distance: 11.2 miles total; Lanesboro to Cheshire, 5.4 miles; Cheshire to Adams, 5.8 miles
Hiking time: Each leg 2.5 hours or more, depending on your pace and conditions
Elevation gain: 0 feet
High point: 0 feet
Map: Department of Conservation and Recreation, Ashuwillticook Rail Trail Map
Information: Department of Conservation and Recreation, Regional Headquarters, 740 South Street, Pittsfield, MA 01201; 413-442-8928; *www.mass.gov/dcr, www.berkshirebikepath.org*

Getting there: Take the Massachusetts Turnpike to exit 2, then follow Route 20 west to Route 7 north to Pittsfield. From Pittsfield, take Route 9 east to Route 8 north. Signs for Ashuwillticook parking areas are located on Route 8. Park at Berkshire Mall Road in Lanesboro, leaving a second car at Church Street in Cheshire, to do the southern leg (south–north). To do the northern leg (north–south), park at the visitor center in Adams, with a second car at Church Street in Cheshire. There's also local bus service available from Berkshire Transit Authority (BRTA), 413-499-BRTA.

The word "Ashuwillticook" (ASH-oo-Will-ti-COOK) is the Native American name for the south branch of the Hoosic River, and it translates to something like "the pleasant river in between the hills." Provided you can pronounce it, the name says it all. The Ashuwillticook Rail Trail offers a happy ramble between three towns set in the valley between Mount Greylock and the Hoosac (not Hoosic!) Mountains. It meanders alongside the Cheshire Reservoir and often parallels the Hoosic (not Hoosac!) River, winding past a lake, wetlands, and woodlands.

While the scenery is delightfully varied along the Ashuwillticook, there's nothing challenging about this walk. For many trekkers here, that's the whole point. "Our local EMS store brings people out to the trail and turns them on to snowshoeing," says Rebecca Barnes, Region Trail Coordinator for the

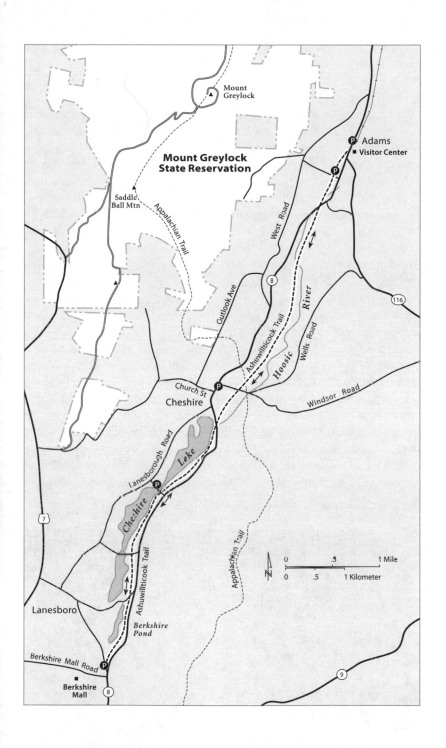

▲ Mount
Greylock

Mount Greylock
State Reservation

Saddle
Ball Mtn ▲

Appalachian Trail

West Road

Outlook Ave

8

Adams
■ Visitor Center

116

Hoosic River

Wells Road

Ashuwillticook Trail

Windsor Road

Church St
Cheshire

Lanesborough Road

Lake

Cheshire

7

Ashuwillticook Trail

Lanesboro

Berkshire
Pond

Appalachian Trail

Berkshire Mall Road

■ Berkshire
Mall

8

9

N

0   .5   1 Mile

0   .5   1 Kilometer

Massachusetts Department of Conservation and Recreation. "This is a good place for your first time out, and a wonderful place to get your 'snowshoe legs' if it's been awhile!" Pick up a map at the Berkshire visitor center in downtown Adams (Route 8 and Hoosac Street) or online.

This 10-foot-wide, 11.2-mile-long multi-use path is open to nonmotorized recreation, including cross-country skiing, jogging, and bicycling. A former railroad corridor, abandoned by the B and M (Boston and Maine) Railroad in 1990, it runs north–south between Lanesboro (south) and Adams. You wouldn't do all of this on snowshoes (and then have to retrace your steps going back), but, happily, you don't have to. There are five places to park, legally, along the trail; one in Lanesboro (near the Berkshire Mall), two in Cheshire, and two in Adams.

From the southern entrance off Berkshire Mall Road, the trail is flanked by wetlands and woods for 2.4 miles. The trail crosses Nobody's Road in Cheshire; here also, the AT crosses, going from the east side of Cheshire Lake to the west side. From Nobody's Road to Route 8 in Cheshire (about 5 miles from the southern entrance), the trail hugs the edge of Cheshire Lake. While the view across the lake is lovely, there's not much vegetative buffer here, so the wind can be biting. Therefore, this section of trail is best for snowshoeing on a calm, sunny day. The next stretch of the rail trail is inviting as well. From Route 8 to Cheshire Harbor Road (about 8.3 miles), the trail follows the winding Hoosic River through wetlands. This undeveloped, expansive area is known locally as the "jungle." Peaceful and quiet, this section is open to the sun and is nicely buffered against the wind. Once you're out of the jungle, the trail declines slightly en route to Adams. This section follows the swiftly moving Hoosic River. If you finish the trail here, you'll pass by Russell Field, a town park, and reach downtown Adams where there are several places to find a snack and a hot beverage. Look for restrooms at the Discover the Berkshires Visitor Center.

The southern end of the Ashuwillticook Trail

--43--
Mount Greylock

Rating: More difficult
Round trip: 6 miles
Hiking time: 5 hours
Elevation gain: 2061 feet
High point: 3491 feet
Map: Mount Greylock State Reservation Trail Map (winter use)
Information: Mount Greylock State Reservation, P.O. Box 138, Lanesboro, MA 01237; 413-499-4262; *www.massparks.org*

Getting there: Take the Massachusetts Turnpike to exit 2, then follow Route 20 west to Route 7 north to Pittsfield. From Pittsfield, take Route 9 east to Route 8 and follow Route 8 north to Adams. In downtown Adams, look for the statue of President McKinley and turn left onto Maple Street. At the cemetery, turn left onto West Road and drive for about 0.6 mile, then turn right onto West Mountain Road. You'll reach the trailhead and parking in 0.9 mile on the right. Pick up a Mount Greylock map at the Discover the Berkshires Visitor Center in Adams (see hike 42).

Climbing the east side of Mount Greylock, Massachusetts' highest peak, via the Gould Trail is one of our favorite hikes, for a couple of reasons. First, there's parking at the trailhead, reachable even without four-wheel-drive; and, second, it's located near North Adams, a town we enjoy for other reasons.

The Gould Trail is named for a local family that still operates a working farm at the base of the mountain in Adams. Even on a perfect, sunny Sunday, this trail is lightly used, so nobody will hear you (other than your hiking buddy) if you huff and puff a little bit as you ascend the steeps. Another nice feature of the Gould Trail: If you run out of steam and decide that maybe you don't feel like tackling the summit, you can hike to the waterfalls at 1.6 miles and head back, feeling like you've accomplished something. You might be tempted to loop back on the Cheshire Harbor Trail, but we wouldn't—it's a snowmobile trail, while the Gould Trail is open to snowshoer hikers only.

We prefer parking at West Mountain Road, even though the trail is reachable via Gould Road, mainly because Gould Road seems to be a gathering place for the snowmobile crowd. Their roaring engines don't provide a happy beginning to a day on the trail.

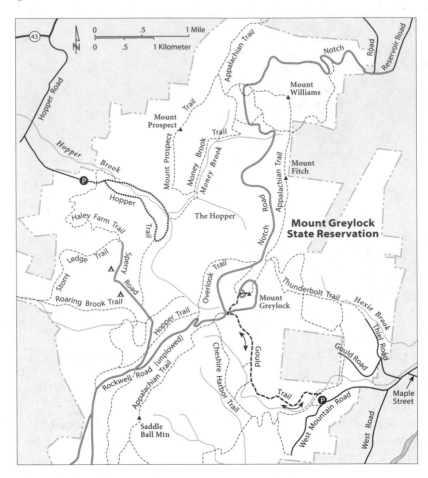

Begin the hike in the woods next to the small parking lot on West Mountain Road. (The parking lot may not be plowed, but you can park along the roadside.) You'll see a sign marking the trail upon entering. From there, you cross a brook onto a wooden bridge and enter a forest of evergreens. At about 0.5 mile, you'll come to an area where a small tornado is said to have touched down—not that you'll notice when everything is covered in white stuff! There's also, they say, a huge rock that was lifted out of the ground by the roots of a tree, on the right side of the trail.

Follow the trail north (right), crossing Pecks Brook. The ice formations and flowing water make this very picturesque—and photo-worthy—in winter. Cross a wooden bridge and continue along the trail, which gradually ascends with several switchbacks. At about 2 miles, a short side trail leads to a waterfall,

Pecks Brook crossing on the Gould Trail

although you may not be able to find it after a recent snowfall; there's no sign, and your only clue is the footprints of other hikers. What you will see is a sign designating the Pecks Brook Shelter; the falls are just southwest of the shelter. You'll definitely hear the gurgling water; if you're a real nature scout, use your ears as your guide.

At this point, though, you may be ready to tackle the bigger goal, the summit of Mount Greylock. Here you ascend 1 more mile to Rockwell Road. Cross the intersection of Rockwell and Notch Roads and follow the Appalachian Trail to the summit, 3491 feet above sea level. With any luck, you'll enjoy dazzling views of the Berkshire Hills and snow-covered valleys. Even on an overcast day, you'll have the wonderful sense of being on top of the world, having earned it with every step!

You'll notice an extensive network of trails on the Mount Greylock State Reservation map. Some of these, like Cheshire Harbor Trail, are used by snowmobilers, so we'd steer clear. The Hopper Trail (reachable off Route 43 and Hopper Road in Williamstown) is a good, strenuous option.

--*44*--
Pine Cobble

Rating: Moderate
Distance: 4.9 miles
Hiking time: 5 hours
Elevation gain: 1400 feet
High point: 2100 feet
Map: *AMC Massachusetts Trail Guide*, Map 1
Information: Appalachian Trail Conference, 799 Washington Street, Harpers Ferry, WV 25425; 304-535-6331; *www .appalachiantrail.org*

Getting there: Follow Route 2 (the Mohawk Trail) to the town of North Adams. This hike isn't a loop, so arrange to be dropped off (or leave a car) in downtown North Adams. Trailhead parking is available near the footbridge to the AT, near the intersection of Route 2 and Phelps Avenue. At the terminus of the trail, there's parking on North Hoosac Road in Williamstown.

Nearly 100 miles of the 2167-mile Appalachian Trail are located in Berkshire County. This section, near the Vermont border, is notable for snowshoe hikers. The trail runs alongside Sherman Brook for a long stretch, so you'll see Mother Nature's ice sculptures in the water and frozen waterfalls. Petes Spring is another highlight, and you'll see numerous deer tracks along the trail. The trail follows the Appalachian Trail for part of the way, but rather than continue your hike into Vermont, you'll circle back on the Pine Cobble Trail, leading to the pretty college town of Williamstown. Leave a car in Williamstown, at the

Appalachian Trail sign

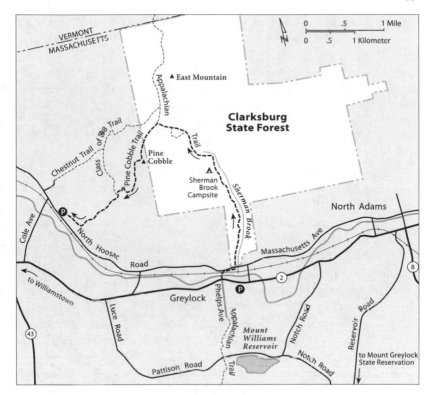

trailhead on Cole Avenue, or arrange for pickup here. Williamstown, home of Williams College, has a lively downtown and several good places to eat, plus lots of options for live music and entertainment.

The hike begins in North Adams, downtown, where there is ample parking. On the north side of Route 2, by the traffic light, look for a footbridge over the B and M Railroad tracks and the Hoosic River. Look for the white, triangular blaze of the Appalachian Trail on a telephone pole. (It's easy to miss it!)

At around the half-mile point, the trail enters the woods and passes over two footbridges. From here, the path climbs steadily upward through hemlock forest. You'll reach Petes Spring at about 1.8 miles, and a blue-blazed side trail to Sherman Brook Campsite (tent platforms and an outhouse). Here, the AT ascends the ridgeline, veering west at 2.4 miles.

You can avoid the next steep, boulder-filled uphill section by taking the 0.3-mile blue-blazed bad-weather bypass. A couple of skinny switchbacks lead to an eastward-facing bluff of East Mountain. On a clear day, you'll get excellent views of the Hoosac Range here. ("Hoosac" is an Algonquin word meaning "place of stones.")

Cross a rocky area and look for the intersection where the AT meets the blue-blazed Pine Cobble Trail. (From here the AT continues right, north, over the ridgeline of East Mountain into Vermont.) The Pine Cobble Trail leads southwest 2.1 miles down the south side of East Mountain, past a rocky outcropping called Pine Cobble. A short downhill segment leads to an overlook, revealing Williamstown (west) and North Adams (east).

Turn right and proceed downhill, steeply at times, to Williamstown.

--45--
Spruce Hill

Rating:	Moderate
Round trip:	3 miles
Hiking time:	4 hours
Elevation gain:	700 feet
High point:	2566 feet
Map:	Savoy Mountain State Forest Trail Map (winter use)
Information:	Savoy Mountain State Forest, 260 Central Shaft Road, Florida, MA 01247; 413-663-8469; *www.mass.gov/dcr*

Getting there: At the intersection of I-91 and Route 2 in Savoy, take Route 2 west to Florida/Savoy town line. Head approximately 7 miles west to Central Shaft Road. Turn left and continue for approximately 3 miles, following signs to Savoy Mountain State Forest. Winter use trail maps are available at park headquarters. From there, a short ride will take you to a turnout on the right of Florida Road, where you can park.

"I knew I'd made it as a ranger when I landed here!" a park ranger told us of his job at Savoy Mountain State Forest. Other rangers, at other Massachusetts state parks, concur: this one is special. Although the park is the fourth-largest piece of public land in the state, it's a hidden gem. Set in the Berkshire Hills at the western edge of the state, this park offers wonderful diversity, with waterfalls, balanced rocks, ponds, and scenic vistas galore. The property is crisscrossed with nearly 60 miles of hiking trails, many of which make awesome snowshoe paths. This hike is set in the northwest corner of the forest.

The Busby Trail (named after a local landowner, George Busby) to Spruce Hill is the most popular trail here. It's great for recreational snowshoe hikers because it is basically a flat, wide woods road, with a short, steep cliff that leads to the summit of Spruce Hill, a distance of 1.5 miles.

Conditions were amazing on the day that we hiked—the Berkshires had been socked with eighteen inches of new snow the night before. Nobody was about—indeed, this forest doesn't get a huge amount of traffic, even in August!—so we were delighted to revel in the solitude of the snow-cloaked stands of maple and spruce.

The first natural feature at the start of the trail is Tower Swamp, obscured by snow during our visit. You'll pass under a couple of powerlines, where the trail starts its gradual ascent. Here, you'll notice some of the strip-cut stands of planted spruce in the forest as you trek through a corridor of maple trees on the hillside. While loggers do have access to some mature trees here, others act as seed-trees.

You'll pass a series of ledges and then encounter a man-made feature, a cellar hole, to the right of the trail, marking a farm that was inhabited until about 1933. After you pass the cellar hole, the trail transforms from a gentle

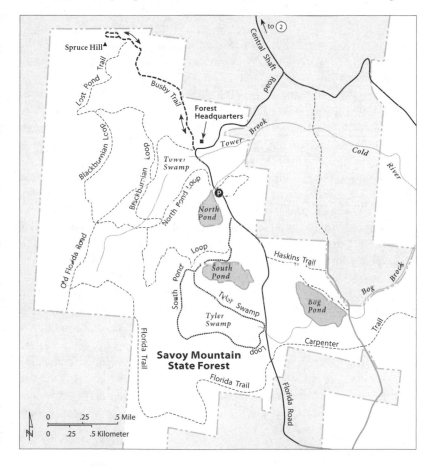

Savoy Mountain State Forest is an undiscovered gem, especially in winter.

logging road to a steeper single track after the first switchback, marking the 400-foot ascent to the summit. You then encounter a stone wall which marks the last leg of the hike (not including your backtrack to the beginning).

Follow the blue blazes to the left for the most direct ascent to the top of Spruce Hill—the steepest section of trail in Savoy Mountain State Forest. The last bit, a 75-foot stretch, is a toughie, so you'll probably ditch the snowshoes and use your crampons to scramble up the last 20 feet of rocky schist to the top. You'll forgive this bit of effort as you emerge from the woods onto the lovely, open summit of Spruce Hill. Check out the views—a glorious panorama that takes in the Taconic Range, the Hoosic River valley, Mount Greylock, even Vermont's Green Mountains and New Hampshire's Mount Monadnock.

If you head to the right at the end of this blue-blazed trail, you can make the last leg to the summit a bit easier. This part of the trail is the route taken by hawk watches that come here in the fall to watch the migration. It's still steep, though, so we'd just head left and go for it!

Up for more? Once you're back at park headquarters, drive south on Central Shaft Road to the state forest camping area (about a five-minute ride). The gates are open all year. The South Pond Loop Trail to Tyler Swamp Loop is about 2.5 miles long and will take you about two-and-a-half hours' time to cover. It's flat, it's easy, and the swamp areas are especially interesting under the cover of winter. Look for eagles' stick nests in treetops, hawks flying overhead, and the eerie, frozen-in-time look of marshland plants like cat-o'-nine-tails, slicked with ice. Although this is a snowmobile route and might show some ruts, it's very lightly used by the snowmobile crowd.

WINTER IN THE BERKSHIRES

City folks are surprised to find that the Berkshire Hills aren't all about summertime pleasures, like Tanglewood Music Festival and Jacob's Pillow. Visit in winter, and you'll discover that this region is a great place to hang out, for a weekend or longer. It's a great destination for snowshoe hikers, with generally plenty of snow and all the trails you can handle (and then some!), especially around Mount Greylock.

North Adams, a former mill town, is undergoing a real renaissance, thanks to the arrival of MassMOCA (Massachusetts Museum of Contemporary Art). You never know what you'll encounter in this restored, nineteenth-century factory space, but It's guaranteed to be intriguing, and sometimes provocative. The cool row houses across the way are The Porches Inn, one of our favorite boutique hotels anywhere, where the funky charms include paint-by-number art, random collectibles, and an outdoor hot tub that's open in winter. From here, you can access numerous snowshoe hikes (the inn is snowshoer-friendly, with loads of trail information) and even walk to dinner.

Other worthy stops in the Berkshires include the family-friendly Berkshire Museum, in Pittsfield; and the Hancock Shaker Village, where the annual winter weekend festivities include nineteenth-century winter traditions like ice cutting and sleighrides.

For more information, contact the Berkshire Hills Visitors Bureau at 800-237-5747; *www.berkshires.org.*

--*46*--

Pleasant Valley Wildlife Sanctuary

Rating:	Easy to strenuous
Round trip:	0.25–0.75 mile, pond loops; 2.5 miles, Lenox Mountain
Hiking time:	30 minutes to 1 hour, pond loops; 4 hours, Lenox Mountain
Elevation gain:	800 feet to Lenox Mountain
High point:	2126 feet
Maps:	Pleasant Valley Wildlife Sanctuary Trail Map; USGS Pittsfield West, MA
Information:	Pleasant Valley Wildlife Sanctuary, 472 West Mountain Road, Lenox, MA 01240; 413-637-0320; *www.massaudubon.org*

Getting there: From the intersection of Routes 7 and 20 in Lenox, drive 3 miles north to West Dugway Road, on your left. Follow West Dugway Road just under 1 mile to the intersection with West Mountain Road. The sanctuary entrance and parking are 0.8 mile in on West Mountain Road. Fee charged. Maps are available at the sanctuary office.

Beaver lodges, winter birds, and crackling, iced-over ponds—these are the features that draw snowshoe hikers to this lovely, 1400-acre property owned by the Massachusetts Audubon Society, set on the eastern slope of Lenox Mountain. All 7 miles of trails are blazed with blue and yellow, with the blues leading away from the sanctuary office and the yellows leading toward the office. Trail maps are available at the office year-round. You may encounter cross-country skiers here, but chances are there won't be too many. This place is blissfully uncrowded, and its natural features make it a pleasant place to ramble on a snow-dappled day, just as the name implies.

Pikes Pond Trail is an easygoing thirty-minute walk around the wetlands. The trail begins at the sanctuary office, heading southwest across a meadow.

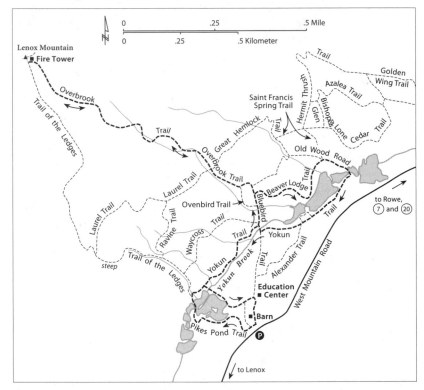

Sanctuary headquarters

At the far side of the meadow, the trail becomes a long boardwalk that extends over swampy areas. You'll follow the south shore of the pond, then cross Yokun Brook on a boardwalk. Complete the loop, or connect with the Yokun Trail/Beaver Lodge Loop, a longer but more moderate route that will take you about an hour. The path takes you past numerous beaver ponds, via a northern hardwood forest with good views of Lenox Mountain and the fire tower that sits atop it.

If you want to get to the summit of Lenox Mountain, talk to sanctuary personnel first about conditions along the Overbrook Trail. Do not, *do not* consider using the Trail of the Ledges in winter! This one is very steep, and we don't recommend it as a snowshoe hike. The Overlook Trail, while quite steep and strenuous, is a better choice. The trail meanders through a hardwood forest along a small stream. You'll hike about 800 vertical feet to the summit. Views take in the Taconic Range to the west and, if the sky is very clear, the Catskill Mountains to the southwest. Plan at least four hours to make the 2.5-mile round trip and, again, confirm weather and trail conditions with sanctuary personnel before you attempt this hike.

CENTRAL MASSACHUSETTS

--47--
Douglas State Forest

Rating: Easy
Round trip: 4.5 miles
Hiking time: 4 hours
Elevation gain: 110 feet
High point: 700 feet
Maps: Douglas State Forest Map; USGS Webster, MA
Information: Douglas State Forest, 107 Wallum Lake Road, Douglas, MA 01516; 508-476-7872; *www.mass.gov/dcr/parks*

Getting there: Take the Massachusetts Turnpike (I-90) to exit 10 in Auburn, and take Route 395 south approximately 10 miles to exit 2 in Webster. Then take Route 16 east for 5 miles to Douglas State Forest. The parking lot with trailhead is on the right.

"Aww, we'll have to come back in the summer!" That was our reaction to this pretty, easygoing loop trail around Douglas State Forest. This gently lovely area of forests, kettle ponds, and wetlands is proof that one doesn't need to conquer a summit to enjoy great scenery. In wintertime, the American chestnut trees that flank the park are nicely turned out in a sparkling cloak of white, and the kettle ponds (formed by retreating glaciers) are visions of shimmering, crackly beauty.

This 4640-acre park, bordering Rhode Island and Connecticut on the southern border of central Massachusetts, is also known for its Atlantic white cedar swampland and its collection of glacial boulders. In addition to all this is Wallis Pond's old stone dam with small waterfalls. Historically, the site has been used for ice harvesting (from Wallum Lake) and as a granite quarry. It was cleared as parkland by the Civilian Conservation Corps in 1934.

This northerly trek, the Whitin Reservoir Loop Trail, is a pleasant, woodsy walk with great views of Whitin Reservoir. The trail is lollipop-shaped; you'll start at the stick of the lollipop and follow it counterclockwise. Be careful at the end of the loop, when you venture onto the stick again; it's easy to miss it and you can get lost (like we did) and add an extra 6 miles to your hike. Otherwise, the hike is well marked but not heavily used—always a great combination!

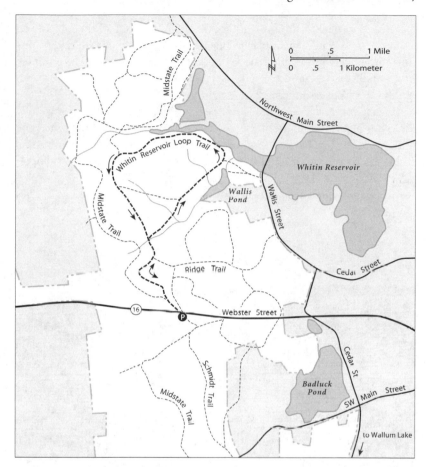

You'll park on the south side of Route 16 (Webster Street), then cross the road to get to the trailhead on the north side, where you can pick up a trail map (also available online). The hike begins on the Midstate Trail, which crosses Route 16 here. This 92-mile interstate footpath extends from Rhode Island to Massachusetts, connecting with the Wapack Trail in New Hampshire. For information, visit *www.midstatetrail.org.* Marked with yellow triangles, the Midstate Trail crosses some paved roads and private property, in addition to natural sites like Mount Wachusett, the path's highest point. There are five designated shelters, including one here at Douglas State Forest.

The Whitin Reservoir Loop Trail is wide and well-blazed with red. Cross two bridges in succession, and then bear right at the next trail intersection. Turn left at the fork (at around the 1-mile mark), heading up a hill, and then go right at the next fork. This is where you begin the loop of the lollipop. In about 0.5 mile, you'll encounter Wallis Pond and its stonework dam. Continue to follow the shoreline. The reservoir will be on your right. In about 0.5 mile, you'll reach a peninsula. This is a great spot for a picnic or snack with views of the lake surrounding you.

When you reach the end of the reservoir, head left, and ascend a small hill that leads west away from the water. Now you've reached the other side of the loop, heading back. Go right at the fork where the Spur Trail intersects the loop and keep going straight at the next intersection to rejoin the lollipop stick. (Jog right, and you'll join the Midstate Trail.)

Retracing your way back from the loop, you'll soon cross the two bridges you saw earlier, and the right-hand turn that will lead back to Route 16 and the parking lot.

Lichen on trees—or clams that took a wrong turn?

--*48*--

Oxbow National Wildlife Refuge

Rating: Easy
Round trip: 1.9 miles
Hiking time: 1–2 hours
Elevation gain: 33 feet
High point: 248 feet
Map: U.S. Fish and Wildlife Service, Oxbow NWR Interpretive Trail Map
Information: Oxbow National Wildlife Refuge, 7 Weir Hill Road, Sudbury, MA 01776; 978-443-4661; *www.oxbow.fws.gov* or *www.refuges.fws.gov*

Getting there: From Route 2 in Littleton, take exit 38 (Route 110/111) south toward Harvard; bear right to stay on Route 110 at Harvard Center, passing a general store. Turn right onto Still River Depot Road. The refuge parking area is at the end of the road, past the railroad tracks.

The theme on this easygoing family hike is beavers. Evidence of beavers is everywhere, from three huge beaver lodges to the countless felled trees and tree stumps gnawed by these toothsome critters. Where are the beavers? Tell the kids that they do not always build stick lodges. In rivers and lakes, they also live in tunnels dug into the banks. Kids get a kick out of all this, and it keeps things lively on this interpretive snowshoe walk.

Located 40 miles west of Boston, this 1667-acre refuge lies along about 8 miles of the Nashua River. When this part of Massachusetts was first settled, English colonists grew crops and hay in the well-watered river meadows. To carry hay out of the wet meadows, they used a causeway trail—now part of the interpretive trail at the refuge. In the early 1800s, a coach and carriage road, known as the Union Turnpike, ran east–west through what is now refuge property. For generations, one family owned a large tract of land here. In 1917, Camp Devens was established, later becoming Fort Devens, an army base. The refuge was part of Fort Devens until the mid-1970s, when it was turned over to the Fish and Wildlife Service. You won't see tanks along Tank Road, but you may well hear target practice as you hike—quite a contrast to an otherwise quiet, peaceful walk in the woods.

This interpretive trail begins at the parking area, and then follows the riverbank, crossing two oxbow ponds, and returns along Tank Road. Highlights

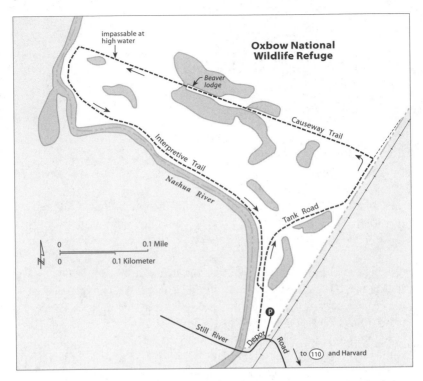

include views of the Nashua River, forest and wetland habitats, and a beaver pond. Allow about two hours to do this in snowshoes, and prepare to be flexible—high water can make the loop impassable in any season, so you may need to head back the way you came when you reach Marker 6 on the trail. You can still see the beaver lodge from here, even if the ice is too thin to cross over to get to it. Also keep in mind that this trail can get a bit icy in winter, thanks to the melt-and-freeze routine that is typical of Massachusetts in winter. You can either walk right alongside the riverbank, or bear slightly to the right of it, depending upon conditions. Either way you do it, it's a pleasant walk, and you'll catch lots of evidence of beaver activity.

The first 0.2 mile or so will take you along the 56-mile Nashua River, a tributary of the Merrimack River, which it joins in Nashua, New Hampshire. Look for beautiful patterns of ice, mosaic-like, along the water, and sparkling ice crystals hanging like gems on strands of plants on the riverbank. To your right, you'll see a pond with a beaver lodge in the middle. The strange contraption you see at trailside is a "beaver deceiver," which drains water from the pond without making much noise. The sound of flowing water makes beavers want to build dams, and that would be a nuisance in this spot, where a road intersects with the trail.

You probably wouldn't choose to hike it in summer, but under cover of snowfall, Tank Road is pleasant and wide, and might offer easier footing than hiking directly along the often-icy riverside. Before the trail jogs to the left, you'll see the tracks of the B and M Railroad to your right.

A short distance ahead, you'll approach the highest distance on the trail, running through a stand of white pine trees. These 200-year-old trees reach heights of 150 feet here, and they frame the trail nicely. Now you've reached the Causeway Trail, the old Colonial trail used by farmers and, later, for stagecoach passage. You'll really notice the work of beavers as you wander, with the unmistakable pencil-point gnaw marks on the trees. According to refuge literature, an adult beaver cuts an average of one tree every two days, and they actually eat the bark (during the summer, beavers switch to salads, dining on aquatic vegetation).

If the boardwalk between the river and the slough isn't flooded over, you can hike to the beaver lodge directly in front of you (Marker 6 on the interpretive signage). If you're able to keep going at this point, you'll pass through a riparian (riverside) forest lined with shagbark hickory, and still more evidence of industrious beavers.

The final half of the loop will take you along the river and back to the parking area off Still River Depot Road.

Peeling bark gives this birch tree a barber-pole appearance.

--*49*--
Upton State Forest

Rating: Easy
Round trip: 3.3 miles
Hiking time: 3 hours
Elevation gain: 100 feet
High point: 550 feet
Maps: Upton State Forest Trail Map
Information: Upton State Forest; 508-529-6923; *www.mass.gov/dcr /parks*

Getting there: From I-90 (Massachusetts turnpike), take exit 22 to I-495 south. Take I-495 south to exit 21B, Main Street, in Upton. Drive west on Main Street/Hopkinton Road. Turn right onto Westboro Road and drive 2 miles to the state forest entrance on the right. Maps are available at the parking lot.

The first time we ever hiked here, in springtime, we were greeted by an unusual sight: A parade of people dressed in Renaissance garb spilled out of the woods—a role-playing group, the Society of Creative Anachronism, all done up in brocades and velvets, not the typical shorts-and-wicking-tee-shirts crowd. And we thought we were the ones who'd discovered this pine-scented, boulder-studded 2660-acre forest!

So it isn't completely unknown, but Upton State Forest is still quite pristine—and pretty much overlooked in winter. This thickly forested paradise of white pine and maples is circled with a pretty 3-mile loop trail that can be shortened if you choose to follow the unpaved Park Road to Dean Pond and circle back on Loop Road. It's easy for beginners and kids, with just a slight climb up the Hawk Trail.

Start at the map and gate at the parking lot, turning right onto Park Road. After about 0.5 mile, turn left onto the Whistling Cave Trail. Heading downhill here, you'll reach level ground and then pass by a stack of boulders (that's the Whistling Cave).

At about 1 mile, you'll reach the junction of the Whistling Cave Trail and Middle and Loop Roads. Turn right and take a brief walk to Dean Pond. Head back from the pond the same way, and take the middle fork to, appropriately, Middle Road. Turn right onto the Hawk Trail. After a brief, uphill jaunt, you'll reach Loop Road, where you take a quick left, then an almost immediate right onto the Grouse Trail. Take the next left onto the Mammoth Rock Trail. A small spur to the right will take you to Mammoth Rock, a set of glacial boulders so big you can stand between them.

Now you'll have to take a left onto a paved road, Spring Street. Either trek along Spring Street and take a left into the park road and the parking lot, or take Spring Street only as far as Swamp Trail, then take a left onto Swamp Trail and a right onto Park Road to the parking lot.

You'll want to come back in the springtime, post-mud season but early enough so that the bright green things are just popping out in the marshlands and the spring peepers are singing their riotous song. In our view, there's no place better to welcome—and smell—the freshness of spring than at Upton State Forest.

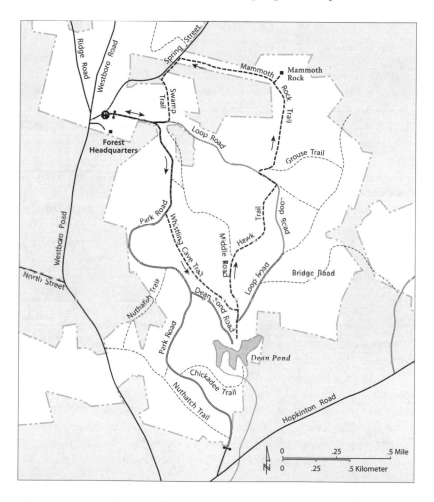

--*50*--
Wachusett Mountain State Reservation

Rating: Moderate
Round trip: 4 miles
Hiking time: 4.5 hours
Elevation gain: 806 feet
High point: 2006 feet
Maps: Wachusett Mountain State Reservation Trail Map; USGS Sterling, MA
Information: Wachusett Mountain State Reservation, Mountain Road, P.O. Box 248, Princeton, MA 01541; 978-464-2987; *www.mass.gov/dcr/parks*

Getting there: From Worcester, head north on I-190. Take exit 5 to Route 140 north in West Boylston. Turn left on Route 62 west toward Princeton, then left again onto Route 31 south. Turn right onto Mountain Road, past the gazebo, and drive about 3 miles. Turn left at the sign for Summit Road and the visitor center, where you can pick up a map.

Wachusett Mountain is home to a busy alpine ski area, but who cares when the rewards of trekking are so sublime? Bag the 2006-foot peak of Mount Wachusett, and you'll enjoy a bird's-eye view of the Boston skyline to the east, Mounts Tom and Greylock to the west, Worcester to the south, and New Hampshire's Mount Monadnock to the north. You may even see a hawk or eagle soaring above. This spot is one of New England's top birding destinations, especially during the fall migration, when people come from miles away to see the raptors. At the height of the action, in October through November, up to 20,000 birds of prey fly overhead. (If you don't see birds on your visit, stop by the nature center and check out the stuffed mounts of New England birds.)

About 3.9 miles of the long-distance Midstate Trail pass through the park. (Portions of this route are part of the yellow-blazed Midstate Trail.)

This hike, a figure-eight loop around Mount Wachusett (including the summit), is a great choice if you want a good workout and great scenery but don't want to totally exhaust yourself (you'll need to reserve some energy to hit the ski lodge for a bowl of chowder and a Pats game, post-hike). There's a short, steep downhill section at about 3.5 miles, but you can avoid it by exiting the Loop Trail segment and taking the Mountain House Trail to the Bicentennial Trail.

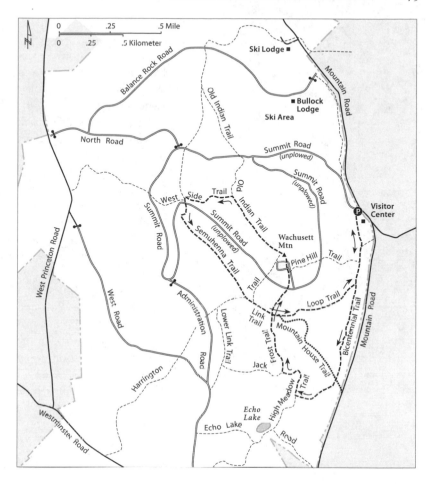

A sign at the south end of the parking lot will direct you to the blue-blazed Bicentennial Trail. Heading south, you'll pass junctions to the Pine Hill Trail, Loop Trail, and Mountain House Trail (look for a stone wall just before the Mountain House Trail intersection). After passing a clearing, turn right onto the High Meadow Trail. You'll follow a steep uphill grade here at around 1 mile. Turn right onto the Jack Frost Trail, which follows the ridgeline through a grove of hemlocks.

At about 1.5 miles, turn left onto the Link Trail, then make an immediate right onto the Mountain House Trail, uphill. You'll cross the Summit Road here. In approximately 0.5 mile (2 miles from the start) you'll reach the summit of Mount Wachusett. Enjoy the stunning panorama from this monadnock—a stand-alone peak, independent of a mountain range (but of course, you knew

Along the trail at Wachusett Mountain

that). You'll see an old fire tower and the ski lift overhead, as well.

To head back down, pass through the summit parking lot and ski lift, and follow the Old Indian Trail's switchbacks, heading northwest off the mountain. (The peak will be on your left.) After about 0.5 mile, turn left onto the West Side Trail. Make another left at the picnic table near the intersection with the Summit Road onto the Semuhenna Trail. You'll make a left onto the Harrington Trail for a short, steep uphill jaunt, then turn right onto the Link Trail. Connect with the Loop Trail here, at 3.5 miles, for a very steep, 0.2-mile descent, and then bear left onto the Bicentennial Trail and retrace your steps to the visitor center. (Or avoid this steep section if you wish, and take a right onto the gentler Mountain House Trail, from which a left will get you back to Bicentennial Trail.)

--51--
Walden Pond State Reservation

Rating:	Easy
Round trip:	1.7 miles
Hiking time:	2 hours
Elevation gain:	110 feet
High point:	270 feet
Map:	Walden Pond State Reservation Trail Map, Massachusetts Forest and Park Service
Information:	Walden Pond State Reservation, 915 Walden Street (Route 126), Concord, MA 01742; 978-369-3254; *www.mass.gov/dcr/parks*

Getting there: Take Route 128 to Route 2 in Concord; follow Route 2 to Walden Street (Route 126) and signs for Walden Pond, on the left. Drive a quarter mile on Walden Street to the reservation headquarters and parking. There is a $5 parking fee. Maps are available outside the gift shop.

Walden Pond, once home to author Henry David Thoreau, is a beloved local landmark. In summer, it is perhaps a bit *too* beloved—so many people throng to this swimming hole (a kettle pond) on a hot summer day, cars are turned away once capacity is reached. As many as 600,000 people visit the reservation each year, mostly in July and August, with crowds tapering off during fall foliage season. Poetry readings, kids' junior ranger activities, Thoreau walks, and, of course, swimming, hiking, and picnicking, draw families from Boston and the 'burbs during the bustling high season.

Then there's winter, when the crowds dwindle, and it becomes easier to understand how Thoreau could embark on a simple life here, studying natu-

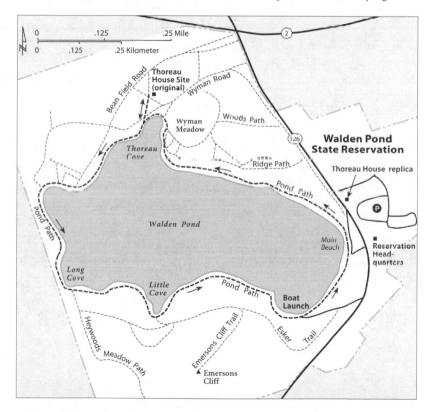

ral history and writing. Of moving to a one-room cottage on Walden Pond, he wrote, ". . . my friends ask what I will do when I get there? Will it not be employment enough to watch the progress of the seasons?" In the winter, it's very easy to notice the little things, like the stumps of white pine trees that were leveled by the hurricane of 1938, located above Thoreau's actual house site (the house is now gone, but markers reveal the location). You might also discover, as we did, tiny snowmen along the trail, sort of a winter version of the cairns left by summer hikers.

Thoreau arrived here to live and work in 1845, staying for two years. He kept a journal of his thoughts about nature and society and eventually published his observations in 1854 in his book, *Walden*. Of course, you can pick up a copy in the reservation's gift shop, and you can check out a replica of the simple cabin he lived in, built alongside the parking lot. And how wonderful to tour this 411-acre property in the simplest possible way, on snowshoes!

Start your walk by parking in the lot (make sure you have a fiver for the fee collection machine). Take a peek at the Thoreau House replica first, and then walk across the street to the water's edge. You could simply tromp around on the perimeter of Walden Pond, as many people do, including the occasional ice fishing enthusiast, but we like the white-blazed Pond Path. You'll easily notice the path, heading to the right, along the wooded shoreline. (You could also head clockwise around the pond, but our way will get you to Thoreau's

A replica of Thoreau's tiny cabin at Walden Pond State Reservation

house site sooner.) Other paths intersect here and there, but it's quite simple to just circle the pond. The wire fencing alongside the trail is definitely lacking in charm, but it's meant to keep people on the path and forestall erosion.

This is a fairly flat walk, and doable for children, with some gentle ups and downs on either side of the pond. You'll reach the house site pretty quickly, even if you jog off on the Ridge Path briefly. An inscribed piece of fieldstone marks the hearth site (the foundation was excavated in 1945, 100 years after Thoreau moved to Walden).

From here, you'll meander through the mixed woodlands and enjoy pleasant views of the frozen pond and—if it's a pretty, warmish day—families and couples enjoying an escape from the brownish slush of the city. On our last visit, we saw young children thrill to the sight of snowmen built along the trail and a couple sitting in the snow on the shoreline, bundled up in puffy parkas but locked in a warm embrace. Maybe a beautiful winter day in Walden Woods brings out the best in all of us.

--52--
Great Brook Farm State Park

Rating: Easy
Round trip: 3 miles
Hiking time: 2 hours
Elevation gain: 66 feet
High point: 246 feet
Map: Great Brook Farm State Park Trail Map, Massachusetts Forest and Park Service
Information: Great Brook Farm State Park, 984 Lowell Road, P.O. Box 829, Carlisle, MA 01741; 978-369-6312; *www.mass .gov/dcr/parks*

Getting there: Take Route 128 south to exit 31B in Lexington, heading west on Route 225. Drive 8 miles to Carlisle. At the rotary in Carlisle Center, take a right onto Lowell Road (look for the bright yellow-painted general store on your right). Go about 2 miles on Lowell Road to Great Brook Farm park headquarters and the sign for Great Brook Farm Ski Touring Center, on your right. There is a parking fee.

After a heavy, wet snow, Great Brook can be like a kayaking trip through Florida's mangrove swamps—a lovely, tangled adventure. You'll tunnel your

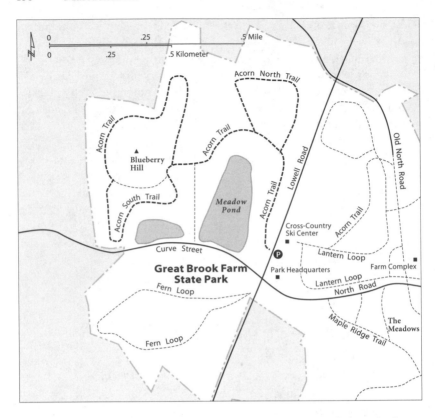

way under dense canopies of brush, and duck under arbors of snowy limbs, to emerge near wide-open pastures. Okay, so maybe it's not exactly like kayaking amidst the mangroves, but it is a similar sensation when the conditions are right!

A mere forty-minute ride from Boston, this is a rather unusual state park among the 100-plus parks and state reservations in Massachusetts. Until 1974, the 1000-acre property was a private home and dairy farm. Then the park service purchased it to preserve a little piece of New England's farming history. Although you won't really notice in winter, there are still farms on the land, leased dairy farms complete with grazing Holsteins and earthy aromas. You'll discover some old stone walls as you wander the main trail. Even older stone walls, dating back to the 1600s, may be seen on the other side of the park, in an area called "The City." You'll have to cross-country ski to get there, though; the snowshoe set isn't allowed on that side of the park, as we were told, quite firmly.

Don't even bother to get out of your car at the state park if you have snowshoeing on your mind. The ski center grooms the trails for cross-country skiing, and state park personnel won't listen to your pleas of, "But we won't mess up the trails, we promise!" Instead, simply do as they tell you, and drive to the ski touring center, just down the street past the intersection with North Road. The section of the state park that's assigned to the snowshoe crowd and hikers is accessible from the ski touring center, and it's the only place for snowshoers to park and access the state park's ungroomed trails.

Great Brook Farm Ski Touring Center operates the cross-country ski center, where you can pick up a can of soda and a state park trail map. They charge a fee for using their groomed cross-country ski trails, but you'll be using the state park's ungroomed trails.

Park at the ski center, then cross the street to the snowshoe/winter hiking side of the state park at the northwest corner. You'll easily see the trailhead for the Acorn Trail, marked with blue blazes and acorn icons on blue tags. Happily, the route is well marked and fairly easy to follow. You take a right to enter the trail, then make a loop around Acorn North. Back on Acorn, you trek past a pond (look out for slushy areas), then walk Acorn South in a loop that connects with the main trail.

What will you see as you loop around the property? Stone walls, a pond, pasture lands, a brook, and snow-frosted sweeps of forest, with the gentlest of climbs around Blueberry Hill. In spite of all the cars in the parking lot, everybody seems to head out to the cross-country side of the place, so you'll likely have this sweet slice of pastoral New England all to yourself.

Old stone walls are among the features at pastoral Great Brook Farm.

--*53*--
Mount Holyoke/Skinner State Park

Rating: Easy to more difficult
Round trip: 1.6 miles
Hiking time: 2 hours
Elevation gain: 1000 feet
High point: 940 feet
Map: *AMC Massachusetts Trail Guide,* Map 6
Information: J. A. Skinner State Park, Route 47, Hadley, MA 01035; 413-586-0350; *www.mass.gov/dcr/parks*

Getting there: Take the Massachusetts Turnpike (I-90) to exit 5, Route 33 north. Follow Route 33 to Route 116; take Route 116 north to Route 47 in Hadley. Head north for approximately 4 miles. The Skinner State Park main entrance, Mountain Road, is on the right. Park here, at the base of the summit road.

"Nobody knows we're out here! It's all about Boston, Cape Cod, and the Berkshires," complained a local innkeeper. 'Tis true, alas. This area of the state doesn't get a lot of attention. It is better known for local colleges (UMass–Amherst, Amherst College, and Hampshire College among them) than it is as a hot destination for outdoor pursuits. Most people who discover it have a "Who knew?" reaction.

So, we'll let you in on a little secret: The Mount Holyoke range is great for hiking and snowshoeing. Most of the land around the peaks is protected as part of 390-acre Skinner State Park, Holyoke Range State Park, and town conservation lands. The western part of the range has three summits: Mount Holyoke (940 feet), Mount Hitchcock (1002 feet), and Bare Mountain (1014 feet). The white-blazed long-distance Metacomet–Monadnock Trail winds around the ridgelines of the Holyoke Range for about 9 miles, adding to its enticements.

The dense forests and wide-open ledges make this an inviting place for summer hikers. In winter, we like trekking the summit of Mount Holyoke. In addition to offering lovely, panoramic views, this hike offers some options—the more challenging (but short) Halfway Trail and the easier, but more popular Summit Road, which is closed to cars in winter. More experienced snowshoers who are looking for a good cardio workout also have the option of connecting with the M–M Trail and leaving the weekend walkers (and snowmobilers) far behind.

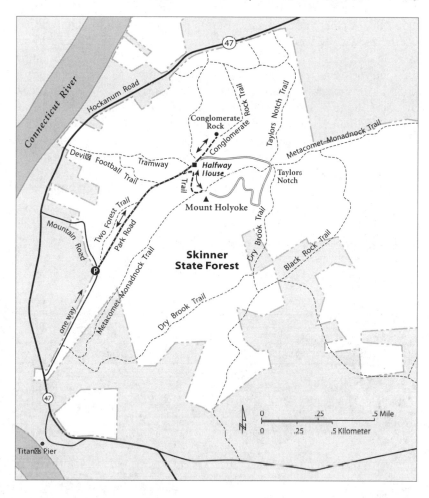

After parking at the main entrance of Skinner State Park, head left up the summit road to the north of the parking area. You'll have to carry your snowshoes for this segment, alas, since they plow the trail up to Halfway House and the caretaker's office. This will get you warmed up for what's to come, since it's fairly steep!

Look for the entrance to Halfway Trail on your right. You'll go up some snow-covered stairs, then head straight up into the trees. The trail will then head left and begin to climb. Careful here; it's a fairly narrow path, barely wide enough for a set of snowshoes.

You'll follow a series of switchbacks and do some moderate climbing, but it's a pretty route—to your left, you'll look into the Connecticut River valley.

In less than a mile, you'll reach the summit road and see, in front of you, the Summit House atop Mount Holyoke. This white, yacht-like building is closed in winter, but is surrounded by picnic spots and shelters. And the views! From this spot, you'll enjoy panoramic vistas of—on a clear day—New Hampshire's Mount Monadnock, and, closer in, the thick, blue ribbon of the Connecticut River. A quick peek at the interpretive sign at the summit will tell you that these glorious views have long inspired artists and writers alike, including Longfellow and Sylvia Plath. Once reachable by stagecoach for fashionable Bostonians, this is said to be the oldest summit house in the U.S. (operated as a hotel from 1851 to 1938).

After admiring the views, consider making a day of it by connecting with Taylors Notch Trail (yellow blazes, on the right-hand side of the summit road). From there, head left to connect with red-blazed Conglomerate Rock Trail to get back to the summit road. This route is about 2 miles round trip.

The old summit house atop Mount Holyoke

Or, you can connect with the Metacomet–Monadnock Trail here, and take the more strenuous, ridgeline route back to the parking area (you'll have to hike along a paved road for a bit to get back to the parking lot if you choose this 2-mile option).

If it's icy, you can simply stick to the summit road to get to the top of Mount Holyoke, a round trip of 1.6 miles. On sunny weekends, you'll see plenty of other folks doing exactly that (we even saw a woman on crutches do this!). After you pass Halfway House, the road is unpaved, so you'll be able to snowshoe again (and get lots of envious looks from those wearing sneakers to do the summit). Alas, you might see snowmobiles and ATVs along here, but you can ditch them at a small shortcut near the summit (you'll see it on your right) and find a secluded spot for lunch at the top of the mountain.

GOING THE DISTANCE

Sure, a day hike is all well and good. But are you ready for something a bit more… extreme? The white-triangle-blazed Metacomet–Monadnock Trail (M–M Trail, as it's called) runs 114 miles. The trail begins near the Connecticut–Massachusetts border (it's a continuation of Connecticut's Metacomet Trail), traversing Mount Tom and the Holyoke Range before it enters New Hampshire. The trail terminates at the 3165-foot summit of Mount Monadnock.

Up for more? Connect with the 51-mile Monadnock–Sunapee Greenway Trail to the 2743-foot summit of Mount Sunapee. From here, a connecting trail, the Sunapee–Ragged–Kearsarge Greenway, heads northeast on a 75-mile loop. The path traverses public and private land, and crosses paved highways at several points, with campsites and shelters along the way. In winter, we'd recommend exploring these long-distance trails as day hikes.

(In Massachusetts, we like the section of the M–M called the Seven Sisters, a series of peak climbs stretching between Mount Holyoke, at 940 feet, and Bare Mountain, at 1014 feet, in J.A. Skinner State Park. This is very difficult, rugged terrain, with great overlooks. At 9 miles, it's too long to do in one short winter's day, so choose a section, and then backtrack.)

For trail maps and current conditions on the Metacomet–Monadnock Trail, contact the AMC Berkshires Chapter at *www.amcberkshire.org/mmtrail*. For a copy of the Monadnock–Sunapee Greenway Trail Guide, contact *www.msgtc.org*. For descriptions of the Sunapee–Ragged–Kearsage Greenway, visit *www.srkg.com*.

--54--
Mount Toby

Rating: Moderate
Round trip: 5.5 miles
Hiking time: 4–5 hours
Elevation gain: 1040 feet
High point: 1269 feet
Map: *Guide to the Robert Frost Trail* (with color topos),
Amherst Area Trails Committee
Information: UMass Department of Forestry and Wildlife; 413-345-1799

Getting there: Take the Massachusetts Turnpike to exit 5, Chicopee; head north on Route 33 to route 116 north, heading toward Amherst. From Amherst, follow Route 116 north for 8 miles; turn right onto Main Street (Route 47) in Sunderland. Turn right on Reservation Road to park.

If you're looking for a good day hike that really delivers in terms of scenery, summits, and a solid workout, you won't do better than this Pioneer Valley favorite. In the summer, Mount Toby State Reservation, owned by the University of Massachusetts, is fringed with forty-plus varieties of ferns and dazzling orchids. Wintertime offers less color but more solitude, with rewarding views of distant peaks and the Connecticut River Valley in shades of white and blue.

This hike includes a portion of the Robert Frost Trail, begun in 1982 as a way to link Amherst conservation properties. More than 40 miles long, the Robert Frost Trail takes in some pretty country, including the 1000-acre Lawrence Swamp.

Heed this word of warning, though: Get a decent map, from the AMC or the Amherst Area Trails Committee (available at bookstores, EMS stores, and other outfitters in the valley) and follow it carefully. It is extremely easy to walk around in circles here; trail blazes are difficult to see in winter, and they can be confusing when you do see them (whose idea was it to use red and orange on the same trail system?). Fortunately, the physical landmarks here, like the mountain, the brook, and the old cabin, will enable you to determine where you are if you do take a wrong turn, or miss one. Please rely on our description only as a general guide; you really, truly need a detailed map here!

Starting from the parking lot at the reservation entrance off Route 47, follow the orange-blazed Robert Frost Trail. You'll enter a lovely forest of conifers and hardwood, ascending slightly. After about 0.5 mile, you'll head right at the junction, and then right again, through a section of hemlock forest. At about 1 mile, turn right (south) and hike under the telephone lines toward Mount Toby. At the next fork in the road, keep to the right to stay on the Robert Frost Trail (the Upper Link Trail is blazed in red).

The last 0.7 mile of this hike is a rather steep climb to the top of Mount Toby (1269 feet). The summit knoll is a great place to catch your breath and enjoy views, on a clear day, of Mount Monadnock in New Hampshire, Vermont's Mount Ascutney, Mount Greylock to the west, and Mount Wachusett to the east. The 360-degree panorama is great, whether or not you choose to climb the nine-story observation tower.

Descend along Summit Road, heading left about 1.2 miles from the summit where the Robert Frost Trail splits right (south). (There are other options, but the Summit Road is the easiest to follow.) The trail runs alongside Roaring Brook (so named because it roars with spring runoff) and passes Metawamp Cabin, a bit of a ruin that's filled with old bottles and splintered wood. Even though there's a fireplace, it's not much of a place to hang out.

Cross the brook and take a steep, short climb to the summit of Roaring Mountain. From here it is about 1.3 miles back to the trailhead, via Summit Road. Cross the brook again and head right on the road, following it back to Reservation Road.

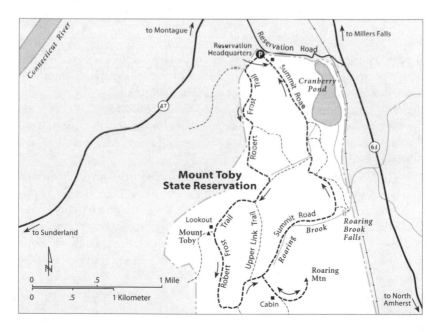

NORTH OF BOSTON

-- 55 --
Bradley Palmer State Park

Rating: Easy
Round trip: 3 miles
Hiking time: 2–2.5 hours
Elevation gain: 100 feet
High point: 150 feet
Map: Bradley Palmer State Park Trail Map (winter use), Massachusetts Department of Environmental Management
Information: Bradley Palmer State Park, Asbury Street, Topsfield, MA 01983; 978-887-5931; *www.mass.gov/dcr/parks*

Getting there: From Route 128, take exit 50 (Route 1 north) toward Topsfield. Turn right onto Ipswich Road. In 1.2 miles, turn right onto Asbury Street. You'll see a sign for Bradley Palmer State Park. Turn left at the stone gate marking the main entrance. Follow the entrance road to the parking area, on the right, and park headquarters where you can pick up a map (in a box to the right of the building).

Bradley Palmer is one of the best-loved and easiest-to-locate parks on the North Shore. Local kids have happy memories of this park in summertime, when the wading pool (sort of a countrified version of the open fire hydrant) is turned on, and parents plop down on surrounding hillsides with picnic goodies. Of course, you can create some fine memories here in winter, too! The main road into the park is, happily, plowed, and there's plenty of parking.

The interpretive trail, where we begin this hike, is just as nice in the winter as it is in summertime, offering up bits of nature fact and tree identification. This very manageable walk traces the Ipswich River for awhile, and passes rhododendron bushes that hold the snow and drape gracefully at the trailside. There's a wide-open field, where you can climb up and over the hills wherever you like (avoiding any cross-country ski tracks, of course), and bridle paths that loop back to the parking area.

Keep your map handy, because you may well find you have energy to burn and decide to explore more of the park. The good news is, there are

An old stone mansion—with a cherry red door—is one of the intriguing sights at Bradley Palmer State Park.

numbers posted on trees all over the property, so a quick glance at the map should reveal exactly where you are.

We should note that cross-country skiers use some of these trails, as do snowmobilers; we've purposely picked out a route that doesn't get much use by the former, and is off-limits to the latter.

You'll start at the beginning of the self-guided walking tour, heading gently to the right (north) behind park headquarters. Before you get going, though, take a look at the beautiful stone mansion, located on your left just past the park headquarters. The house, and the surrounding 5 square miles, was once the private estate of Bradley Webster Palmer (1866–1946), a prominent Boston lawyer. He held great parties in the mansion, and created a steeplechase course for horse racing. Ultimately, Palmer donated the estate, called Willowdale, to the state of Massachusetts. The property extends to neighboring Willowdale/Cleaveland Farm State Forest.

After admiring the mansion, with its leaded glass and vivid red door, head back to the nature trail. You'll cross over a small wooden bridge, draped with rhododendron on either side. The path is marked with blue triangle blazes with a bear pawprint logo. Heading left, the path runs parallel to the Ipswich River. Around Marker 5, you'll pass a wood and stone bridge on your left. Stay on the trail, and you'll next notice a sign marking land protected by the Essex County Greenbelt. Bear right, slightly uphill, and right again, onto an open path. You're back on state land again.

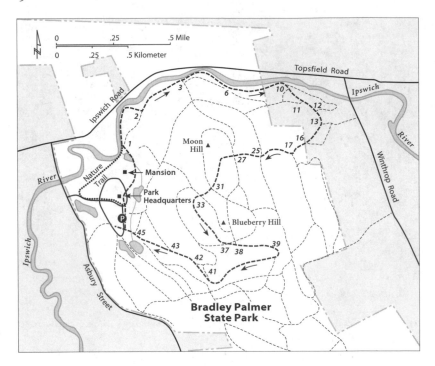

Cross the dirt road, around Marker 25, and head toward the open field. You'll notice two small hills, Moon Hill and Blueberry Hill; walk downhill between them. At the bottom of the hill, bear right at Marker 33; follow the wide, flat path as it curves to the left, then right at Marker 39.

Take a right at the fork at Marker 43; there will be a small pond to your left. Once you've reached the main road, take a quick right back to the parking lot.

--56--
Weir Hill Reservation

Rating: Easy
Round trip: 1.9 miles
Hiking time: 2 hours
Elevation gain: 100 feet
High point: 250 feet
Map: Weir Hill trail map, The Trustees of Reservations
Information: The Trustees of Reservations, 978-682-3580; *www .thetrustees.org*

Getting there: From points south, take I-93 north to exit 41. Turn right onto Route 125 north. (The road veers to the right at light just past Merrimack College.) Turn right onto Andover Street. Fork right, across the North Andover town common, to Great Pond Road, then make an immediate left onto Stevens Street. Park along Stevens Street, alongside the reservation entrance on the right side of the road.

During the warmer months, Lake Cochichewick is abuzz with activity. Students from the nearby Brooks School ply the waters of the 592-acre lake in sailing dinghies or sculls, while residents jog the lakeside trails or ramble about with their rambunctious canines. In winter, though, it's a snow-hushed and peaceful scene, with just a few diehard dog-walkers on the trails and lakeside footpaths.

Set on a 200-foot double drumlin, this gentle walk offers lovely views of surrounding hills at its highest point, then scoops into woodlands and follows

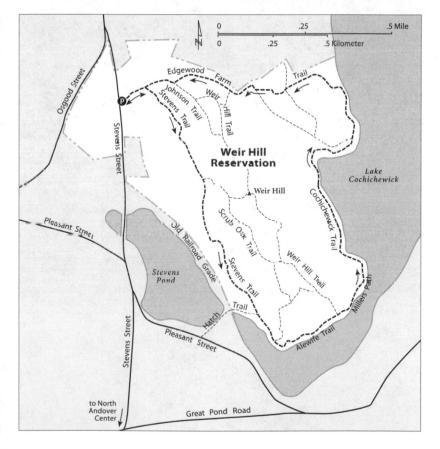

the lakeshore of Cochichewick. It's perfect for kids, who are always the first to spot rabbit tracks in the snow, or an owl standing sentry on a tree limb—both common occurrences here!

Weir Hill is named for weirs, the latticework structures used by Native Americans for fishing. These underwater fences worked so well that European settlers caught onto the concept and began to build weirs on local rivers. As for Cochichewick, it was known as "The Great Pond," until the early 1900s. Cochichewick means "the place of great cascades," a name used by native local tribes, like the Penacooks, who moved up and down the Merrimack River here.

Trail maps are posted in the reservation, and available online from The Trustees' website. You'll start at the parking area on Stevens Street, walking

Travis Kelley surveys the scene at Weir Hill.

uphill past the reservation sign and heading left, into the woods. The Stevens Trail forks immediately to the right, and you'll begin an uphill climb. At the top of the hillside at 1000 feet is a clearing, with pastoral views of hills and a scattering of homes. A stone bench marks the spot.

From there, head down the hill and under a powerline, back into the woods. You'll soon cross a small stream (narrow and probably iced over) and drop downhill. Continuing the loop, you'll trace the edge of Stevens Pond and, rather than cut up inland, head toward the shoreline. (These trails have names, but they're unmarked, so your best bet is to simply follow the tracks around the lake, ignoring the trails that lead to the left.)

You'll follow the lakeshore for some time—about nine-tenths of a mile or so—and cross a wooden boardwalk. Notice the pretty views of the lake and the white house, jutting into the water, that blends perfectly with its surroundings. You'll see some remnants of stone walls, evidence of sheep- and cattle-grazing here, centuries ago.

Look for a posted trail map, and turn right, continuing along the shore; follow the trail (now the Edgewood Farm Trail) as it leads uphill and away from the lake. When you see a sign marking the reservation boundary, take a left on the trail (you'll see a private house toward the right), then cross another boardwalk. Bearing right, you'll follow the trail for a short distance and emerge back at the parking lot.

SNOWSHOE-FRIENDLY DIGS: MASSACHUSETTS

Make it a weekend getaway, and stay at one of these friendly inns. Not only are they located in appealing destinations (with good, casual restaurants and museums or galleries in the 'hood), but their proprietors know all the great places to snowshoe nearby. They'll happily share their secret spots, copy maps for you, and maybe even pick you up at the end of the trail (if you ask nicely!).

Allen House Victorian Inn, 599 Main Street, Amherst, MA 01002; 413-253-5000; *www.allenhouse.com*

Applegate Bed and Breakfast, 279 West Park Street, Lee, MA 01238; 413-243-4451; *www.applegateinn.com*

Emerson Inn by the Sea, 1 Cathedral Avenue, Rockport, MA 01966; 800-964-5550; *www.emersoninnbythesea.com*

Ivory Creek Bed and Breakfast Inn, 31 Chmura Road, Hadley, MA 01035; 866-331-3115; *www.ivorycreek.com*

The Porches Inn, 231 River Street, North Adams, MA 01247; 413-664-0400; *www.porches.com*

--$\mathcal{57}$--
Ravenswood Park

Rating: Easy
Round trip: 4.8-mile loop
Hiking time: 2.5 hours
Elevation gain: 30 feet
High point: 180 feet
Map: Ravenswood Park Trail Map, Trustees of Reservations
Information: Trustees of Reservations, 978-356-4351; *www
.thetrustees.org*

Getting there: Heading north from Boston, follow Route 128 to exit 14, Gloucester. Follow Route 133 east for 3 miles; turn right on Route 127 south. Drive for 5 miles, then turn into the Ravenswood Park entrance and the parking lot marked with the Trustees of Reservations sign. There is parking for twelve cars (less in winter due to plowing).

Most people think of the sea when they think of Gloucester. This seaport city is, after all, a working fishing port and home to the famous "Fisherman at the Wheel" statue on Stacey Boulevard, sculpted in 1923. This landmark, along with the more recent (and poignant) "Fisherman's Wives" statue, honors the 15,000-plus Gloucester fishermen lost at sea, and the families they left behind. The monument is a constant reminder of the power of nature, something you'll see evidence of at Ravenswood Park, although in less dramatic fashion.

Ravenswood Park is a 600-acre glacial moraine. Thousands of years ago, retreating glaciers left giant boulders, or erratics, all over the park. In the winter, these giant, snow-covered boulders look like giant snowballs. Other features of the property tend to disappear under heavy snowfall, like the kettle ponds and Great Magnolia Swamp, a glacial bog. The park's variety of trees look gorgeous draped in snow; you'll tromp past oak, birch, beech, maple, eastern hemlock, white pine, mountain laurel, and even the sweetbay magnolia (uncommon around here).

You can devise loop trails in three or four ways here, depending on conditions. Keep in mind that while there are numbered markers (wooden posts) along the trails, these can be obscured in the snow, and you definitely won't see blazes. So, if you have any uncertainty about following the longer route described here (Magnolia Swamp Trail to Fernwood Lake Trail, 4.8 miles round trip), just stick with Old Salem Road, the carriage road that begins at

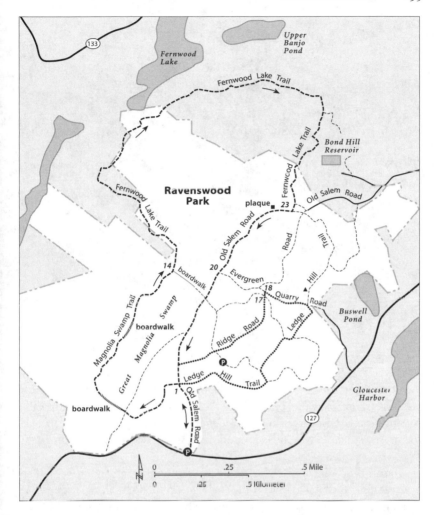

the park's entrance. You can make a nice hike from Old Salem Road to the
Ledge Hill Trail (at Marker 25), connecting with Quarry Road (Marker 18),
and then following Ridge Road (Marker 17) back to Old Salem Road. That
loop is about 2 miles long. We recommend the Magnolia Swamp to Fernwood
Lake loop, a longer, pork chop–shaped route with fairly open views of a small
lake. This one is less used than the shorter loops and Old Salem Road, and we
always find it more fun to walk through the woods than travel a logging road.

For all hikes, you'll start at the Trustees of Reservations trailhead, off
Route 127. There are trail maps in a box here; you can also download one from
the Trustees' website. Start your walk on Old Salem Road, heading north, and

Lisa Hollis chooses among the trail options at Ravenswood.

then take a quick left onto Magnolia Swamp Trail at Marker 1. You'll begin a pleasant, meandering trail into the woods and over two sections of boardwalk, passing several fallen trees and many enormous boulders (even a balanced rock). At Marker 14, continue along the trail, which becomes Fernwood Lake Trail here, marked by blue dots.

From this point, those marker posts are nonexistent, so you'll have to look carefully for blue blazes on the trees. The park boundary stops here, so you'll be hiking on private property for a while. You'll get nice, fairly unobstructed views of the lake as you pass by the top of the "pork chop" at around 2 miles. If you go off-trail, you can hike down to the shoreline. (We'd stay off the lake, though. After several trips here, we've found that the ice is rarely safe to walk on.)

Stay on the Fernwood Lake Trail to trail junction 23. According to your trail map, the Hermit's Plaque is supposed to be here, at the fork of Old Salem Road and the Fernwood Lake Trail. Surprise—it's actually a few yards down along Old Salem Road, to the right, a verdigris brass plate on a boulder. (Good luck finding it under heavy snow cover!) We will tell you that the hermit was Mason A. Walton, who built a cabin here (you can still see remnants of stone walls) in the late 1800s. He became an expert in the flora and fauna of the park, and wrote several books and articles on the subject before his death in 1917.

From here, continue on Old Salem Road and complete the loop along this old logging path (favored by dog walkers and joggers), just over 1 mile. You'll pass a junction at Marker 20 with Evergreen Road. Be sure to stay on old Salem Road, and follow it back to the parking lot.

--58--
Harold Parker State Forest

Rating: Easy
Round trip: Varies
Hiking time: 1–2 hours
Elevation gain: 0
High point: 0
Map: Harold Parker State Forest Trail Map, Massachusetts Forest and Park Service
Information: Harold Parker State Forest, 1951 Turnpike Road, North Andover, MA 01845; 978-686-3391; *www.mass.gov/dcr /parks*

Getting there: From I-495 take exit 42 in Andover and go east on Route 114 for 6 miles. Turn right on Harold Parker Road and turn left at park headquarters.

Only 25 miles north of Boston, this 3000-acre state forest is virtually unknown to those outside the area. Even in the height of summertime, campsites (in the western section of the park) can often be had at the last minute, on sultry August weekends (try doing that anyplace else in the state!). Why is this? The Harold Parker State Forest is certainly pretty enough. Park lands spread to Andover, North Andover, North Reading, and Middleton, and include forests of hardwood, hemlock, and white pine, circling eleven ponds (nine of them man-made).

The property offers 35 miles of trails and logging roads to ramble, shown on the state forest map (available at forest headquarters and online). For snowshoe hikers looking for a nice, woodsy walk, it can't be beat, since unpaved roads (closed to vehicles in winter) make an easygoing ramble, and you can head off-trail and roam around the frozen ponds and pristine forests. It won't be too difficult to find your way back to one of the main roads that crisscross the property.

Lightly used Harold Parker State Forest offers skinny paths and unpaved roads for snowshoeing.

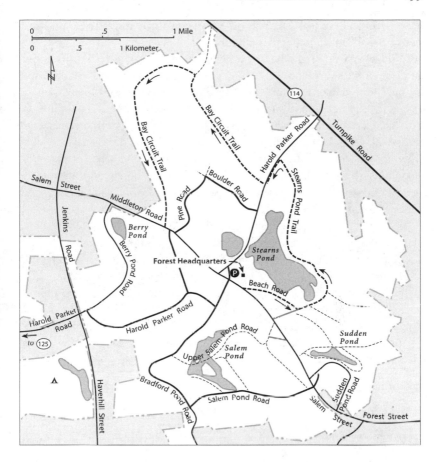

As a warm-up, you can start from forest headquarters on Harold Parker Road (no staff in winter, typically, but a porta-potty and small parking lot), and then cross the street to the trailhead. Follow the trail marked with acorn signs. The trail bears to the left, with interpretive signs that won't be of much interest; they're either covered with ice, or alluding to things you can't see in winter, like beech leaves.

You'll loop back to Beach Road, where you'll cross and go around a gate to (unpaved) Stearns Pond Road, leading to—surprise!—Stearns Pond. From there, you can follow the Stearns Pond and Bay Circuit Trails around the northern edge of the park, looping back to Middleton Road (paved). From there a short walk along the road will get you back to the parking lot.

Or, from Stearns Pond you can follow any of the small side trails leading to Sudden Pond; from there you can retrace your steps back to forest headquarters.

West of forest headquarters, trails off Middleton Road and Berry Pond Road lead to Berry Pond, another pleasant hike.

In our view, though, the best way to enjoy this park is to simply ramble, and not worry much about the official trails which aren't well marked and are hard to find in any season. (We thought winter was the problem; then we visited in summer, and it was still virtually impossible to find the trailheads. We asked a park official, who told us, "Oh, those trails haven't been cleared for twenty years.") So, we'd stick to the unpaved roads here. They're plenty wide, easy to find on the map, and will provide a good sense of place for you amidst this sprawling property. The park's eleven ponds, all reachable off Berry Pond Road, Walker Road, and Harold Parker Road, will provide good landmarks as you go.

This park is even prettier in winter than in summer. Blanketed in snow, Harold Parker State Forest is all towering pines, scampering mammals, and frozen ponds, wrapped in silence (amazing to think that three million people in Boston and environs are so nearby). We tend to meander off the trail, following deer tracks and the long, loping prints of the snowshoe hare. Animal tracks are everywhere, further proof that this place is an undiscovered gem. The only people tracks you'll likely encounter here will be your own. So, wander off the unpaved roads when the whim occurs, and simply retrace your own footprints back.

A winter walk in New England will tune you into the small stuff, like the peeling bark of a birch tree.

VERMONT

SOUTHERN VERMONT

--59--
Griffith Lake and Baker Peak

Rating: Moderate to difficult
Round trip: 5.6 miles to Baker Peak; 6.6 miles to Griffith Lake; 8.1 miles loop via AT/Long Trail connector
Hiking time: 5 hours
Elevation gain: 1947 feet
High point: 2850 feet
Maps: Green Mountain National Forest Map, Griffith Lake/Baker Peak via the Lake Trail; USGS Danby, VT
Information: Manchester Ranger District, Green Mountain National Forest, Routes 11 and 30, 2538 Depot Street, Manchester Center, VT 05233; 802-362-2307; *www.fs.fed.us/r9/gmfl/*

Getting there: From Manchester, take Route 7 north approximately 10 miles until you reach a Green Mountain National Forest sign (on the right.) About 500 feet north of this sign, turn right onto Forest Road 259 (aka South End Road); you'll see a cemetery on a knoll on the right. Drive 0.4 mile down Forest Road 259 to the trailhead parking on the left.

"This is the coolest thing I've ever done!" proclaimed our friend Nancy, virgin snowshoe trekker, as she took on the Lake Trail to Baker Peak. Nance was hooked. Indeed, we couldn't have planned a better first-time outing. Temps were warmish (twenty degrees or so, balmy by January-in-Vermont standards), with a bluebird sky—a perfect backdrop for the gorgeous views of Otter Creek Valley and Dorset Mountain in southern Vermont's Green Mountains.

Nancy Bergeron bushwhacks a trail to Baker Peak.

If you're looking for more great snowshoe hikes than you can possibly squeeze into a weekend—or even a week—look no farther. The Green Mountain National Forest offers an embarrassment of snowshoe riches, from waterfall hikes to lake hikes to Long Trail summits to valley treks tucked between the mountains. The folks at the Manchester Ranger District office are happy to arm you with trail maps and advice. Post-hike, the Manchester area has several inviting places to dig in to hearty pub grub and hoist a warm beverage or a Vermont-brewed Long Trail Ale. Towns here, like Arlington and Manchester, are postcard-pretty and loaded with cozy inns that will spoil you between snowshoe outings. No need to go fancy anywhere—they're used to folks dressed for the weather here, wherever you go. No matter how many hikes you fit into your visit, make sure this one's on the list. It's a great workout that rewards you with lovely views, and it never gets boring.

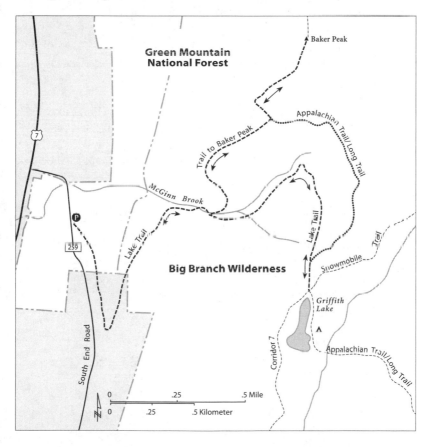

From the parking area, follow the blue-blazed trail as it passes through a mixed hardwood/softwood forest alongside McGinn Brook. At the brook crossing, about 2 miles in, the trail divides, with the Baker Peak trail heading left and the Griffith Lake trail heading right. Baker Peak is 0.8 mile from this point; Griffith Lake is 1.3 miles from here. You have three options: You can head left toward the summit for an out-and-back hike to Baker Peak (5.6 miles round trip), or right for an out-and-back hike to Griffith Lake (6.6 miles round trip). Or, you can make it a two-fer, scenery-wise, and hike down 2 miles of the Appalachian Trail/Long Trail to Griffith Lake (8.1 miles round trip). Be sure you have adequate daylight if you choose to make the loop.

You'll gain elevation pretty quickly as you wind your way up the narrow, rocky route toward Baker Peak. (You'll see a sign denoting the Big Branch Wilderness Area of the national forest.) The steeps aren't grueling, though, especially when you look to your left and watch the mountains emerge through tree branches. You'll enjoy lots of great scenery even before you reach the summit, as you hike past the looming Taconic Mountains and peer into the valley with sloping farmlands in the distance. That will only encourage you to keep going, because the views from the top, at 2850 feet, are even better.

From there, you can head back down the way you came on Baker Peak Trail, or continue right for 2 miles on the Appalachian Trail/Long Trail connector, to Griffith Lake. (For more on the Long Trail, see the sidebar "Footpath in the Wilderness.") From the lake, catch the Lake Trail again to get back to the parking lot.

--*60*--
White Rocks Recreation Area

Rating: Moderate
Round trip: 1.6 miles
Hiking time: 2 hours
Elevation gain: 180 feet
High point: 1300 feet
Maps: USGS Wallingford, VT; Green Mountain National Forest Map, White Rocks/Ice Beds Trail
Information: Green Mountain National Forest, Manchester District, Manchester, VT; 802-382-2307; *www.fs.fed.us/r9/gmfl*

Getting there: From Manchester, take Route 11/30 west to Route 7 north. Take Route 7 to Wallingford Four Corners. Take a right onto Route 140 east, drive 2.1 miles, and then bear right onto Sugar Hill Road. Follow Sugar Hill Road for a short distance to Forest Road 52, on the right, and drive 0.5 mile to the picnic/parking area at the end of the road, following signs to White Rocks National Recreation Area.

Who can resist a trail with an intriguing name like "ice beds"? This short, energizing hike, easily accessible from the tourist hub of Manchester, offers sweet rewards for little effort. You'll enjoy cool views of boulder slides and the ice beds, where ice remains even in summertime. (Granted, this is a bit more thrilling a concept when it's hot outside!)

From the White Rocks picnic/parking area, cross the road and head left (slightly back where you came from) to the trailhead. Follow the blue-blazed Ice Beds Trail into the woods. Cross a brook, and begin a steep hike up a staircase to a series of switchbacks. This can be a bit of a rocky zigzag, so this trail is best undertaken after a heavy snowfall. Otherwise, you'll encounter some exposed rock and ice (and will probably want to take off your snowshoes for portions of the hike).

At 0.2 mile, a short spur trail to the left leads to an overlook of the northwestern side of White Rocks Cliffs—your first peek at the white rock slides. Keep going, just another 0.1 mile, and enjoy a more wide-open vista of the cliffs to the

Enchanting views of the ice beds, where the snow never melts

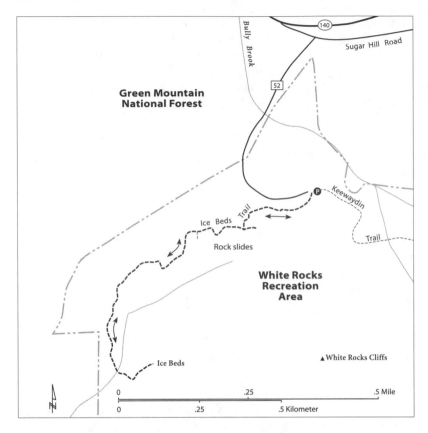

west. This is a good photo-op/snack stop. The rockfall is on your left. To the right, you'll see the valley, the Taconic Mountains, and the talc mine in South Wallingford.

From here, follow the blue-blazed trail, crossing a stream, and walk down to an off-road-vehicle trail. After a short uphill trek, you'll reach the ice beds, a tumble of piled Cheshire quartzite chunks that have slid off the cliffs over the centuries. The cliffs themselves were sheared by glaciers about 12,000 years ago, they say. Native people once quarried stone from the site for their tools. Like much of the Green Mountain region, the area was used for grazing cattle, and, later, for logging. Happily, it is now protected as recreation land.

So why the persistent ice? Cool downdrafts of air keep the area cold year-round, so the ice remains. For a longer hike around this unusual geographic gem, take the Keewaydin Trail, a blue-blazed path at the far end of the picnic area. This 3.2-mile trail winds around the northern and eastern edges of the cliff area, and gets a bit steep in places. It meets up with the Appalachian Trail/Long Trail and the Greenwall Shelter.

SNOWSHOE-FRIENDLY DIGS—VERMONT

Who doesn't love a Vermont country inn? When it comes to cozy digs with crackling fires and great food, the Green Mountain State has no peers! One of the real joys of living in New England is the close proximity to scores of inviting inns. Here are some we can recommend that are warm, welcoming to the snowshoe set, and close to some great snowshoe areas:

Arlington Inn, Route 7A, Arlington, VT 05250; 300-443-9442; *www.arlingtoninn.com*

Blueberry Hill Inn, Goshen-Ripton Road, Goshen, VT 05733; 800-448-0707; *www.blueberryhillinn.com*

Kedron Valley Inn, Route 106, South Woodstock, VT 05071; 802-457-1473; *www.kedronvalleyinn.com*

Mountain Top Inn, 195 Mountain Top Road, Chittenden, VT 05737; 800-445-2100; *www.mountaintopinn.com*

The following resorts are also a good bet for snowshoe hikers, and offer lots of options for outdoor fun—and indoor comforts (including hot tubs and massages after a day on the trail).

Smuggler's Notch Resort, 4323 Route 108 South, Smugglers Notch, VT 05464; 800-451-8752; *www.smuggs.com*

Topnotch at Stowe Resort, 4000 Mountain Road, Stowe, VT 05672; 800 451 8686; *www.topnotchresort.com*

--61--
Bromley Mountain

Rating:	Moderate to more difficult
Round trip:	5.4 miles
Hiking time:	4 hours
Elevation gain:	1380 feet
High point:	3200 feet
Maps:	USGS Peru, VT; Green Mountain National Forest Map, Bromley Mountain
Information:	Manchester Ranger District, 2538 Depot Street (Route 11/30), Manchester Center, VT 05255; 802-362-2307

Getting there: From Route 7 in Manchester, take Route 11/30 east for approximately 5 miles to the Appalachian Trail/Long Trail crossing. The parking area is on the north side of Route 11/30.

The parking lot doesn't look promising: You'll probably see at least a couple of trucks with trailers attached. "Uh, oh!" you'll think; "Snowmobilers!" And, in fact, this trail intersects with Corridor 7, a major snowmobile route. But early on, once you pass Bromley Brook, you probably won't see or hear them at all. You'll be deep, deeper, deepest into the woods, en route to the summit of Bromley Mountain.

This is an extraordinarily peaceful hike, not heavily used in winter, perhaps because of its length and the fact that it is rated moderate to difficult. Plus, Bromley Mountain is home to a bustling ski resort, which might make it seem like you'll be dodging downhill skiers as you go. Not so, as we discovered. The ski resort is actually southeast of the trail. If you're lucky, the only company you have will be your hiking buddy and a couple of pileated woodpeckers as you attack the 3260-foot summit of Bromley. We actually sang as we hiked, something we wouldn't have done if we thought anyone would hear us!

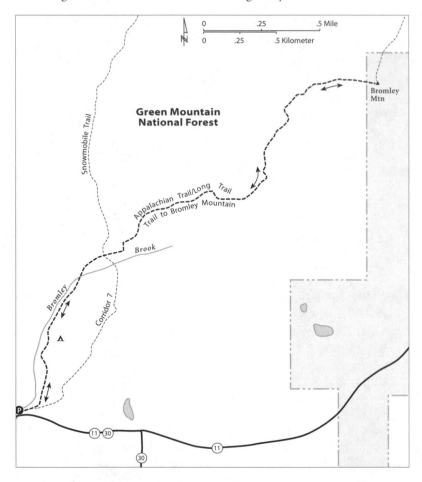

Signs point the way to the Bromley summit.

This is an easy trail to find, and to follow, for the most part. Just past the parking lot, you'll head left at the trailhead for the Appalachian Trail/Long Trail, and follow the white blazes all the way. You'll enter a mixed northern hardwood forest and cross over a narrow bridge. At about 0.5 mile, the trail follows Bromley Brook.

At nearly the 1-mile point, you'll cross over a road, Corridor 7, the snowmobile route we mentioned. If you want to make a short loop of it, just take a right and follow the road back to the parking lot. (We wouldn't recommend this on a weekend, when there's lots of snowmobile traffic, although you could just traipse through the woods alongside the road.)

At this point, Corridor 7 heads north while you hike to the northeast, along a rocky trail that has been climbing pretty steadily from the get-go. At about 1.6 miles, you'll notice the trail becoming steeper. There's one confusing spot to look out for: After you see the Bromley shelter to your right, it will appear as though the summit trail goes straight ahead, and up into a series of boulders. The blaze is poorly located, plus you'll probably see footprints from other hikers who mistakenly went off-trail here. Since these boulders are fairly insurmountable in winter, you'll quickly realize you need to head right, here, to stay on the trail.

At this point, you may well be wondering, "When will this thing end?" It seems to take a long time to get to the top. On our last hike up Bromley, we were trying to out-hike a major snowstorm, which really added some pressure to get the heck up the mountain!

Just when you're getting discouraged, not to mention tired, the views begin to unfold around you—lovely, snow-dusted panoramas of Stratton Mountain to the south and Mount Equinox to the west. The ski trails carved onto Stratton's face look like lava flowing down a volcano (or else we were just really tired and hallucinating). You might be tempted to stop here, but if you keep going to the tip-top, the views will just blow you away—as will the wind if you're not careful! Happily, it's a fairly quick romp back to the parking lot, since it's downhill all the way.

CENTRAL VERMONT

--62--
Mountain Top Inn

Rating: Easy to moderate
Round trip: 6 miles
Hiking time: 4 hours
Elevation gain: 550 feet
High point: 2174 feet
Maps: Mountain Top Inn Nordic Ski and Snowshoe Center Trail Map; USGS Chittenden, VT
Information: Mountain Top Inn, 195 Mountain Top Road, Chittenden, VT 05737; 802-483-2311 or 800-445-2100; *www.mountaintopinn.com*

Getting there: From Route 89 north, take exit 1 toward Woodstock and Rutland, onto Route 4 west. Travel on Route 4 toward Pico Resort; 5 miles past Pico, take a right onto Meadow Lake Drive (just past Sugar and Spice Restaurant). Turn right onto Chittenden Road. Go 2.6 miles past the church and fire station. Look for the Mountain Top Inn sign; go left on Holden Street, right at the Civil War monument onto Mountain Top Road. The inn is 1.8 miles up on the right.

Bet they don't get much drive-by traffic here! The last you'll see of civilization is a Civil War statue and a few lonesome homes. From there, you go up, up, up, to a sprawling inn that once hosted President Eisenhower. Surrounded by languid peaks and backed by a mountain lake (okay, it's a reservoir, but "mountain lake" sounds more romantic), the Mountain Top Inn is an outdoor lover's paradise. Snowshoe hikers can show up, park the car, and spend a weekend away from it all. The bustling alpine ski areas of Pico and Killington are just a few miles away, but you'll be far from crowds and lift lines here. Cross-country ski and snowshoe trails climb to 2174 feet at the peak, with nearly 50 miles of trails meandering through forests, along the hillside, and deep into the valley. You won't mind sharing the scenic trail up to the top and along the ridge with a cross-country skier or two, since the views are so great. (From that point, you can link with an ungroomed trail where skinny skiers seldom venture.)

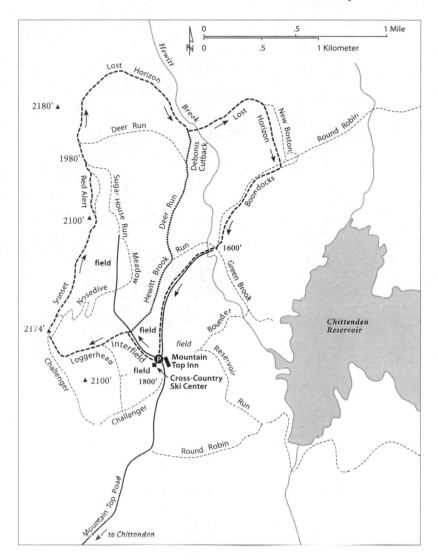

Just in case you don't knock yourself out completely, there's a lighted ice-skating rink (lovely under a starlit sky), a sledding hill, dogsled rides, and horse-drawn sleigh rides. Chef Shaun Casey's food makes it worth hiking an extra trail or two, just to feel you've earned those fried pumpkin raviolis! Even if you just come up for the day, stick around for dinner. Those who stay can sign on for the ski and snowshoe package; they'll throw in a ski/snowshoe pass with your room and breakfast.

Snowshoer Paul Kelley contemplates taking a nose dive at Mountain Top.

From the Nordic center, you'll head straight up, heading left at the trout pond, to the Interfield Trail. This short-but-steep trek will get you warmed up for the rest of the hike, which heads mostly down into the valley.

From Interfield, you'll connect with the Loggerhead Trail, still heading up but leveling off with rolling terrain. Next comes the Sunset Trail, a pretty stretch with views of Chittenden Reservoir and, on a clear day, peaks as distant as the Adirondacks to the west. This is one of the great things about snowshoeing; when the trees are filled in, these views are shrouded in foliage.

If it sounds like a lot of trail-switching, not to worry; this place is amazingly well marked, with "you are here" signage everywhere. You can travel the entire property and never feel lost.

From here, it's Red Alert, a gorgeous trail that winds through evergreens. So far, you've hiked on groomed trails—now, you'll connect with the Lost Horizon Trail, an ungroomed stretch that's often dotted with the tracks of white-tailed deer. We were here in the heart of the winter, during a holiday period, and saw no people tracks along Lost Horizon. The entire trail loops down to the valley floor—about 3.7 miles in all, but you can cut it off if you wish, and make a shorter loop, taking Deer Run to Hewitt Brook Run (part of the Catamount Trail System).

The Lost Horizon Trail will remind you why you love snowshoeing, especially if you visit after a heavy snowfall. You'll feel like you're bushwhacking at times, slipping beneath archways of snow-laden tree limbs. As you make tracks in fresh snow, and step over snow-covered bridges, you'll notice something that perhaps you hadn't noticed before: silence. You won't hear cars, snowmobiles, anything but the pleasant plod of snowshoes in fluffy white stuff. That—and the good food at the inn—makes this an easy call: a trip to Mountain Top, well worth the drive. It's a fun destination for winter adventure.

--63--
Mount Tom, Woodstock

Rating: Easy
Round trip: 2.6 miles
Hiking time: 2.5 hours
Elevation gain: 200 feet
High point: 1300 feet
Map: Woodstock Ski Touring Center Trail Map
Information: Marsh-Billings-Rockefeller National Historical Park, 54 Elm Street, Woodstock, VT 05091; 802-457-3368; *www.nps.gov/mabi/pphtm*; Woodstock Ski Touring Center; Woodstock Inn, 14 The Green, Woodstock, VT 05091; 802-457-6674; *www.woodstockinn.com*

Getting there: From I-89 north, take exit 1 for Woodstock, Rutland, and Route 4. At the bottom of the ramp, turn left onto Route 4 west and travel 10 miles to the Woodstock Village Green (traffic rotary). From the Village Green, take Route 12 to Prosper Road. You'll pass a small cemetery; the parking lot is just past it on the left. Trail maps are available at the trailhead, or from the Woodstock Ski Touring Center where you can buy a trail pass. There is a fee for trail use ($14/day, $10/half day).

Woodstock is the quintessential Vermont town, postcard-perfect, with handsome homes tucked around a village green, some enchanting inns, and even a covered bridge. You couldn't ask for more. Or could you? A terrific place to snowshoe, perhaps? Woodstock has at least a couple of summit hikes, including Mount Tom (in the center of town) and Mount Peg (on the east side, across the Ottauquechee River). These aren't the loftiest peaks in the Green Mountains, by any means, but they're scenic summits and quite doable. As a result, they're local favorites with folks on Nordic skis and snowshoes.

While the main trails are groomed by the Woodstock Ski Touring Center (with signs warning skiers and snowshoers to pay or not play), snowshoe hikers can easily wander off into the woods and catch up again at landmarks like Mount Tom's south summit and The Pogue, a high mountain lake.

Mount Tom is part of the conservation-themed Marsh-Billings-Rockefeller National Historical Park, the only national park in Vermont. Many of the trails in the park were first cut as carriage roads in the 1880s. The forests here comprise Vermont's first tree farm, and some of them are among the oldest forest plantations in the country. While skiers tend to glide right past them, a snowshoe

Panoramic views from the summit of Mount Tom

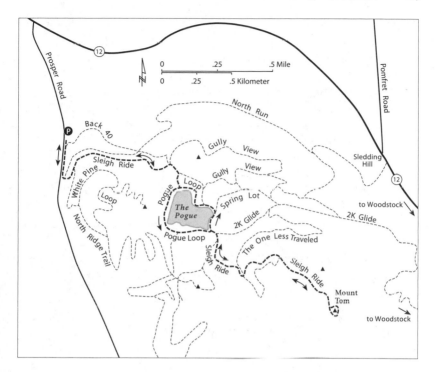

hiker can really enjoy the sensation of wandering amid the towering Norway spruce trees here (planted in 1887), and enjoy the play of sunlight and shadow in the forest.

Local folk will tell you to park at Faulkner Park downtown, but resist the temptation. That may work during summer, but in winter parking on the side of the road (necessary here) is just asking to be sideswiped. Instead, head west on Route 12, and take a left on Prosper Road. You'll quickly pass a cemetery on your left, then the trailhead parking lot. This is a great place to pick up the Sleigh Ride, the classic 2-mile hike or ski to the summit of Mount Tom.

Call it the perfect Sunday afternoon snowshoe walk: it's pretty and park-like, it's easygoing, and there are nice benches along the way so you can stop and have lunch. You'll follow the signs at the right-hand side of the parking lot to the Sleigh Ride. You'll hang a left and follow the signs into the pines, including white, Scotch, and red pine. Some of these stately trees are more than a century old. The trail is wide, groomed, and fairly flat, winding through the woods.

After about a mile of gentle climbing, you'll reach The Pogue, a pretty, snow-covered lake, circled by a 0.6-mile loop trail. There's also a bench there, and if you sit, be prepared to be a welcoming committee to other snowshoe hikers and cross-country skiers. We said, "Yes, isn't it a beautiful day?" a half-dozen times while we parked there.

Back on the Sleigh Ride, you'll trek an open area and then make a left turn into a dark hemlock forest (you'll see other trails heading off to your right and your left). Even if you wander off a bit, you can easily find your way to the south peak of Mount Tom, and if you're not sure, just ask; there's usually someone on the trails here on weekends. Signage is good, too.

Soon, you'll reach an open area with good views into the valleys below and the village of Woodstock. You'll know you're almost at the summit. If you've wandered off onto the snowshoe trails, you'll reconnect with the ski trail here, and follow it to the top, where benches are perfectly placed to gaze at the peaks and valleys of central Vermont and beyond to Mount Ascutney, Killington, even New Hampshire.

Tip: Before you hit the trail, head to the Woodstock Farmers' Market (Route 4 West, close to the green) for a sandwich. Try the smoked turkey with Vermont cheddar and apples. Trust us, this will be the best sandwich you've ever had.

SNOWSHOES YOU SIT ON

You've probably seen them at ski resorts, those benches with the tall, spiky backs, made from old skis. Fun to look at, perhaps, but not so hot in the comfort department.

Then there's snowshoe furniture. Settle back into a rocking chair with a webbed back that looks like an old-fashioned snowshoe. It kind of conforms to your back—mmm, feels pretty good after a day on a mountain trail! A family-run business called the Vermont Snowshoe Furniture Company makes loveseats, coffee tables, log racks, rocking chairs—including a child-sized version—from Vermont ash and rawhide.

The company, originally owned by Tubbs, a famous name in snowshoes, began in 1928. The new owners continue to make an old favorite, the original snowshoe chair, which folds down to nine inches. Admiral Byrd took these chairs to his South Pole base camp, they say. So, if you're really into the sport, why not give your home a makeover in Snowshoe Style? For information, call 802-365-4636 or visit *www.vtsnowshoefurniture.com*.

STOWE AREA

--64--
Smugglers Notch

Rating: Easy
Round trip: 6 miles
Hiking time: 2 hours
Elevation gain: 200 feet
High point: 2000 feet
Map: USGS Mansfield, VT
Information: Smugglers Notch Area Chamber of Commerce, P.O. Box 364, Jeffersonville, VT 05464; *www.smugnotch .com*; Smugglers' Notch Nordic Center, Smugglers' Notch Resort, 4323 Vermont Route 108 South, Smug glers Notch, VT 05464; 802-644-1173; *www.smuggs.com*

Getting there: From I-89 in Waterbury, take exit 10 and follow Vermont Route 100 N through Stowe to Morrisville. In Morrisville, pick up Route 15 west through Johnson to Jeffersonville. In Jeffersonville, pick up Route 108 south. The resort and Nordic center is located about 5 miles south of Jeffersonville on the left.

Getting to the Smugglers' Notch Ski Resort is a lot more complicated in winter. Because it's located beyond an actual notch in the Green Mountains, they close the wild, hairy passage of hairpin turns (otherwise known as Route 108) that links Stowe to Smugglers Notch. Route 108 is one of two officially designated scenic highways in Vermont. Instead of driving 5 miles or so from Stowe to Smuggs, as the resort is called, it's a good 45-minute drive around the Notch to get to Smugglers' Notch the resort. What's bad news for drivers turns out to be great news for snowshoe hikers, because the closed Notch road becomes a pleasant route for trekking. This two-lane road, left unplowed for a 3-mile stretch, is a thoroughfare for adventure seekers who want to leave the downhill ski crowds behind.

If you're traveling with friends or family who like to ski, Smugglers' Notch is a fun compromise where nobody loses. The ski resort is strongly geared toward families, and they get lots of repeat business, so they're always looking for something new to offer guests. In recent years, one of those options has

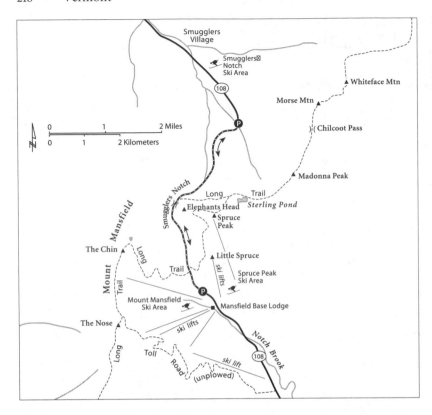

been snowshoeing. There are several miles of dedicated snowshoe trails on the property, plus the center runs learn-to-snowshoe programs and family snow-shoe walks. Themed hikes include moonlight walks, fireworks walks, and "Where's the Bear?" hikes to look for signs of black bears. (The actual bears aren't seen in winter, of course, but it's still fun for kids to see bear claw marks on trees and to learn about bears' habits and habitat.) These walks, along with trail passes, are offered by the resort's Nordic Ski and Snowshoe Center. (Rentals are available, too, including snowshoes for the tiniest of hikers.)

Even if you do all of those things, don't miss a walk through Smugglers Notch, which is named for Vermont smugglers who headed north to trade illegally with Canada in the early 1800s. Leaving the resort, head left on Route 108 until you hit the "Road Closed" barricade. Park your car here, and simply walk down the road. This doesn't sound promising, we admit. But there are a couple of things you can do to make the out-and-back trek more exciting. First, you can head off the road (on the left-hand side) to what they call The Bowls, for some good backcountry hiking. Be prepared for some steep, straight ups

Jarrett Kelley and Connor Bair-Cucchiaro examine woodpecker holes on a tree near Smugglers Notch.

(you're in the shadow of Mount Mansfield and the Greens, remember); then, when you've had enough, head back down to the Notch road. (If you're up for it, you can do the entire road, 3 miles each way; we'd probably turn around halfway.) Beware of skiers and snowboarders barreling down these steeps; many of them crash spectacularly as they hit the road and you don't want to be slammed! We had a great time tromping up steep side trails, and then sliding back down on our backsides (just for fun, not because it was necessary!).

As you head toward Stowe, you'll probably encounter a few folks on downhill skis, heading back up to Smugglers Notch, some boarders, and ice climbers. There's some good climbing here alongside the road, and also at higher elevations. As you get to the Notch, though, you'll no doubt be distracted by the view: As one snowshoe hiker put it, "You're on an ordinary walk, and then suddenly you're surrounded by vast, ice-covered mountains. It really catches you by surprise." The scenery around you is, simply put, stunning. It's worth the long walk along the road to experience this. Smugglers Notch is truly one of the most awesome sights in New England. Sheer granite walls drop dramatically from mountain cliffs to a valley of boulders.

Alas, all that's left, at this point, is to head back along the road and see how much progress the ice climbers have made since you saw them last. If you've ever taken this road in the summer, admiring the green-on-green mountains that rise above you (for a quick second, since you're focused on steering around the humongous boulders that line the roadside), wait 'til you see them in winter! They are truly dazzling. On foot, you can really take in the spiny landscape of the Green Mountains, swathed in shades of white and gray.

FOOTPATH IN THE WILDERNESS

You've noticed the trailheads in the Stowe/Smugglers Notch area, and elsewhere in the Green Mountain State. So how long *is* the Long Trail? Oh, about 270 miles. America's oldest long-distance hiking trail (yes, it pre-dates the Appalachian Trail), Vermont's "Footpath in the Wilderness" was built by the Green Mountain Club between 1910 and 1930. (The Long Trail, in fact, was the inspiration for the AT.) The Long Trail follows the main ridge of the Green Mountains from the Massachusetts state line to the Canadian border, crossing a spine of Vermont's highest peaks. For its first 105 miles, the Long Trail shares the same route as the Appalachian Trail, before splitting off to the north, where it traverses 4083-foot Camels Hump and 4393-foot Mount Mansfield, the state's highest peak, heading north to the Canadian border. The trail system includes 175 miles of side trails and seventy backcountry campsites. Shelters and campsites are located a day's hike apart throughout the trail. About a hundred through-hikers complete the Long Trail every year.

The trail is a visual celebration of Vermont's singular beauty, as it climbs rugged peaks (including creamy white marble summits), pristine ponds, and dense hardwood forests. Many sections of the trail make great snowshoe hikes. The best source for details is the *Long Trail Guide*, published by the Green Mountain Club. Call 802-244-7037 or visit *www .greenmountainclub.org*.

--65--
Little River State Park

Rating: Easy to moderate (due to length, not steepness)
Round trip: 3.5–4 miles
Hiking time: 4.5 hours
Elevation gain: 0
High point: 0
Map: Historical Map of the Little River Area, Mount Mansfield State Forest/Little River State Park
Information: Vermont Department of Forests, Parks and Recreation, 802-476-0170; *www.vtsstateparks.com*

Getting there: From Waterbury, take Route 2 west for 2 miles, then turn right on Little River Road. Drive 3 miles and park at the gate at the top of the dam of the Waterbury Reservoir.

Even in winter, the siren song of the Ben and Jerry's ice cream factory tour is tough to resist! That, and the fact that Stowe is just up the road—a road that's filled with all manner of other treats, from Vermont cheddar to homemade chocolates to apple cider donuts! You know you'll feel better about all that indulgence if you squeeze in a snowshoe hike first. This one's a local favorite, and easily reachable off Route 89. It's relatively flat, and fairly long, so if you take it at a good pace, Stevenson Brook Trail will be a great warm-up for some of the tougher hikes in the Waterbury–Stowe area, like Mount Hunger.

One of the intriguing aspects of this 5110-acre park is its history, and the remnants that exist today. In the late 1700s, pioneers set up settlements here, including farmhouses, schools, and cemeteries. About fifty families lived here, until the younger generations abandoned the hardscrabble life of farming and harsh weather. Later, around 1934, the Civilian Conservation Corps came here, working with the Army Corps of Engineers to build the Waterbury Reservoir. At the height of this activity, 2000 men lived on the property.

What's left today is a ghost town of stone bridges, chimneys, cellar holes, and a sawmill. Remnants of these are much more visible in summer, of course, but you still get a sense of this when the park is covered in snow. You'll still see the ruins of old farmhouses on this loop hike, where the Ricker Basin settlement once stood. The northern side of the park has more trails, but that stretch is favored by the snowmobile crowd, so we prefer the small loop hike that's closer to the entrance road.

Park at the gate near the reservoir (you'll see other vehicles there, and the road ahead will likely be closed) and then walk or snowshoe into Little River State Park. It will be a hike, but there are reservoir views as you go. Inside the park, keep to the left of the entrance buildings (after picking up a map in the wooden bin at park headquarters, if you don't already have one) and walk on the road for another hundred yards or so. Go left around the gate and look for the sign for the Stevenson Brook Trail. An easygoing climb will take you to Stevenson Brook.

You'll cross two bridges, and at about 1.5 miles you'll see the Sawmill Loop Trail, a snowmobile trail, to the right. At this point, you can turn back and retrace your steps, or take a right. After a short jaunt on the snowmobile trail, go right on Dalley Loop Trail, which is part of Little River State Park's History Loop. The area was a farming settlement in the late eighteenth and

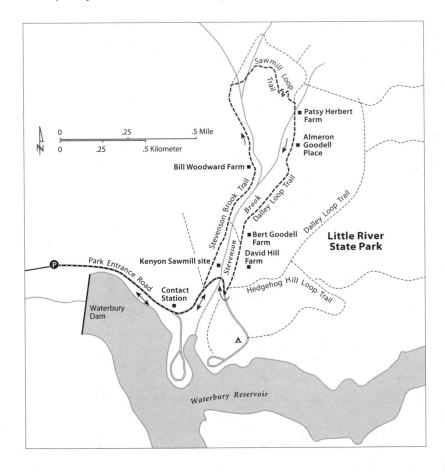

Exposed rock provides a good picnic spot at Little River State Park.

early nineteenth centuries, and the roads were built for horse-drawn carriages. You'll see evidence of the past in the old foundations and remnants of the Patsy Herbert Farm, the Almeron Goodell Place (still standing), the Bert Goodell Farm, and the David Hill Farm, along with weathered implements, stone bridges, and gravestones.

At the end of the trail, go around the gate and turn right on the camp ground road, where you'll see the park headquarters buildings and the park entrance road leading back to your car.

With any luck, Ben and Jerry's will still be open. Incidentally, there's even snowshoeing at the ice cream factory, believe it or not. On weekends during the winter, Stowe-based Umiak Outfitters leads half-hour nature walks on the woodsy trails surrounding Ben and Jerry's. Umiak also offers a Fondue Dinner trip, where hikers rendezvous at Siebeness Lodge in Stowe for cheese fondue. For dessert, what else but chocolate fondue, using Vermont-made Champlain Chocolates? For details, and other specialty tours, contact Umiak Outfitters at 802-253-2317, located about 9 miles north of Waterbury on Route 100.

BURLINGTON AREA/NORTHERN VERMONT

--66--
Mount Philo State Park

Rating: Moderate
Round trip: 1 mile
Hiking time: 40–60 minutes
Elevation gain: 568 feet
High point: 968 feet
Map: Mount Philo State Park Trail Map, Vermont Department of Forests, Parks and Recreation
Information: Ranger Station, Mount Philo State Park, 5425 Mount Philo Road, Charlotte, VT 05445; 802-425-2390; *www .vtstateparks.com*

Getting there: From junction of Routes 22A and 7 in Charlotte, go 6 miles north on Route 7 to Mount Philo Road. Turn right, and drive a short distance to the parking lot.

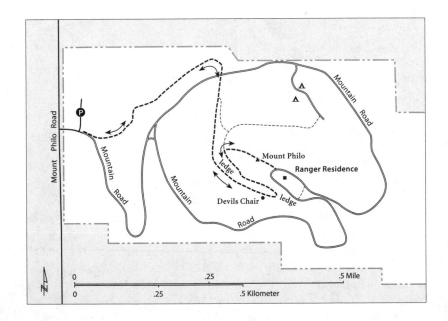

Hiker Paul Kelley sprawls out on a picnic table at the summit.

Who says you need to work hard to enjoy wonderful views? If you can get over the fact that you don't have to suffer to earn a reward (and we New England Puritan types have a very hard time with this!), you'll enjoy this sweet, short hike and the panoramas at the top of Mount Philo, in Vermont's oldest state park.

Mount Philo still bears a few scars from a wicked ice storm in January 1998, when trees were toppled or split down the middle, ravaging much of the forest—here and throughout the Northeast. As a result, the state put in a cleared road to the summit, on the path of an old horse-and-carriage trail. There's also a new parking lot at the top. Picnic tables and grills are every-where and, while this doesn't mean much to the winter hiker, it makes the destination more user-friendly in summertime.

With ample snow cover, you could take the summit road up this little peak, but the trail is a better choice. (The park trail map is available online.) The fairly straight-up climb, with a few small switchbacks, will be a more interesting and energizing route, so you'll feel you've earned some relaxing and sightseeing at the top.

The trail begins just to the left of the parking lot. There's only one path here, so it's easy to locate, even in winter. As is the case with Green Moun-tain hikes, this one heads up quite quickly and steadily, into a straggle of wiry pines. You'll see the harsh effects of that '98 storm, and more recent icy blizzards here—leveled trees, trunks and branches split apart like a collection of ogres' slingshots. About halfway up, the path is intersected by the paved Mountain Road.

The trail continues just a few feet down the road, and begins to follow the ridgeline. You'll bear to the right and encounter a giant (40-foot) jumble of rocks known as the Devils Chair. It can be a bit icy here, so tread carefully. Go around the Devils Chair and get back on the trail, descending as you bear right.

In short order, you'll bear right again (a sign directs you to the summit) and head up a short, steep stretch to the summit. There are plenty of hints of civilization here—a toilet, some cabins, picnic tables, even a soda machine—but, oh, what views! Head directly to the picnic table perched on the ledge for a wide-open look at the crazy quilt that's northern Vermont: farms, fields, ribbons of roadway, Lake Champlain, and, beyond it, New York State and the Adirondacks. If you can tear yourself away from the views, look up; you may well see a hawk in flight. Red-tailed hawks, rough-legged hawks, and northern harriers are seen overhead here, even in winter. On our last visit, in late March, we heard a cacophony of crows, punctuated by a squeaky screech that sounded like a tree frog.

Follow the path to the right, and you'll learn exactly what you're looking at—there's a concrete slab with a railing, and a diagram of the peaks spread out before you. Step away from the ledge for a moment and pirouette around, so you get the full effect of the panorama here—simply spectacular views in every direction.

All this, and a soda machine!

--67--
Robert Frost Interpretive Trail

Rating: Easy
Round trip: 1.2 miles
Hiking time: 1 hour or less
Elevation gain: 30 feet
High point: 1280 feet
Map: USGS East Middlebury, VT
Information: Green Mountain National Forest, 802-388-4362

Getting there: From Middlebury, travel south 4 miles on Route 7 to the intersection of Route 125. Travel east on Route 125 for 5.8 miles. Signs and parking for the Robert Frost Interpretive Trail are on the right. (Note: Not to be confused with the 40-mile-long Robert Frost Trail in central Massachusetts; see hike 54.)

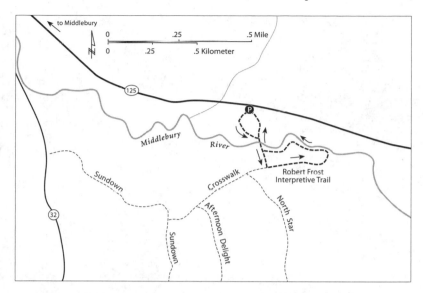

We discovered this one completely by accident. We'd been hanging out around the charming town of Middlebury, and Middlebury College, where poet Robert Frost—who died in 1963—is still a major presence. Frost co-founded Middlebury's Bread Loaf School and the Bread Loaf Writer's Conference in the 1920s. Named Vermont's Poet Laureate in 1961, the four-time Pulitzer Prize winner spent the summers between 1939 and 1962 in nearby Ripton, in a cabin on the Homer Noble Farm.

You'll find yourself thinking about Robert Frost as you drive around the area. You won't be able to help it! Route 125, heading east out of Middlebury, has been renamed The Robert Frost Memorial Drive, and a sign marks the Robert Frost Wayside Area and the cabin where he wrote (now a National Historic Landmark). Head along the lovely, curving Route 125 past the town of Ripton, as it hugs the South Branch of the Middlebury River, and look for a small parking lot that marks the Robert Frost Interpretive Trail.

This short and sweet hike has a wonderful literary bent. You'll hike over a wooden boardwalk to a fork in the road, marked by a sign with Frost's poem, "The Road Not Taken." You'll also encounter "Going for Water," alongside a stream, "The Pasture," and nine other Frostian favorites. To a snowshoe hiker, the best among the twelve poems featured is "Stopping by Woods on a Snowy Evening." Even if you're not a huge fan of Robert Frost, you're bound to be a tad enchanted by the pairing of poetry and nature along the loop trail. The landscape is rural, with mountains (including Bread

The poet would've approved of this simple log bridge along the Robert Frost Interpretive Trail.

Loaf, Bethel Mountain, and Mount Wilson) rising like a painted backdrop to the east. The trail meanders through the woods and traces the river. In winter, the bare trees reveal full views of the 1800-foot hills that surround the property.

Given that this area is set within the boundaries of the Green Mountain National Forest, there are numerous snowshoe hiking options nearby, and most are far more strenuous than this pastoral walk. But what's not to like about a hike that pairs the beauty of the rural countryside with the magic of the written word? If you're a fan of Frost, bring along a book of his poetry and (if it's not too cold to take off your mittens!) stop at a bench and read some favorite poems to your snowshoe companion.

--*68*--
Hogback Mountain/Blueberry Hill

Rating: Easy
Round trip: 3 miles
Hiking time: 2 hours
Elevation gain: 669 feet
High point: 2286 feet
Maps: Blueberry Hill Cross-Country Ski Area Trail Map;
Moosalamoo Outdoor Recreation Map
Information: Blueberry Hill Inn, Goshen, VT 05733; 800-247-6733;
www.blueberryhillinn.com; Moosalamoo Association,
P.O. Box 108, Forest Dale, VT 05745; 800-448-0707;
www.moosalamoo.org

Getting there: From the south, take I-89 to exit 3 in Bethel and turn left onto Route 107 west. Travel west on Route 107 for about 12 miles, then turn right onto Route 100 north and drive for about 7 miles. Make a left on Route 73 west toward Goshen. (If you get to the town of Rochester, you have gone too far.) Follow Route 73 up and over Brandon Gap in Goshen. On the downhill side of the gap, look for the state information sign for the Blueberry Hill Inn. At Goshen Four Corners, make a right onto Hathaway Road, and follow it for 1.3 miles to a three-way junction. Turn right onto Flora White Road and drive 1 mile to a four-way junction. Make a right onto Goshen–Ripton Road (Fire Road 32), and drive 1 mile to the Blueberry Hill Inn on your right.

Until recently, we'd never even heard of Moosalamoo. Yet there we were, snowshoeing like crazy and drinking gloppy Irish ale with the locals on St. Paddy's Day. Located east of Middlebury between Route 125 to the north and Route 72 to the south, the Moosalamoo region comprises 20,000 acres within the Green Mountain National Forest. Moosalamoo, they say, is an Abenaki Indian word meaning, "He trails the moose," or "the moose departs." Red-tailed hawks, black bear, peregrine falcons, and, of course, moose, are among the residents here. And the hiking! Our feet get twitchy just thinking about it. The more we hiked, the more we discovered still more super-inviting trailheads looping around the Brandon/Moosalamoo region of Vermont's Green Mountains.

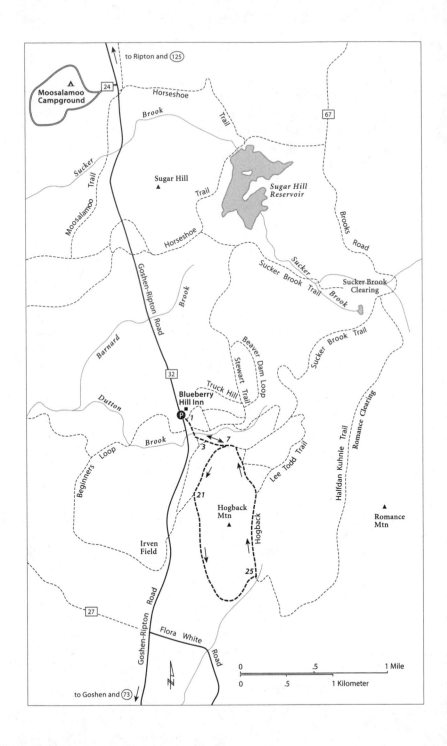

to Ripton and (125)

Moosalamoo
Campground

24

Sucker Brook

Horseshoe Trail

67

Sugar Hill

Sugar Hill
Reservoir

Moosalamoo Trail

Sucker

Horseshoe Trail

Brooks Road

Sucker Brook Trail

Sucker Brook

Sucker Brook
Clearing

Goshen-Ripton Road

Brook

Barnard

Beaver Dam Loop

Stewart Trail

Sucker Brook Trail

32

Dutton

Blueberry
Hill Inn

Truck Hill

P

1

7

3

Brook

Beginners Loop

21

Lee Todd Trail

Romance Clearing

Halfdan Kuhnle Trail

Hogback
Mtn

Hogback

Romance
Mtn

Irven
Field

25

27

Goshen-Ripton Road

Flora White Road

N

0   .5   1 Mile

0   .5   1 Kilometer

to Goshen and (73)

There's the famous Long Trail, of course, Vermont's 50-mile "footpath in the wilderness," and there's a religion-themed (but nondenominational) meditative "spirit walk" (see sidebar, "Walks for the Spirit"), and even a nature trail enhanced by the poetry of Robert Frost (see hike 67). Add to that about a zillion miles of local trails in Banbury State Park that lead to enticing destinations like the Falls of Lana, Ethan Allen's Cave, Silver Lake, and Mount Moosalamo (see hike 69), and you have nothing less than heaven for winter walkers!

Oh, yeah, and great digs, too, if you bunk up at the Blueberry Hill Inn (home of gourmet dinners and the never-empty cookie jar). The Blueberry Hill Inn, with its own ski touring center, is a gathering place for winter recreation mavens of all stripes. They offer 40 miles of cross-country ski and snowshoe trails, plus trail maps, and they're definitely snowshoer-friendly. Plus, you'll need to stay someplace, and the meals here can't be beat.

Located directly behind the Blueberry Hill Inn, Hogback Mountain (2286 feet) was once a small ski area. As an early-season, "get your snowshoe legs" trail, this one is a standout. Just 3 miles long, it will only take you an hour or so, depending upon how long you linger to take in the expansive

Giant boulders rise along the trailside at Hogback Mountain.

views, and whether you decide to take the old road straight up the mountain to the summit proper.

You'll see a small sign pointing the way, and note that there's a numbering system in place. The main thing to know is that the lower numbers lead back to the inn (at #1). Trail intersections as well as the trails themselves are numbered, so read carefully. You'll cross Dutton Brook on a plank bridge, and then pass an open area where an old schoolhouse and cemetery once stood. Take a left at intersection #4, uphill to #7, then head counterclockwise on the trail.

Following the contour of Hogback Mountain, the trail is mostly level. There's a short uphill section beyond #21. You'll tromp through a stand of birch trees and, just when you're thinking this is just another plain old walk in the woods (insert yawn here), you'll reach a clearing that makes you feel like you're on top of the world. Here are glorious wide-open views of the Adirondacks to the west, the Taconic Range (southwest), and the eastern Green Mountains and Brandon Gap (to the southeast). "But we didn't even climb this!" someone will say. "How can there be such amazing views with absolutely no effort at all?"

If you'd like to exert a bit of effort, you can always climb the old road that goes up Hogback, where the views get even better. (Come down the same way.) You won't notice this in winter, except for signage that will tip you off: wild blueberry bushes literally cover the southern end of the slope. (Picking season is late July.) Promise yourself to come back in summertime so you can join the hordes of hikers who tromp back to the inn with purple tongues and blue lips!

Back on the trail, go through the gate and bear left at intersection #25 to head back to the inn.

--69--
Mount Moosalamoo

Rating: More difficult
Round trip: 7.7 miles
Hiking time: 6 hours
Elevation gain: 800 feet
High point: 2,640 feet
Maps: Moosalamoo Outdoor Recreation Map
Information: Blueberry Hill Inn, Goshen, VT 05733; 800-247-6733; *www.blueberryhillinn.com*; Moosalamoo Association, P.O. Box 108, Forest Dale, VT 05745; 800-448-0707; *www.moosalamoo.org*

Getting there: From the south, take I-89 to exit 3 in Bethel and turn left onto Route 107 west. Travel west on Route 107 for about 12 miles, then turn right onto Route 100 north and drive for about 7 miles. Make a left on Route 73 west toward Goshen. (If you get to the town of Rochester, you have gone too far.) Follow Route 73 up and over Brandon Gap in Goshen. On the downhill side of the gap, look for the state information sign for the Blueberry Hill Inn. At Goshen Four Corners, make a right onto Hathaway Road, and follow it for 1.3 miles to a three-way junction. Turn right onto Flora White Road and drive 1 mile to a four-way junction. Make a right onto Goshen–Ripton Road (Fire Road 32). Head north 3.5 miles on Goshen–Ripton Road to Fire Road 24 on the left and the entrance of Moosalamoo Campground. Park in the lot on the right.

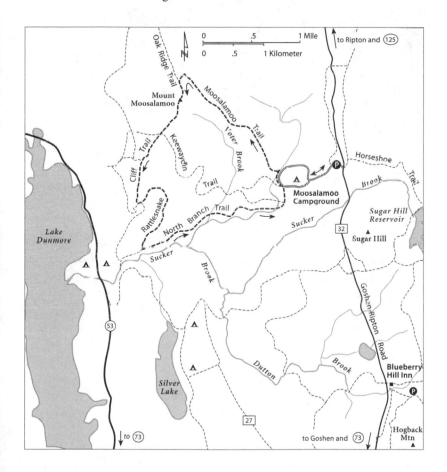

The Mount Moosalamoo hike is demanding, but the rewards are worth the effort.

It's a long day of hiking—say, six to eight hours—and you'll work some, but the trip to the summit of Mount Moosalamoo (2640 feet) is worth the trip. Plan on lots of woodsy walking, some brook crossings, a fair amount of climbing, and one rather steep descent, but the payoff comes with excellent views of the many iced-over lakes that dot this part of Vermont.

Before you head out, pick up a copy of the Moosalamoo Outdoor Recreation Map, available from Blueberry Hill or the Moosalamoo Association.

The Moosalamoo Trail heads north and west from the right-hand parking lot at the entrance of Moosalamoo Campground. You'll climb over a knoll and cross Voter Brook, then climb an old woods road up the eastern flank of Moosalamoo at 2.3 miles.

The summit offers wonderful views to the east and south. (Look for the Goshen Dam Reservoir and the roof of the Blueberry Hill Inn ski touring center.) This gorgeous, sunny spot is a great place to have lunch.

Continuing south along the trail, you'll pass the middle summit of the mountain, with views of Lake Dunmore to the west, Lake Champlain to the northwest, and Lake George to the southwest. The trail follows the ridge to Rattlesnake Point in about 2 miles, with more frozen water views: Silver Lake to the south.

From here, take Rattlesnake Cliff Trail heading south, and then connect with North Branch Trail to the left, following Sucker Brook. (Note: Rattlesnake Cliff Trail may be closed due to peregrine falcon nesting. Please check with the ranger station before you head out.) Soon you'll reach a woods road. Cross it, stay on the trail, and you'll end up back at the campground.

WALKS FOR THE SPIRIT

For us, being in nature often feels like a religious experience. The Spirit of Nature trail system celebrates that concept. Set on 70 acres in the foothills of Vermont's Green Mountains, near the Robert Frost Interpretive Trail (see hike 67), the Spirit in Nature walking paths link spirituality with Mother Earth. Here, you pick a religion (yours, or someone else's—choices include Hindu, Buddhist, Christian, Jewish, and so on) and then walk the path. Most are about 1.5 to 2 miles long, and they end at the Sacred Circle, a 60-foot-diameter ring surrounded by white pines. Along the paths are scriptural references to nature and "nature notes." When the property is covered in virgin snow (as is often the case in the snowy Green Mountains), the effect is definitely serene.

Typically, we find ourselves singing theme songs from 1970s movies and sitcoms when we hike, or spirituals like "Swing Low, Sweet Chariot" when the going gets particularly rough. Walking along the Spirit in Nature trails, though, we realized that we were walking in silence, and contemplating the wonders of the natural world—not a bad way to spend a few hours on a sunny winter afternoon. The trails are open daily, year-round, from dawn to dusk. They request a small donation in return for hiking the paths. For maps and information, visit www.spiritinnature.com, or call 802-388-7244.

NORTHEAST KINGDOM

--70--
Mount Pisgah

Rating: More difficult
Round trip: 3.8 miles
Hiking time: 3 hours
Elevation gain: 1450
High point: 2752 feet
Map: USGS Sutton, VT
Information: Vermont State Parks and Forests, District V-Northeast Kingdom, 1229 Portland Street, St. Johnsbury, VT 05819-2099; 802-748-6687; *www.vtfpr.org/lands/willoughby*

Getting there: From West Burke, drive 5.7 miles north and west on Route 5A 5.7 miles to the sign for Willoughby State Forest and the South Trail trailhead, on the east side of the road just south of Lake Willoughby. The winter parking lot will be on your right, a small plowed area in front of the trailhead.

The fjord-like Lake Willoughby, with sparkling, deep waters reaching depths of more than 300 feet, is considered the jewel of Vermont's Northeast Kingdom. Two sheer-sided rock cliffs—Mount Pisgah and Mount Hor—face each other, towering some 1000 feet or more above the lake. It's a dramatic sight and worth a visit to Vermont's quietest and most remote region.

Pisgah is the biblical summit from which Moses sighted the Promised Land. We know some longtime Vermonters who would indeed consider this region of vast valleys, farmlands, lakes, and mountains their own promised land. We can't vouch for that, but we can tell you that the views from atop the summit of Mount Pisgah (in Vermont) are majestic.

The hike is a moderate jaunt with some steep pitches. For part of the way, you'll travel along the edge of the plunging cliffs as you skirt the western flank of the mountain. For this reason, the hike is definitely not for acrophobics. The granite ledges leading to the summit can also be slippery in winter, so snowshoes with crampons—and caution—are recommended.

From the trailhead, follow the blue blazes as you veer left across a wooden bridge. You'll have nice views of a frozen beaver pond and marshes on this easygoing, flat-beginning section of the hike. The trail follows an old road as it leaves the pond, then turns sharply to begin its climb up the ridge of the mountain. You'll hike a series of steep switchbacks, gaining quick elevation, before it levels to a more gradual ascent.

Follow the edge of the glacier-carved cliffs, with few open views as the forest is dense along this stretch. But, at 0.9 mile, you'll reach the spur trail to Pulpit Rock. The massive rock hangs 650 feet above Lake Willoughby. You'll have great views of the lake and Mount Hor from this perch—even if you can't bring yourself to the edge! The spot is also a favorite area for peregrine falcons, which return each spring to nest in the rocky ledges.

Returning to the main trail, the climb becomes steeper as it crosses the mountain. You'll hike in fits and starts, steep pitches interspersed with gradual climbs. In less than a mile, the views begin to open up. Look back, and you'll be able to see over the treetops, across to the surrounding mountain ranges.

Just shy of the summit, you'll reach an open, rocky area with expansive views. On clear days, Vermont's East, Burke, and Bald Mountains and the

Snow-filled skies and views from Mount Pisgah

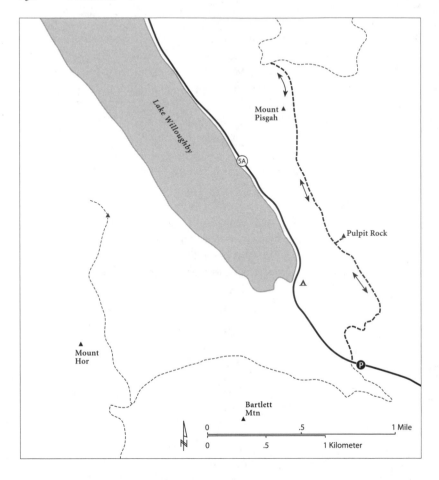

Franconia and Presidential mountain ranges of New Hampshire will be right in front of you. As you look north and south, you'll get a good glimpse of the rocky walls of Mount Pisgah and Mount Hor, home to rare arctic plants deposited by retreating glaciers aeons ago.

If you continue on a short distance (about 0.2 mile) to Mount Pisgah's true summit and the second overlook (off a side trail), you'll have even more fine views. Grab a seat on a rock and take a gander: Lake Willoughby, dressed in its winter blanket of snow, stretches below. Mount Mansfield, Camels Hump, and Jay Peak loom in the distance—and the jagged cliffs of Mount Pisgah plunge below you.

Retrace your steps back to the parking lot—with one final, careful hike out on Pulpit Rock. Hallelujah . . . look at that view!

--71--
Sugar Hill

Rating: Easy
Round trip: 2 miles
Hiking time: 2 hours
Elevation gain: 700 feet
High point: 1700 feet
Map: Hazen's Notch Association Winter Trail Map
Information: Hazen's Notch Association, P.O. Box 478, Montgomery Center, VT 05471; 802-326-4799; *www.hazensnotch.org*

Getting there: From Montgomery Center, take Route 58 (Hazens Notch Road) 1.5 miles east. The Hazen's Notch Association Center is on the left as you come from Montgomery Center. Parking for trail users is just past the building. Note: Hazens Notch Road is plowed from Montgomery Center to the Hazen's Notch Welcome Center, but not far beyond.

If you're looking for stunning scenery and solitude, a trip to this pristine area in northern Vermont is well worth it. The Hazen's Notch Association, a nonprofit organization, manages the area, including more than 2000 acres of private conservation land. More than thirty landowners cooperate to keep open 40 miles of trails in the winter, across fields and meadows filled with forests, beavers, ponds, orchards, and mountains. While all of the trails are open to snowshoers and cross-country skiers, you'll also find 10 miles that are ungroomed and dedicated for snowshoeing only. Note: It's always good to call ahead to check on trail conditions. If there's light snow cover or recent thaws, the center and all trails may be closed.

Stop by the converted farm building that serves as the welcome center and offices for the association to pick up trail maps, get information on trail conditions, and to enjoy the views of the craggy Jay Mountains on the northwest horizon. The center also has cross-country ski equipment and snowshoes for rent, and a small retail area with snacks, nature and trail guidebooks, photo postcards of the area—even pure Vermont maple syrup from the nearby High Ponds Farm.

There are several nice hiking loops here. The 0.8-mile Coyote Meadow snowshoe loop circles open fields and around beaver ponds, before returning to the welcome center along Spruce Brook. But one of our favorites is the short climb to the bare top of Sugar Hill for views of the classic Vermont villages of Montgomery and Montgomery Center, nestled in the expansive Trout River Valley.

From the Welcome Center, cross the road and take the Lower Woodfern cross-country trail that veers to the right. Turn left on the Spruce Brook snowshoe trail and follow it a short distance to the Sugar House Trail. Head straight on this trail and begin a gradual ascent through open fields, passing a sugar house and the intersection with the Beaver Ponds cross-country trail. Look for the Sap Run Trail that enters on your right.

Follow the Sap Run Trail as it pushes gently up the side of a large stand of sugar maples. The maple forest is decorated with bright-colored tubes that are strung from tree-to-tree, carrying the sap down the hill to the sugar house. You'll see now why it's called Sugar Hill! This is a very active and productive maple sugaring forest; it's interesting to see here how the gravity-fed system is laid out. The colored tubes not only lend a festive look to the hillside, they also tend to take your mind off the climb.

At about 0.7 mile, you'll leave the forest for open ledges, as you make your final, gradual ascent to the summit of Sugar Hill. The last time we hiked

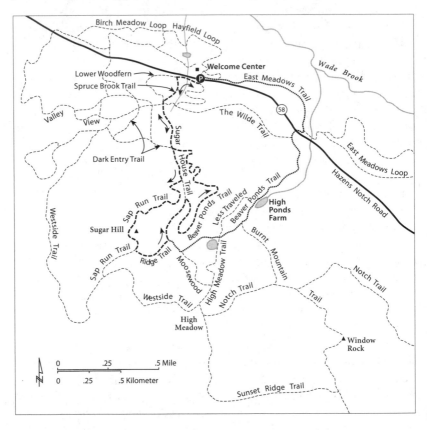

this trail, it was a gorgeous, sunny winter day. We sat at the top of Sugar Hill, under robin's egg blue skies, looking into the sweeping valley and silhouetted mountains beyond.

You can either retrace your steps back down the hillside, or continue over the summit connecting with the Ridge Trail. If you like quick descents, take the Beaver Ponds cross-country trail to the left as it zigzags down the hillside, connecting back with Sugar House Trail. Another option would be to follow the Beaver Ponds Trail to the right as it gently loops around the picturesque High Ponds Farm area. You'll have open field-to-mountain views along the way. The trail stops at the (unplowed) Hazens Notch Road; cross the street and follow the East Meadows Trail back to the center.

--72--
Burnt Mountain

Rating: Most difficult
Round trip: 4.6 miles
Hiking time: 5 hours
Elevation gain: 1800 feet
High point: 2800 feet
Map: Hazens Notch Association Winter Trail Map
Information: Hazens Notch Association, P.O. Box 478, Montgomery Center, VT 05471; 802-326-4799; *www.hazensnotch.org*

Getting there: From Montgomery Center, take Route 58 (Hazens Notch Road) 1.5 miles east. The Hazens Notch Association Center is on the left as you come from Montgomery Center. Parking for trail users is just past the building. Note: Hazens Notch Road is plowed from Montgomery Center to the Hazens Notch Welcome Center, but not far beyond.

Ready for a workout? You'll get one on this steep trek up to the summit of 2800-foot Burnt Mountain in northern Vermont. It's a 4.6-mile up-and-back hike, but you can choose to opt out sooner, if you like. Window Rock, with nice views of Hazens Notch, is about halfway up the mountain. Continue the strenuous hike to the bare peak, and views open up even more to reveal surrounding mountain ranges, and on a clear day, Mount Mansfield and Lake Champlain.

The good thing about this hike is that it's pretty much unheard of, so you're likely to have the trail and the mountaintop to yourself. The more

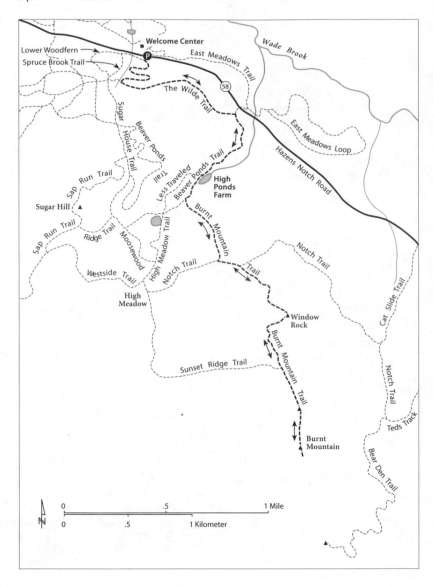

popular hikes—Mount Mansfield to the south and rugged Jay Peak to the north—draw hardy winter peak-baggers, leaving this pretty, remote peak to those in the know.

You'll use the Hazens Notch Association Center's cross-country ski trails and snowshoe trails to access the Burnt Mountain trailhead. The nonprofit

Open views on the way to Burnt Mountain

organization manages the area, including more than 2000 acres of private conservation land open to winter hikers and skiers (see hike 71 for more on the Hazens Notch area). Hikers climbing Burnt Mountain are asked to sign in and out at the center for their own safety. Also, if you don't have ski poles, consider renting a pair here before you head out. They'll come in handy when negotiating the steep pitches. Note: It's always good to call ahead to check on trail conditions. If there's light snow cover or recent thaws, the center and all trails may be closed.

Start at the center to pick up a map, check on trail conditions, and stock up on snacks and fluids; you're going to need them! Cross Hazens Notch Road and follow the Wilde Trail as it weaves through the meadow on relatively flat terrain. At less than a quarter mile, turn right onto the Beaver Ponds Trail as it climbs to pretty High Ponds Farm, a working farm producing maple syrup (see hike 71). You'll skirt a pair of frozen ponds, in the shadows of surrounding mountains, as you climb out of the open fields into a healthy sugar maple forest. Turn left onto the Burnt Mountain Trail as it ascends the forests and meets up with the Notch Trail. Turn left to follow the Notch Trail briefly, then bear right to continue on the Burnt Mountain Trail. Now, wasn't that easy? The tough part is yet to come.

The Burnt Mountain Trail now begins its unrelenting, steep climb up the north side of the mountain. Push up and up for nearly half a mile (it will feel like a lot more) until you reach the bare ledge known as Window Rock. Spin around, and you'll have views in all directions. You could stop here and be perfectly satisfied; we have in the past. Or, push forward!

The next half a mile or so is an unforgiving huff-and-puff, up steep pitches and slippery slopes. You'll have a quick breather as the trail follows the ridgeline for a short distance, but just as you regain your momentum, you'll begin the final climb to the 2800-foot summit.

Burnt Mountain is a fine roost. From the top, you'll see a series of surrounding mountain ranges, rolling hillsides, and deep valleys. The splendid view is just reward for your effort.

Appendix

NEW HAMPSHIRE CONTACTS:
Ammonoosuc Ranger Station, NH
Box 239
Bethlehem, NH 03574
(603) 869-2626

Androscoggin Ranger District, NH
80 Glen Road
Gorham, NH 03581
(603) 466-2713

Appalachian Mountain Club
Pinkham Notch Visitor Center
Route 16 (P.O. Box 298)
Gorham, NH 03581
(603) 466-2721
www.outdoors.org

Pemigewasset Ranger Station, NH
RFD #3, Box 15, Route 175
Plymouth, NH 03264
(603) 536-1310

Saco Ranger Station, NH
RFD #1, Box 94
Conway, NH 03818
(603) 447-5448

White Mountain National Forest, NH
P.O. Box 638
Laconia, NH 03247
(603) 528-8722
www.fs.fed.us/r9/white/

MAINE CONTACTS:
Acadia National Park
P.O. Box 177
Eagle Lake Dr.
Bar Harbor, ME 04609-0177
(207) 288-8800
www.nps.gov/acad/index.htm

Baxter State Park
64 Balsam Drive
Millinocket, ME 04462
(207) 723-5140
www.baxterstateparkauthority.com

Evans Notch Ranger Station
18 Maryville Road
Bethel, ME 04217-4400
(207) 824-2134

Grafton Notch State Park
1941 Bear River Road
Newry, ME 04261
(207) 624-6080
www.state.me.us/doc/parks

MASSACHUSETTS CONTACTS:
Appalachian Trail Conference
799 Washington St.
Harpers Ferry, WV 25425
(304) 535-6331
www.appalachiantrail.org

Massachusetts Audubon Society
208 South Great Rd.
Lincoln, MA 01773
(781) 259-9500
(800) AUDUBON
www.massaudubon.org

Massachusetts Department of Conservation and Recreation
251 Causeway St.
Boston, MA 02114
(617) 626-1250
www.mass.gov/dcr

The Trustees of Reservations
Northeast Regional Office
Castle Hill/Crane Estate
290 Argilla Rd.
Ipswich, MA 01938
(978) 356-4351
www.thetrustees.org

VERMONT CONTACTS:
Green Mountain Club
4711 Waterbury-Stowe Rd.
Waterbury Center, VT 05677
(802) 244-7037
www.greenmountainclub.org

Green Mountain and Finger Lakes National Forests
231 North Main St.
Rutland, VT 05701
(802) 747-6700
www.fs.fed.us/r9/gmfl

Manchester Ranger District
Green Mountain National Forest
2358 Depot Rd.
Manchester Center, VT 05233
(802) 362-2307

Moosalamoo Association
P.O. Box 108
Forest Dale, VT 05745
(800) 448-0707
www.moosalamoo.org

US Fish and Wildlife Service
1849 C Street, NW
Washington, DC 20240
(800) 344-WILD (wildlife refuge information)
www.fws.gov/refuges

Vermont State Parks
103 South Main St.
Waterbury, VT 05671
(802) 241-3655
www.vtstateparks.com

Index

About the Authors

Diane Bair and Pamela Wright believe they have the world's most fun jobs: They play outside and get paid for it! The travel writing team has co-authored more than two dozen books, including *Adventure: New England; Wild Encounters: The Best Animal-Watching Adventures in the U.S.; Unofficial Guide to Best Campgrounds in the Northeast;* and *Fun Places to Go With Children in New England.* They are contributing authors of *Lonely Planet's Hiking USA; Fodor's Golf Resorts;* and *Fodor's Healthy Escapes.* The duo also writes a weekly outdoor adventure column for *Foster's (NH) Daily Democrat.* They've written for a variety of newspapers and magazines, including *The Miami Herald,* the *San Francisco Chronicle,* the *Boston Globe Sunday Magazine, Yankee Magazine, FamilyFun, Backpacker, Cruise Magazine,* and *Diversion.* They've also written several books for children, including a series of wildlife-watching guides.

Between them, Diane and Pamela have tried almost everything, from ice-diving and caving to glider-flying and hot air ballooning. They've appeared on national television and radio as travel experts, which they discovered is far more terrifying than swimming with hammerhead sharks in the Galápagos. They're always planning the next adventure. Diane lives with her family in Beverly, Massachusetts, while Pam resides with her family in Durham, New Hampshire.

THE MOUNTAINEERS, founded in 1906, is a nonprofit outdoor activity and conservation club, whose mission is "to explore, study, preserve, and enjoy the natural beauty of the outdoors. . . . " Based in Seattle, Washington, the club is now the third-largest such organization in the United States, with seven branches throughout Washington State.

The Mountaineers sponsors both classes and year-round outdoor activities in the Pacific Northwest, which include hiking, mountain climbing, ski-touring, snow-shoeing, bicycling, camping, kayaking, nature study, sailing, and adventure travel. The club's conservation division supports environmental causes through educational activities, sponsoring legislation, and presenting informational programs.

All club activities are led by skilled, experienced instructors, who are dedicated to promoting safe and responsible enjoyment and preservation of the outdoors.

If you would like to participate in these organized outdoor activities or the club's programs, consider a membership in The Mountaineers. For information and an application, write or call The Mountaineers, Club Headquarters, 300 Third Avenue West, Seattle, WA 98119; 206-284-6310. You can also visit the club's website at *www.mountaineers.org* or contact The Mountaineers via email at *clubmail@mountaineers.org*.

The Mountaineers Books, an active, nonprofit publishing program of the club, produces guidebooks, instructional texts, historical works, natural history guides, and works on environmental conservation. All books produced by The Mountaineers Books fulfill the club's mission.

Send or call for our catalog of more than 500 outdoor titles:

The Mountaineers Books
1001 SW Klickitat Way, Suite 201
Seattle, WA 98134
800-553-4453
mbooks@mountaineersbooks.org
www.mountaineersbooks.org

The Mountaineers Books is proud to be a corporate sponsor of The Leave No Trace Center for Outdoor Ethics, whose mission is to promote and inspire responsible outdoor recreation through education, research, and partnerships. The Leave No Trace program is focused specifically on human-powered (nonmotorized) recreation.

Leave No Trace strives to educate visitors about the nature of their recreational impacts, as well as offer techniques to prevent and minimize such impacts. Leave No Trace is best understood as an educational and ethical program, not as a set of rules and regulations.

For more information, visit *www.LNT.org*, or call 800-332-4100.

MORE WINTER ACTIVITY BOOKS YOU MAY ENJOY . . .

SNOWSHOEING: From Novice to Master, 5th Ed.
Gene Prater, Dave Felkley
The definitive instructional for the activity.

CROSS-COUNTRY SKIING:
Building Skills for Fun and Fitness
Steve Hindman
Includes everything you'll need to
know to begin striding
and sliding.

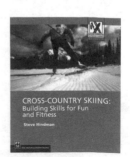

FREE-HEEL SKIING: Telemark
and Parallel Techniques for All
Conditions, 3rd Ed.
Paul Parker
The all-time most popular how-to book for
free-heeling.

WINTER HIKING AND CAMPING:
Managing Cold for Comfort
and Safety
Michael Lanza
Advice from the experts at *Backpacker* magazine.

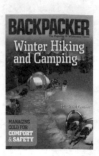

CONDITIONING FOR OUTDOOR
FITNESS: Functional Exercise and
Nutrition for Every Body, 2nd Ed.
David Musnick, M.D., Mark Pierce, A.T.C.
Pick a sport; find the exercises that will
get you fit to participate.

MOUNTAIN WEATHER: Backcountry
Forecasting and Weather Safety for
Hikers, Campers, Climbers, Skiers,
Snowboarders
Jeff Renner
Written by a weatherman with a fixation for
outdoor sports—he's got this topic covered.

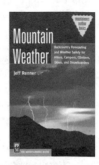

The Mountaineers Books has more than
500 outdoor recreation titles in print.
Receive a free catalog at
www.mountaineersbooks.org.